A Black Educator in the
Segregated South

A Black Educator
in the
Segregated
South

Kentucky's
RUFUS B. ATWOOD

Gerald L. Smith

THE UNIVERSITY PRESS OF KENTUCKY

The publication of this book has been aided by a
grant from Kentucky State University.

Editorial and Sales Offices: Lexington, Kentucky 40508-4008

Library of Congress Cataloging-in-Publication Data

Smith, Gerald L., 1959-
  A Black educator in the segregated South : Kentucky's Rufus B. Atwood /
Gerald L. Smith.
    p.   cm.
  Includes bibliographical references (p.) and index.
  ISBN 0-8131-1856-5 : (alk. paper)
  1. Atwood, Rufus B., 1879 –   .   2. Kentucky State College
(Frankfort, Ky.)—Presidents—Biography.   3. Segregation in higher education—
Kentucky—History.   I. Title.
  LC2851.K417 1929.S63 1994
  378.1′11—dc20   93-5993
  [B]

To my wife, *Teresa,*
my parents, *Romanno and Mary,*
and the memory of my best friend, *William Lewis*

Contents

Acknowledgments

While writing and researching this book, I received significant advice and support from several people. Thus, I take this opportunity to convey my appreciation for the contribution they made toward the completion of this study. Humbert S. Nelli has been my teacher and friend. He directed this study as a doctoral dissertation, and when I was a graduate student he fine-tuned my research skills and demonstrated unwavering confidence in my academic abilities.

I am especially appreciative of the comments and suggestions I received from James C. Klotter, Joe M. Richardson, and George C. Wright. Each read the manuscript carefully and provided invaluable insights as to how it might be improved. While their comments contributed to bettering the quality of this work, they are not responsible for any of its weaknesses.

Several other scholars read part or all of the manuscript at various stages. Thomas H. Appleton, Jr., Margaret M. Caffrey, Aingred Dunston, Kenneth W. Goings, and Robert Randall made important and helpful comments regarding my work on Atwood. I believe the book also benefited from constructive criticisms offered by members of the University of Kentucky's History Department as well as by participants in the faculty seminar at Memphis State University.

While researching this book I received noteworthy assistance and cooperation from the following institutions: Paul G. Blazer Library, Kentucky State University; the Department of Special Collections and Archives and the Oral History Program, University of Kentucky; Drain-Jordan Library, West Virginia State College; Ekstrom Library, University of Louisville; Frederick Douglass Library, University of Maryland—Eastern Shore; Forrest C. Pogue Library, Murray State University; Fisk Memorial Library, Fisk University; John Willard Brister Library, Memphis State University; John Grant Crabbe Library, Eastern Kentucky University; Kentucky Department For Libraries and Archives, Frankfort; Louisville Free Public

Library; the Library of Congress and the National Archives, Washington, D.C.; W.R. Banks Library, Prairie View Agricultural and Mechanical University; and Western Kentucky University Libraries, Bowling Green.

The following people assisted my efforts to ascertain library sources: Dorthy Bailey, Terry Birdwhistell, Deborah Brackstone, Donald Bradsher, Elizabeth Buck, Bill Cooper, Charles Hay, Karen McDaniels, John Moore, Elizabeth Scobell, Frank Stanger, Jeff Suchanek, Venita Swetnam, and Joyce Thornton. Had it not been for their familiarity with the holdings in their respective libraries I may have overlooked important sources.

Memphis State University played an important role in this study. A Faculty Research Grant and travel funds from the History Department allowed me to visit repositories and collect valuable information. My research efforts would have been more difficult had it not been for these resources. I am also grateful for financial support from the University of Kentucky.

Although I found writing and researching a book to be a lonely and challenging experience, it was made easier as a result of the encouragement I received from friends, family, and those who knew Rufus Atwood. A special appreciation is extended to the descendants of the Atwood family. Rufus Mitchell, Roy Mitchell, and Marilyn Nelson Waniek generously opened family archives and engaged in conversations that enhanced the success of my research.

Along the way, my colleagues Linnea Burwood and Katherine Jellison listened to my worries and tolerated my anxiety attacks as I completed the manuscript. Thus, to them I say, thank you. I am also appreciative of the support I received from my cousin, Darrell Williams, who welcomed me into his home during my research visit to Washington, D.C. As I worked on this study Darrell was always willing to engage in stimulating telephone conversations about my work on Atwood or any other issues relating to African-American history. Unfortunately, my best friend, William Lewis, who was like a brother to me, did not live to see this book published. Dedicating the book to his memory is an expression of my appreciation for our friendship and the genuine interest and support he demonstrated while I worked on the manuscript.

Finally, I acknowledge my appreciation to my family, in recognition of their support and patience as I worked on this book. I can truthfully write that they were always there when I needed them most. I am especially grateful for my wife, Teresa, who encouraged my work and yet, somehow, managed to shoulder the responsibilities of motherhood and maintain a successful career even while I was busy writing or researching. I also want to thank my mother and father, Romanno and Mary Crawford, my grandmother, Mamie Mayfield, and my mother- and father-in-law, Clifton and Octavene Turner, who believed that this book would one day be published. My daughter, Elizabeth, is too young to remember the many hours I spent working on this book, but her presence gave me the added incentive I needed to complete this volume. Thank you, Elizabeth. I hope you will one day be proud of your father for having written this biography.

A Black Educator in the
Segregated South

Introduction

Ralph Ellison wrote in his classic 1952 novel *Invisible Man* a critical analysis of a black college president named Dr. Bledsoe. As one of the central characters of the book, Bledsoe intimidated faculty and students and abused his "power and authority" at the expense of the black community. He was rude and deceitful with blacks yet obsequious and patronizing with whites. He was not an educator but the caretaker of an educational institution controlled by white philanthropists.

Yet Bledsoe was no fool. He had thoughtfully crafted his relationship with whites to protect the college's existence and maintain his job. He was an actor and politician around whites and an ambassador of the black community who understood the complications of his precarious postion.[1]

Although Dr. Bledsoe was a literary figure, his style of leadership was not imaginary. There were black college presidents who were strict overseers of their campuses. Louis Harlan revealed that Booker T. Washington "repressed" the writing and speaking activities of the students, faculty, and alumni of Tuskegee. According to Harlan, "teachers at Tuskegee dreaded the sound of carriage wheels in the night that signaled the return of Booker T. Washington to the campus, for they knew that the following morning he would be out inspecting every nook and cranny of his institution with an obsessive appetite for detail."[2]

President R.S. Grossly of Delaware State College in Dover also monitored faculty activities. He tactfully placed a curfew on his faculty by locking the chained entrance to the campus driveway at twelve o'clock midnight. Since he was the only person with a key to the lock, faculty who stayed out past midnight had to ring a bell to wake him up to open the gate. As far as Grossly was concerned, any teacher who returned to the campus after twelve deserved an early morning teaching schedule for the following semester.[3] At South Carolina State College in Orangeburg, President Benner C. Turner did not permit any criticism of his administration. Regarded by his subordinates as an "insufferable tyrant," Turner discharged faculty and expelled students who dared to publicly defy his leadership.[4]

While some ran their institutions like dictators, there were black college presidents who ingratiated themselves with racist whites. According to Harlan, Booker T. Washington "sought an identity of interest with, rather than a challenge of, the dominant white leadership."[5] Additionally, Robert Russa Moton, Washington's successor at Tuskegee, and William H. Council of Alabama Agricultural and Mechanical College in Huntsville adopted a similar relationship with the white community.[6]

To be sure, black college presidents throughout the segregated South held significant influence in their respective states. They spoke at commencements, inaugurations, and religious services. They published articles in black newspapers and journals to express their opinions on issues that affected the lives of black people. The schools they administered were responsible for educating the teachers, ministers, politicians, and businessmen who served the needs of the black community.

Because they were visible black leaders as well as vulnerable employees, southern whites placed high expectations on black college presidents. They were designated to serve on various committees, to campaign for whites in elections, and to help resolve racial disturbances. Clearly, the leadership role they played was shaped by the era of segregation. Historian David Goldfield writes that "racial etiquette created a system of behavior that served to reinforce the supremacy of the white race and the inferiority of the black. . . . The tone of speech, the gesture, what was said and not said, where and how one stood or sat became parts of the rituals of southern personal relations."[7]

The oppressiveness and inconveniences that resulted from racism make for an interesting study of the leadership of black college presidents. With the exception of Harlan's excellent biography on Booker T. Washington and a few other publications, scholars of African-American history have not carefully examined the roles black college presidents played in their communities. This is especially true of state college presidents who never achieved national reputations comparable to that of Washington.[8] This study seeks to fill that void. It is a biography and case study of the most influential black educator in Kentucky during the pre–civil rights years, Rufus Ballard Atwood.

Atwood served as president of Kentucky State College in Frankfort from 1929 to 1962. As the chief administrator of the state's foremost black educational institution, he worked closely with the Kentucky Negro Education Association, the Conference of Presidents of Negro Land Grant Colleges and the Association of Colleges and Secondary Schools for Negroes.

Atwood was frequently selected by whites as a qualified representative from the black community to sit on various boards and commissions. In 1944 Governor Simeon Willis commissioned him a member of the Post-War Advisory Committee. In 1950, Governor Earle Clements made him a member of the Kentucky Committee, Mid-century White House Conference on Children and Youth. In 1951, Governor Lawrence Wetherby appointed him to the Hospital Advisory Council. These appointments, combined with numerous others, gave Atwood access to the state political and educational power structure. It also gave him prestige and influence in the black community and throughout the state of Kentucky.

Atwood's responsibilities and the demands he faced created dilemmas that troubled him during the course of his thirty-three years in Frankfort. During the movements to desegregate schools in Kentucky and integrate segregated businesses in Frankfort, Atwood was trapped in a perplexing position of leadership. Blacks wanted him to serve as a spokesman for racial equality while white state officials expected him to avoid conflicts over racial issues since he depended on their support for school appropriations. Atwood knew if he responded inappropriately to either group, he risked criticism and retaliation. He desperately searched for some middle ground—safe ground on which he could continue to build his school and maintain his high profile in the black community.

Atwood was not alone in confronting his dilemma; other black college presidents of state and private schools shared the same problem. Frederick Patterson, president of Tuskegee Institute, a black private college in Alabama, admitted that he had "to bow to the exigencies of race relations. When I saw things that made me angry," recalled Patterson, "I didn't react as strongly as I felt. I did not want to tarnish the image of Tuskegee Institute, and so I couldn't be a spitfire."[9] President Benner C. Turner of South Carolina State College was criticized by the students, however, when he failed to take a stand against racial discrimination. He was hanged in effigy by the students because he refused to break school contracts with local storeowners affiliated with the white citizens council.[10]

H. Council Trenholm, president of Alabama State College in Montgomery, became "angry and visibly shaken" when he learned one of his faculty was organizing the 1955 bus boycott. According to JoAnn Gibson Robinson, who taught in the English Department, Trenholm eventually endorsed her role in organizing the protest. "He cautioned me, however," recalled Robinson, "to be careful, to work behind the scenes, not to involve the college, and not to neglect my responsibilities as a member of the faculty of Alabama State College."[11]

F.D. Bluford, president of North Carolina Agricultural and Technical College in Greensboro, encountered strong expectations from blacks and whites. Bluford chose not to publicly denounce the racist practices of the South. He also discouraged his students and faculty from participating in civil rights activities out of fear of losing state funds. Because Bluford accommodated white racist expectations, blacks in the community referred to his on-campus residence as "Uncle Tom's Cabin." Yet, writes William Chafe, "for the Blufords of Greensboro, the ultimate question was not what felt best, but what could be done to help the community."[12]

Because Kentucky was an economically impoverished rural state that had never valued education, Atwood's situation was extremely challenging. In 1941, the state's per capita income was less than half the national average. In the 1943-44 school term, Kentucky ranked forty-first among the forty-eight states in funds spent for education. Kentucky children attended classes an average of 159 days out of the year compared to the national average of 176. In 1944-45 Kentucky allocated $150,000 for black higher education while West Virginia spent more than $600,000 despite having a smaller percentage of black residents. These alarming statistics led *Colliers* magazine to publish a scathing article in its March 30, 1946, edition that described Kentucky as a "backward state."[13] Atwood had to face all the disadvantages of this environment as well as the additional problems of racism and bigotry.

Furthermore, Kentucky State was located in Frankfort, the state capital, which made it difficult for him to remain aloof from political activities. The governor reserved the right to appoint the school's board of trustees, which in turn appointed a president for the institution. By the time Atwood arrived on the campus, the board had established a reputation of choosing a president who supported the governor's election to office. Thus the school's presidency became a political plum, awarded to black educators with significant political influence.

Atwood was the school's sixth president. He accepted the position with the intention of removing Kentucky State from politics. When he retired, Atwood proudly proclaimed that he did not participate in politics.[14] However, the paradox of his leadership is that several of his accomplishments as president were the result of his own shrewd political activities.

This study will assess Atwood's political dealings and contacts with white state officials; appraise his contributions to Kentucky State College; examine his efforts to improve black education in the state and nation; discuss his relationship with faculty and students; and evaluate his contributions to the civil rights movement in Kentucky. It will also review his early teaching assignments, military career, and family background. However, it should be noted that I have chosen to focus on Atwood's professional career more than his personal life.

In writing this book I have tried to examine Atwood's life within the context in which he lived in order to explain the complications surrounding each decision he made. I hope to prove, at least, that Atwood was a gladiator in the arena of black education. He did whatever necessary to protect his job and to promote the interests of Kentucky State. While he was not an outstanding scholar, he was a capable administrator.[15] And, even more important, Atwood was a skilled interracial diplomat.[16] He maintained successfully close ties with white educators, politicians, and federal officials in order to achieve whatever gains he could toward the advancement of racial equality in Kentucky and the nation.

The leadership of Atwood and other black college presidents served as bridges that enabled civil rights activists to walk away from the accommodationist ideals of Booker T. Washington toward the nonviolent methods of Martin Luther King, Jr. Had it not been for the efforts of some black college presidents, according to Christopher Jencks and David Riesman, "the years of complete segregation would have been even more stifling than they were, for by drawing on their connections with cosmopolitan whites they were able to create at least some breathing space in the Negro community."[17]

1

The Homeplace

It's the ragged source of memory,
a tarpaper-shingled bungalow
whose floors tilt toward the porch,
whose back yard ends abruptly
in a weedy ravine. Nothing special:
a chain of three bedrooms
and a long side porch turned parlor . . .
—Marilyn Nelson Waniek

On April 26, 1962, University of Kentucky president Frank Dickey telephoned Rufus Atwood at the Sheraton Hotel in Louisville during Atwood's meeting with the board of directors of the Kentucky Council on Human Relations. Dickey informed Atwood that he had been chosen by the Committee on Sullivan Awards to receive the Algernon Sydney Sullivan medallion, one of the highest awards presented by the University of Kentucky. The news came as a surprise to Atwood who had recently announced his decision to retire as president of Kentucky State College. Atwood told Dickey that he would be honored to receive the distinguished award at the university's graduating ceremonies.[1]

On June 11, 1962, the day of the university's commencement, Atwood felt mixed emotions. He was proud of his heritage and his accomplishments as an educator. Yet he "wondered" what blacks and whites thought of his recognition from the University of Kentucky. Did blacks think of him as an "Uncle Tom" since he was the first black to receive the award from the institution that originally did not want to admit them? Were whites merely honoring him because of the "humble circumstances" from which he had risen?

To Atwood these were pertinent questions that would no doubt someday be asked in order to assess properly his contributions to black education and the civil rights movement in Kentucky. In spite of his concern, Atwood did not allow his personal worries to spoil the excitement of being recognized for his work. As he sat on the platform stage in Memorial Coliseum on the campus of the University of Kentucky, Atwood proudly reflected on his life experiences, which began in Hickman, Kentucky.[2]

Located in the extreme southwestern part of the state, Hickman is a small rural community on the banks of the Mississippi River. Some consider Hickman as the part of the south "where Dixie begins." Supposedly, Mark Twain once described the community as "the most beautiful town on the river." Because of its rich lands and convenient location, Hickman exported large quantities of tobacco, corn, wheat, and cotton. With the constant arrival and departure of steamboats and flatboats, Hickman was a busy community during the nineteenth and early twentieth centuries.

By 1900 slightly more than fifteen hundred persons lived in Hickman, including a small number of African-Americans. While growing up in Hickman, Atwood learned that African-Americans must remain in "their place" if they wished to overcome segregation and racial violence. Since the Atwoods were long time residents of Hickman they were familiar with the community's attitude toward and treatment of African-Americans. "We knew our place," wrote Atwood in later years, "and we stayed in it."[3]

According to his unpublished autobiography, Atwood's paternal grandmother was a Jamaican slave named Diverne. Diverne was brought to Clinton, Kentucky, and sold in a slave auction to the Atwood family of Franklin County. The Atwoods later gave Diverne as a wedding present to their daughter, Sallie, who had married into the Rogers family of Hickman, Kentucky.[4]

While serving Sallie Rogers's household during the Civil War, Diverne gave birth to two children: Rufus King, who was nicknamed "Pomp," and a daughter named Harriet. Whether the children had the same father is unknown; regardless, Diverne decided to give them the surname of her first master—Atwood.[5] Her decision to adopt Atwood as a last name for her children was not an unusual practice among slaves who had been separated from or sold by their original owner. As Herbert Gutman explained in his brilliant study, *The Black Family in Slavery and Freedom*, slaves sometimes accepted the last name of a previous master because they did not feel close to their new owner. Other slaves used their original owner's last name in order to identify with "an immediate slave family."[6]

To be sure, Diverne wanted her children to have a sense of family in spite of the oppressive institution of slavery. Yet the reality of making this dream possible was rendered even more difficult by the Civil War. As the war intensified, the Rogers family fled Hickman, leaving Diverne and her children to settle with Sallie's sister, Mary Cowgill.

After the war, Diverne remained in Hickman and maintained a close relationship with the Cowgill family. For some unexplained reason, Diverne was also a friend of Henry Tyler, a white Confederate soldier who had served with General Nathan Bedford Forrest. Tyler bought Diverne a five-room house on Cedar Street in a section of Hickman known as Shelby Hill. Why Tyler bestowed such generosity on Diverne is unclear. There is the possibility that he was the father of one or both of Diverne's children, but there is no evidence to support such a claim.[7]

Nonetheless, Diverne did not raise Pomp and Harriet alone; she married twice. When Pomp was nine she married Alf Hammock. Their relationship lasted ten years before it ended in divorce. Diverne's second marriage was to Val Matson, a local blacksmith. Whether Diverne continued to work for the Cowgill family while she was married is unknown, but in all probability she did since there were limited employment opportunities for blacks after slavery.[8]

Pomp and Harriet were most likely among the black children in Hickman who went to work in the cotton fields at an early age to help supplement their family's income. Their chances of receiving an adequate education were hampered by the state's reluctance to provide equal funding for black schools. For several years after the war, taxes collected from the black community went into a separate fund, which was used to support black paupers as well as black education in the state. Not until 1882 did the Kentucky legislature vote to integrate the funds used for educating black and white children. After that, black schools continued to receive insufficient funding.[9]

Since Kentucky failed adequately to support the education of black children the chances of Pomp and Harriet receiving a good classroom education were remote. Pomp, however, did learn the rudiments of reading, writing, and arithmetic from the Cowgill children. He furthered his education by attending classes in the basement of the Thomas Chapel C.M.E. Church, where he completed the eighth grade. Because Diverne did not want him to leave her and go away to school, Pomp stayed in Hickman, never having the chance to attend a higher learning institution.[10]

While he was a young eligible bachelor, Pomp met Annie Parker.

Annie had been born a slave in Bemis, Tennessee, in 1862, the daughter of Lockie Moore Parker, a slave who died when Annie was nine years old. After Parker's death, Annie was sent to live with an uncle in Nashville. When this arrangement failed, Jane Allen, a friend of the family, agreed to become Annie's guardian. "Aunt Jane," as she was called by everyone who knew her, operated a boarding house in Hickman. As a teenager Annie spent much of her time cooking and cleaning for the men who patronized Aunt Jane's establishment. As a result of her work schedule, Annie had limited opportunity to obtain an education; she went no farther than the fifth grade. Aunt Jane never forgot Annie's faithfulness, however; when she died in May 1929, she left her house on Moscow Street to Annie. The house stayed in the Atwood family for many years. It became the "Homeplace," where Rufus would go in later years to enjoy restful visits with friends and relatives.[11]

Diverne and Aunt Jane were very upset with Pomp and Annie's decision to get married. Diverne was very close to Pomp, her only son, and Jane had become quite dependent on Annie's assistance at the boarding house. Realizing the family opposition to their relationship, Pomp and Annie eloped to Newborn, Tennessee, and got married in 1880. Afterward the young couple returned to Hickman to live with Diverne in the house she owned on Cedar Street.[12] Pomp first worked in the shipping department of the Hickman Wagon Company while Annie worked as a laundress to supplement their income. Although both were born into slavery, they raised children who overcame race prejudice. This was no easy task considering the racial oppression blacks faced in Kentucky and throughout the South during the late nineteenth and early twentieth centuries.[13]

Pomp and Annie had six daughters: Ray, Blanche, Geneva, Annie, Rosa, and Mildred. Rufus, the sixth child and only son, was born March 15, 1897. To support this large family Pomp worked at a variety of businesses including the Mengel Box Company. Established in 1901 on thirty-five acres of land, the company employed the services of one hundred men. Pomp earned one dollar each day he worked, which amounted to six dollars per week.[14]

The establishment of the Mengel Box Company was considered a reflection of economic growth developing in Hickman. In June 1898 the Hickman *Courier* published a special edition highlighting the progress and modernization of the community. According to the paper, Hickman was "one of the most stable towns in the state. Not a business failure in 30 years." The water works and electric lights were owned by the city. Furthermore, observed the *Courier*, Hickman was "populated by a people of refinement and culture. Noted for their hospitality."[15]

The Hickman *Courier* significantly contributed to the public image of the town. On September 19, 1902, the *Courier* observed that "Hickman numbers among its other blessings a colored population vastly ahead of its race in all virtues. The leaders of that race in Hickman inculcate the lessons of industry and thrift, and are in great measure endowed with the intelligence born of superior educational surroundings and moral environment."[16]

The *Courier* cited W.F. Crowell as an example of Hickman's thriving "colored population." Crowell operated a four-chair tonsorial parlor, "the leading and largest" in the community. "He is the Booker Washington of his race" and "stands for morality, law, and order," printed the *Courier*.[17] Crowell must have been one of the blacks in Hickman who knew his place, thereby qualifying for such dubious recognition from the white community.

Crowell's business was not the only successful one owned by Hickman blacks. The *Courier* also spoke favorably of the "splendidly managed" Hickman Joint Stock Company which was incorporated on December 27, 1890. The company was organized for the purpose of "buying and selling at retail, groceries, wares and merchandise." According to the company's articles of incorporation, capital stock was set at eleven hundred dollars and business transactions were to begin after 50 percent of the stock had been paid. The names of twenty-two black shareholders were listed in the articles of incorporation, and each had agreed to invest fifty dollars.[18]

Pomp Atwood's name headed the list of black investors. It is unclear how he acquired the fifty dollars needed to invest in the company. He may have acquired a loan through his association with the Cowgill family, who had operated a successful drug store and soda fountain in Hickman since the 1870s and had owned him, his mother, and his sister near the end of slavery. Yet, there is also the possibility that Pomp saved his money from picking cotton and working at the Hickman Wagon Company, which enabled him to invest in the Joint Stock Company.[19]

Certainly, Pomp was an industrious worker. He owned a coal and ice company that, according to his son Rufus, eventually failed because of his lenient credit policy toward customers. Pomp also ventured into real estate, a profession he was involved with until he died. For a man who had a limited education, Pomp managed to establish quite a business reputation in Hickman. Blacks in the community often called upon him to cosign the loans on their homes, groceries, and even medical bills.[20]

Because he had a relatively large family to provide for, Pomp made sure his children contributed to the needs of the household and learned to appreciate the value of hard work. All of the Atwood children were encouraged to get jobs. This expectation probably did not sit well with Rufus since it meant he could not spend as much time fishing, swimming, and hunting as he wanted. At one time or another, Rufus and each of his sisters worked in the cotton fields; however, at an early age, Rufus began assisting his mother with her laundry business. He was responsible for making laundry deliveries and pickups for his mother's white customers.[21]

After working a while for his mother, Rufus got a job as a janitor at the Farmers Bank of Hickman for fifty cents a week. This was his first real job and one, he observed years later, which he "hated . . . because of the ordeal of cleaning the spittoons with a day's accumulation of tobacco juice in them." Atwood also worked for the William Boltzer family in Hickman. He took care of their horse and buggy and furnished coal and firewood during the winter months. Although Rufus later described the Boltzers as "kind" employers, his job with them was not as interesting as was the clerking he did in the general store owned by the Hickman Joint Stock Company. "I used to marvel," recalled Atwood, "at the clothing, the language, and the manner of the whites who patronized the store. . . . They usually had large accounts with us, and this is where the trouble arose—collecting from whites." Since blacks did not have the power to demand that whites pay their debts, some accounts were never liquidated.[22]

Pomp Atwood did not speak out against the financial problems whites caused him or other blacks in the community. For instance, each Sunday afternoon former slaves who lived near the Atwood family would stop by the house so Pomp could check their grocery and clothing bills to see if they had been treated fairly. "I remember Papa sitting for hours and hours going over his neighbor's grocery bills looking for mistakes," wrote Atwood in his memoir. "Most of the time there were mistakes." Instead of directly confronting the proprietor with the evidence of his wrongdoing, Pomp advised those who were overcharged to stop patronizing the establishment and go elsewhere to shop.[23] This was probably the best option available to blacks living in a southern town the size of Hickman.

By 1910 several new buildings had been built in Hickman, including a bank, a library, and a courthouse. While describing his family's home and neighborhood, Atwood recalled that their house was "an ordinary frame house." It sat atop a large hill on unpaved Cedar Street. A long hall divided the house. The three rooms on the left side of the hall included the kitchen, the dining room, and his parents' bedroom. Each had doors that opened into the hallway. As far as the other two rooms were concerned, one was used as a parlor while the other was divided into a bedroom for Atwood and one for his sisters. Draperies hung across the hall between the kitchen and Rufus's room. Although Rufus got the portion of the house that was actually a bedroom, there was enough space available to give his six sisters their own corner of the house.[24]

According to Rufus, the Atwoods "were never hungry." Pomp raised vegetables and Annie canned them in preparation for the winter months. The family also owned a smokehouse behind their home. Each year Pomp would purchase four or five pigs, allow the animals to get fat, and then slaughter them.

"'Hog killing time' was really something," remembered Atwood: "Huge kettles of water were set to boiling over large fires in the yard; each hog was shot right between the eyes, and dipped into the boiling water. The skin was peeled off the animal's body and his insides removed. Then the meat that was to be stored was covered with salt and hung in the smokehouse. The women collected the liver, heart, chitterlings, and other edibles from the animals' insides and cleaned them . . . . We were always well stocked for the winter months."[25]

The Atwoods were a socially active family. At least once or twice during the week they would gather after supper around the piano in their parlor and sing songs. The Atwoods also shared activities with the other families living on Cedar Street, all of whom were black with the exception of one white family, the Hunzikers. Atwood and the Hunziker children played together throughout their neighborhood.[26] This experience influenced Atwood's belief that blacks and whites could live and work together in a friendly atmosphere. He maintained this belief throughout his lifetime. But considering the daily oppression blacks faced in Hickman, Atwood knew the chances of convincing whites to accept racial integration were remote.

Throughout the late nineteenth and early twentieth centuries there were several cases of racial violence in Hickman and surrounding communities in western Kentucky. In 1880, Henry Seay, a black Republican who was active in local politics, was attacked by whites and forced to leave Hickman. A couple of years later, other black Republican activists whom the Democratic party considered politically threatening surrendered their right to live in Hickman after they were attacked by racist whites.[27]

George Wright, in his exhaustive study of racial violence in Kentucky, wrote that the Night Riders played a significant role in forcing blacks to move out of several western Kentucky communities, including Hickman. The Night Riders were a band of white tobacco farmers who were members of the interracial Planter's Protective Association of Kentucky, founded on September 24, 1904. The association had been formed in reaction to an agreement between the American Tobacco Company and several tobacco partnerships in Europe which fixed the prices offered to farmers for their crops. To offset the power of the tobacco trust, the association set prices it believed farmers should receive for their crops. The organization also attempted to unite farmers into holding their crop until the trust agreed to offer the price demanded by the association.[28]

Several independent farmers believed the price set by the association was too high and refused to affiliate with the organization. This situation led to the formation of the Night Riders, a select group of the association's membership that decided to employ coercive means to recruit support. Dressed like the Ku Klux Klan, the Night Riders initially burned the tobacco barns and destroyed the crops of dissenting tobacco farmers. However, by the spring and summer of 1908 there were increasing attacks on African-Americans who had no connection with the production of tobacco. These attacks were launched against "uppity" blacks who, according to the Night Riders, had to be put in their place.[29]

When Rufus was eleven years old the Night Riders rode into Hickman and lynched David Walker and his family. Their reason for attacking the black family is unclear. Supposedly, Walker became involved in a dispute with a white woman. Considering the racial climate of the period, whites believed Walker had stepped out of his place. The Night Riders paid a visit to his farm during the night of October 3, 1908. After surrounding his home, they ordered Walker to step outside. When he refused to comply, they saturated his house with coal oil and set it aflame. Although Walker pleaded with the mob to spare him and his family, he was gunned down when he opened his door. When his wife came to the door, also pleading for mercy, she too was shot and killed, along with the couple's infant child who was in her mother's arms. Three children followed their parents out the door and met the same fate. The eldest son remained in the house and was burned to death. According to Wright, "Nothing was done to bring the lynchers of the seven Walkers to justice. Fulton County whites justified the lynchings by explaining that David Walker had a bad reputation and was a 'surly negro.'"[30]

Incidents involving the Walker family and others reinforced young Rufus's willingness to remain in his place, regardless of the status his father had in the African-American community. This is best illustrated in Atwood's autobiography when he recalled a personal encounter he once had with the town's chief of police, John Wright, nicknamed "Skullbuster" by the black community because of his violent behavior toward them. During the summer of 1916, while Rufus was working as a shoe-shine boy at the downtown barbershop, Chief Wright sat down at his stand and told Rufus to shine his shoes. At the time Rufus was finishing business with another customer and was preparing to give him change. Yet Chief Wright decided to use the moment playfully to impose his authority over Rufus. As Rufus kneeled forward to make change for his customer, Wright took his knees and trapped the boy's head between them. The room grew quiet as Wright added pressure. Rufus of course was terrified by the chief's unexpected action. Finally, Wright released his knees and burst into laughter, but for Rufus the incident was one he never forgot.[31]

In spite of the racial oppression that existed in Hickman, Pomp Atwood firmly believed a good education would increase the opportunities available to his children. Although all of the Atwood children did not graduate from college, Pomp encouraged each of them to continue their education after completing grade school. "Yet he did not try to force us into something we did not feel we were capable of doing," recalled Rufus. "He wanted it to be our decision." Ray, the eldest child, followed her father's advice and graduated from Lane College in Jackson, Tennessee. She returned to Hickman to teach the local black children at Riverview School. Blanche graduated with honors from Fisk University in 1909. Mildred, the baby, would years later finish her education at Kentucky State while her brother, Rufus, was president of the school.[32]

Because Pomp believed in the importance of having a good education he was active on Hickman's black school board and at one time served as its president. The black school board's responsibilities were limited to one school, the Riverview School. The facilities at Riverview were not as modern as those provided for white students. When Rufus attended the school, it was merely a two-room building located on a bluff overlooking the Mississippi River. However, teachers such as Ray Atwood, Onie Jenkins, Beatrice Nichols, Ada Yates, and Hertha Nichols, were committed to providing the black children of Hickman with an opportunity to receive an education. The principal-superintendent was George Towne Halliburton, a graduate of the normal department of Roger Williams University, a Baptist college in Nashville, Tennessee.[33]

According to Atwood, Halliburton "was a neat, brown man, whose head seemed too large for the size of his body, and whose feet turned out in opposite directions. His lips were thick and partly covered by the heavy mustache he wore; and his front teeth—like polished pearls—gleamed as he talked or laughed. No matter what the occasion, Professor Halliburton was always immaculately dressed." It was Halliburton's teaching ability, however, especially in English and American literature, that most impressed Atwood. "He could speak for hours about the great authors, their works and lives, or read and recite their contributions aloud, doing some from memory alone."[34]

Atwood developed an appreciation for history and biography as a result of reading books from Halliburton's personal library. Halliburton also motivated him. The principal made sure Atwood and his classmates were aware of the possibilities of higher education. For instance, Halliburton ordered tenth grade study material from the College Preparatory Department at Fisk University in Nashville, Tennessee, so Atwood and other students at the same grade level could continue their education.[35] There was never any doubt that Atwood would continue his education upon completing the tenth grade. His family took for granted that he would further his education like his older sisters had chosen to do. Rufus's major concern, then, was choosing which college to attend. Annie, who was a student in the college department at Fisk, finally persuaded him to attend college with her.[36]

In 1913 Rufus and another one of Halliburton's promising students, Charles Adkisson, traveled to Nashville to take the examination for admission into the College Preparatory Department of Fisk University. All students were required to pass grammar and arithmetic before they were admitted to the school. The College

Preparatory Department was actually a four-year high school that prepared students for admission to college. The examination proved no challenge to the two former students from Riverview, however. Atwood received the highest and Adkisson the second highest score of the sixty students who took the examination. When the school year began that fall, Atwood and Adkisson were among the thirty-four senior middle (third year) students enrolled in the department.[37] For two years Atwood took classes in the preparatory department before being admitted to the college program in 1915.

With the exception of visits home during school vacation, Atwood would never live in Hickman again, but the experiences he shared with his family would always remain an important part of his scrapbook of memories. Atwood's mother and sisters, no doubt, spoiled him since he was the only boy in the family, but it was his father who had the greatest influence on the development of his character and personality once he had left home. Pomp was a community leader who had compassion for his friends and family. He was a confident and ambitious businessman who knew the value of having white contacts in important political and economic circles. Rather than openly challenge racial customs, Pomp merely remained in his place relative to whites. Because of the restrictions African-Americans faced as a result of segregation, Pomp had struggled to obtain a lifestyle somewhat equal to that of whites within the boundaries of this system. Atwood inherited many of his father's characteristics as well as his approach to dealing with racist whites. His disposition toward racial issues would be further shaped by the education he received as a student at Fisk.

2
Goodbye, "Skullbuster"

On September 22, 1915, at ten o'clock in the morning, the students and faculty of Fisk University assembled on the campus in front of Jubilee Hall to mark the beginning of a new academic year. The ceremony included a selection of songs, a brief address by President Fayette Avery Mckenzie, and the raising of the American flag over Jubilee Hall. In his remarks, Mckenzie explained to the audience how the flag symbolized "obedience" and "perfection." "The flag of Lincoln," observed Mckenzie, "is the flag of the North, and the flag of the South, the flag of the white and flag of the black. As Fisk shall improve the stars will shine more golden in a brighter sky for a nation more pure and more perfect."[1]

Although Rufus was beginning his third year at Fisk, the ceremony marked his first year enrolled in the college program. There were sixty-eight members in his freshman class, and they came from various cities and towns scattered throughout the South, including: Memphis, Tennessee, Charleston, South Carolina, Meridian, Mississippi, and Albany, Georgia, among others.[2] Like Atwood, many of the students probably had friends or family members who had gone to Fisk and had since highly recommended the school.

Fisk was one of the more prominent institutions of higher learning for blacks. Although its facilities were not comparable to those for whites, the conditions were better than those available at other black schools. In 1917 Fisk received a significant appraisal from Thomas Jesse Jones, the director of research for the Phelps-Stokes Fund. Jones conducted a study for the Federal Bureau of Education on the status of black schools. His research revealed that Fisk, Howard, and Meharry Medical School were the only three black schools that deserved the distinction of being recognized as "colleges." According to the study, each of these institutions had the equipment, faculty, funding, and student body required to be recognized as such.[3]

Fisk University had been in operation for over fifty years by the time Jones's study was published. The American Missionary Association, out of a concern for the need to train black teachers, had opened the school on January 9, 1866. In its early years Fisk offered students elementary, normal, and college courses, but the founders wanted it eventually to become a college.[4]

Despite serious financial difficulties, the school's college program continued to expand during the late nineteenth century. There were fifty-four students enrolled in the program in 1898. Students were encouraged by the faculty to help uplift their race by becoming doctors, lawyers, teachers, and clergymen. By 1915 close to 50 percent of Fisk graduates were teachers. According to Joe Richardson in his examination of the school's history, "Fisk students considered themselves a part of the talented tenth and as future leaders of their people."[5]

Blacks and whites recognized the significant role Fisk played in education. Black students from throughout the country were attracted by the educational opportunities the school offered and the national exposure the school received. Former President Rutherford B. Hayes, Admiral George Dewey, Frederick Douglass, and Theodore Roosevelt had been among the many distinguished visitors to the school between 1885 and 1900. Booker T. Washington had spoken at commencements and had visited the school on numerous occasions. He even served as one of the school's trustees from 1909 until his death in 1915.[6]

Fisk had an impressive history when Rufus Atwood matriculated in the college program. It held significant pride and prestige within black communities. The school's traditions and activities had been passed down to each class entering the institution, and an alumni association was intact, prepared to recruit new students to the school and place graduates in highly professional jobs.

Fisk clearly had all the necessary ingredients to attract good black students. Four different courses of study in the college program were offered for new students like Atwood to choose from: classical, scientific, education, and home economics. According to the school's catalogue, the classical course was designed for students who wanted a liberal education. Influenced by Professor Halliburton's appreciation of the classics, Atwood first majored in this field with a special interest in Latin and Greek[7] before eventually deciding to pursue a bachelors degree in biological science.

In 1915 tuition for Fisk students was thirteen dollars for the first semester and twelve dollars for the second term. This charge did not include room and board, which cost fourteen dollars a month and had to be paid in advance. At times Pomp took out loans to assist his son in paying his expenses. But, most often, Rufus paid his own bills by working various odd jobs. During the school year, he cleaned classrooms or "collected" and "delivered" laundry at Fisk. He spent summer vacations working in Chicago as a porter and dining-car waiter on one of the trains operating out of that city.

Atwood's work schedule did not prevent him from participating in campus programs. As early as his freshman year he became involved in several extra-curricular activities. He joined the Extempo Club, which was the oldest literary club in the college department. The club held various programs that allowed members the opportunity to discuss current events and to engage in extemporaneous speaking. Each member was encouraged to "go forth into the world fitted to take their places not only as learned men, but as those who can benefit the communities in which they live, and by their lives be examples for their less favored brothers."[8]

In addition to joining the Extempo Club, Atwood sang baritone with the Mozart Society and played on the football and basketball teams.[9] He enjoyed sports as both a spectator and a college player. Long after he had graduated from Fisk, Atwood continued his interest in this American pastime.

While Atwood was adjusting to college life, Fisk and the Nashville community were becoming acquainted with the institution's new president, Fayette Avery Mckenzie. Mckenzie was selected by the board of trustees to head the school in February 1915. A native of Montrose, Pennsylvania, Mckenzie was a graduate of Lehigh University and the University of Pennsylvania. Before accepting the position at Fisk, Mckenzie had taught sociology at Ohio State University where he conducted research on American Indians.

As president of Fisk, Mckenzie worked to increase the university's endowment to a million dollars and to improve the curriculum by placing more emphasis on the physical and social sciences. However, to the dismay of some members of Nashville's black community, who believed blacks deserved more administrative opportunities at the university, Mckenzie continued to hire whites to chair departments.[10] In his study of black education in the South, James Anderson claims that Mckenzie was viewed very favorably by industrial philanthropists. "More than any of his predecessors, Mckenzie sought to make Fisk acceptable to the white South and northern philanthropist." According to Anderson, "he urged Fisk

Rufus Atwood, number 19 (far right), as a member of the Fisk basketball team. Courtesy of the Atwood family.

students and graduates to eschew political and social questions and concentrate on interracial cooperation and economic development."[11]

President Mckenzie was a firm disciplinarian. He retained old campus rules that prohibited card playing, gambling, and the use of tobacco. Because the founders of Fisk wanted to establish strong Christian values at the institution, attendance at religious services was a requirement for all students. Mckenzie also added new campus regulations that, though apparently intended to ensure the safety of students, were viewed by students as outdated and dictatorial. These rules declared that students possessing electric irons, extension cords or any other appliance in their dorm rooms could be suspended.[12]

The Mckenzie administration was especially concerned about the social relationships between male and female students. Women were not allowed to leave the dining hall with the men after they had finished their meals. Instead, they were required to wait ten minutes in order to make sure the men were in their rooms. Dress regulations for women were so rigid that they filled three pages in the university's catalogue in 1920. Male and female students could be expelled for walking together on the campus, even in the middle of the day, regardless of how close they were to each other. Despite the severity of these regulations and others, Mckenzie was confident that strict rules were in the students' best interest. "I am convinced," he noted, "that fidelity to school and college youth requires unfailing and constant insistence on regularity, reliability, and fidelity."[13]

Although rules were enforced to keep the sexes separate, chaperoned social events allowed the students to mingle. While work and school kept him very busy, Atwood managed to acquire time for female friendships. He had matured into a handsome young man. At the age of twenty Atwood stood close to six feet tall and was slenderly built. He had brown eyes and a light brown complexion. He was a snappy dresser, styled more like a professional male model than a college student.

Because he had grown up in a family of girls, Atwood felt naturally comfortable around young women. He dated as regularly as his time and money permitted. But this kind of social life changed during his sophomore year. He met and later fell in love with Mabel Edith Campbell, a petite, attractive, very fair-skinned young freshman. "From the first time that I saw Mabel," Atwood later recalled, "I knew she was the girl for me." Mabel was the only child of Roger and Carrie Campbell, a black middle-class family from Petersburg, Virginia. Roger operated a barbershop that successfully attracted a large white clientele.

In spite of Mckenzie's strict campus rules Rufus and Mabel found ways to engage in a relationship. They communicated with their eyes by exchanging glances of affection. They also managed to hold discreet conversations on the campus when one of them walked behind the other. Gradually Rufus and Mabel cultivated a relationship that eventually led them to the marriage altar.[14] In the meantime, however, their relationship and Atwood's college education were put on hold as a result of the United States' entry into World War I in 1917.

Blacks throughout the country volunteered to serve in the war and were initially rejected. The passage of the Selective Service Act in May 1917, however, proclaimed that all American men between the ages of twenty-one and thirty-one had to register. Consequently, black men continued to volunteer their services in large numbers. Many of them wanted to serve as officers but found that there was no officers training camps for blacks. The NAACP and the black press adamantly supported the training of black officers. Students at Fisk, Howard, and Tuskegee also lobbied for the establishment of a black officers training camp. The prudential committee at Fisk even voted that all male students should be required to have military training one hour each week.

Eventually Congress agreed to establish a camp in Des Moines, Iowa, to train black officers. More than six hundred black men were commissioned as officers on October 15, 1917. Prior to this event,

Atwood in uniform during
World War I. Courtesy of
the Atwood family.

Newton D. Baker, secretary of war, had appointed Emmett J. Scott, former secretary to Booker T. Washington, to serve as his special assistant. As "confidential advisor," Scott was responsible for promoting the interests of the black community and making sure that Selective Service regulations were fairly administered.[15]

The army was the only branch of the service that permitted blacks to serve in different units. They could serve in the infantry, labor battalions, medical corps, and signal corps, among others. In November 1917 the War Department established the 92nd Division specifically for black troops. The men of this division were sent to seven different camps scattered throughout the country.

On February 3, 1918, Atwood enlisted in the United States Army. He was sent to Fort Oglethorpe, Georgia, where he stayed for almost a week. There he took his oath for military service, received several vaccinations, and was given his army uniform.[16] Meanwhile an "Important Military Notice For Colored Men" was published in the *Fisk University News* from the headquarters of the 92nd Division. The notice was the result of a campaign to recruit skilled blacks such as plumbers, electricians, pharmacists, typists, civil engineers, and radio and telegraph operators into the armed services. Forty-two young men from Fisk joined Atwood in volunteering to serve their country in February 1918.[17]

Initially Atwood thought he would be treated the same as white soldiers fighting for democracy; however he soon learned that blacks would serve in segregated units and would be denied the same privileges as whites. This fact became most apparent to Atwood as the two races shared the mess hall at Fort Oglethorpe. Blacks were ordered to move to the back of the meal line no matter how much earlier they had entered than whites. Because the policy of Fort Oglethorpe stipulated that the last person dining would clean the area, it was black soldiers who generally got that assignment. Atwood quickly realized the situation and thereafter made it a practice to arrive late to meals. Since he was going to be eating after whites anyway, he decided that it made no sense to rush to the mess hall. After spending a few days in the racist atmosphere of Fort Oglethorpe, Atwood was transferred to Camp Sherman in Chillicothe, Ohio, for training. Though he found conditions for blacks better in the North, they were still treated unfairly.[18]

In June 1918, Atwood and the other members of the 92nd Division embarked for France where they received additional training. It was not until September that Atwood, as a member of the signal corps, was assigned to the front near Pont-a-Mousson. There he was a member of B Company of the 325th Field Signal Battalion. Within a few months of fighting in France, Atwood became a military hero. During the morning of November 10, 1918, the building that housed the battalion's switchboard was struck by enemy shell fire, severing the lines of communication. According to a citation by a Major General Martin: "Sergeant Atwood rendered valuable assistance to the officer in charge in reconstructing the switchboard and connecting new lines under heavy shell fire. When the ammunition dump began to explode in the same neighborhood, he remained on the job, tapping new connections. After repairs were made from the first explosion, there were two to follow which completely wrecked the room and tore out all the lines which were newly fixed. Sergeant Atwood was left alone and he established a new switchboard and the same connections they had at first."[19]

For his "coolness" in handling the situation, Atwood was

Atwood (second from right) and fellow soldiers during World War I.
Courtesy of the Atwood family.

awarded a bronze star. His heroics were described in the *Fisk University News*. The Hickman *Courier* even printed a front page article praising the hometown hero. "The *Courier* delights to give credit to our boys whether white or black," read the article, "who did their whole duty as soldiers and as Kentuckians on the bloody fields of France."[20]

After serving six months in France, Atwood returned to Fort Oglethorpe. During a medical examination, doctors discovered a spot on his left lung. For several months Atwood remained in the hospital while his doctors continued to watch his condition. They eventually diagnosed him as having arrested tuberculosis. He was given an honorable discharge with a disability of 15 percent, and for the remainder of his life his medical condition was closely monitored.[21]

The patriotism demonstrated by black war heroes like Atwood did not alter the racist perceptions many whites held of blacks. Segregation and racial violence continued to be significant problems in American society. In December 1918, less than a month after the signing of the armistice to end the war, Charles Lewis, a black veteran, was lynched in Hickman. He was accused of resisting arrest and assaulting the sheriff. His attackers also claimed that he had murdered a white man several years earlier. By 1919 seventy-seven blacks nationwide had been lynched, including a black veteran from Georgia who was beaten to death while still wearing his uniform.[22]

In February 1919, while still waiting for his dismissal from Camp Taylor in Louisville, Kentucky, Atwood's father advised him not to wear his uniform home. In a concerned letter to his son, Pomp Atwood wrote: "Rufus, men are coming home from the war on every train. For the whites its [sic] good, but for colored men its [sic] different. Chief Wright is meeting all the trains and telling the colored veterans to get out of their uniforms and into their coveralls. You know what can happen to a Negro that crosses skullbuster. So son, take your bonus money and buy an ordinary suit and wear it home. This way you won't have no trouble with skullbuster."[23]

The request bewildered Atwood, who had attained the rank of sergeant first class. He could not understand how a town, which earlier recognized his bravery on the front page of the local newspaper, would allow the chief of police to threaten black veterans. Yet Atwood did not want to create any problems for himself or his family and so he did as his father advised. He was dismissed from Camp Taylor on September 2, 1919. He returned home in a civilian suit with his uniform packed in his suitcase. Once inside his home he put the uniform on so the family could see its soldier. It was the first and only time his relatives saw him wear his uniform. He never wore it outside the house. As for "Skullbuster," he died a few years after the war.[24]

With an honorable military career behind him, Atwood returned to Fisk to complete his college work. He also resumed his interest in campus activities. He wrote sports related articles for the *Fisk University News* and became a key member of the debating team. In a spring 1920 debate with Knoxville College, Atwood argued that foreign laborers should not be prohibited from emigrating to the United States. He claimed the country needed them as laborers. Fisk's negative team, of which Atwood was a part, won this debate. According to the *Fisk University News*, Atwood "handled his subject with perfect ease and astonishing power."[25]

On May 27, 1920, commencement exercises were held for Fisk's largest graduating class since its founding. Thirty-eight students were presented undergraduate degrees. Atwood received a bachelor of arts degree in biological science. He was not among those students recognized for outstanding academic achievement. Yet

Atwood (second from left) during his senior year at Fisk with classmate Henry Arthur Kean (far left). Courtesy of the Atwood family.

Atwood must have felt especially proud to be among the two lines of seniors parading into Fisk Memorial Chapel as Guilmant's "Nuptial March" resounded from the pipe organ. He had withstood the pressures of racism and war. That it had taken him five years to receive his degree did not diminish the fact that he too could now be counted among the "talented tenth." [26]

Four months after graduation Atwood enrolled in Iowa State Agriculture and Mechanical College in Ames, Iowa, to begin study for a second undergraduate degree. Because of his disability discharge from the army he could afford to meet the fifty-dollar registration fee for nonresidents of Iowa. Established in the mid-nineteenth century, Iowa State was a leading institution in the field of agriculture. Many of its graduates had gone on to accept jobs with the federal government. One of the school's distinguished alumni was George Washington Carver, the famed black scientist who taught at Tuskegee Institute. An expert on plants, Carver had won acclaim for his research on peanuts and sweet potatoes.

When Atwood arrived at Iowa State, he met a group of young black men who were also attending the college. They had rented an entire floor above a ten-cent store at 202 ½ East Main Street, about a mile from the campus. The men had recently formed an organization they called the Interstate Club. The president of the club was Frederick D. Patterson, who would years later become president of Tuskegee Institute in Alabama as well as the founder of the United Negro College Fund.

Mabel Campbell Atwood
as a student at Fisk.
Courtesy of the Atwood
family.

Atwood met Patterson and asked if he could share the floor with the group. At sixteen dollars a month, the rent was relatively inexpensive since it would be divided among those living in the house. Without hesitation, Patterson, or "Pat" as he was often called, accepted Atwood's offer and directed him to a place where he could purchase a bed mattress.

The floor the group lived on, which was recognized as the clubhouse, consisted of a living room, kitchen, and dining room. An elongated hall served as the bedroom. Members lined their cots side by side "army barracks style" in order to make room for each other. According to J.R. Otis, one of the original members of the Interstate Club: "At times there were as many as twenty-seven students at the Club, but sometimes there were so few that the Club could hardly be maintained."[27]

Although Atwood claims the Interstate Club was already organized when he joined, J.R. Otis considered him to have been an original member. Club members alternated the responsibilities of cooking, washing dishes, and cleaning the house, yet Patterson did most of the cooking because of his excellent culinary skills. Often club members would take Patterson's turn at washing dishes or cleaning house so that he could continue cooking. The Interstate

Club provided an important social outlet for Atwood and his friends and created friendships between young black men who came from various backgrounds but had common social and cultural interests. Patterson and Atwood remained friends over the years even into their careers as leaders in education.

In 1920 few black students attended Iowa State College. Patterson recalls that: "Most of them were discharged army personnel and had some veteran's benefits that they used to take vocational programs, mostly below the college level."[28] However, the small black community residing in Ames befriended the students and welcomed them into their homes for social gatherings. Atwood and the other black students most assuredly appreciated this hospitality since segregated restaurants and theaters existed in the town of Ames.[29]

While a student at Iowa State, Atwood first majored in poultry husbandry with an emphasis on incubation. He had grown up with an affection for animals and the outdoors and decided to apply his education to something he definitely enjoyed. Atwood believed his work in poultry husbandry would provide an opportunity for him to establish a day-old chick business. The trade involved hatching chickens and mailing them to buyers across the country. Because it was a mail-order venture, Atwood assumed he could obtain white trade since customers had no way of knowing his race.[30] Cognizant of his father's business activities and the problems he had with some of his white customers, Atwood was looking for a means of achieving personal economic success by circumventing the racial discrimination facing blacks. His interest in becoming self-employed was stimulated at Fisk since President Mckenzie had also encouraged students to pursue economic growth. During his first year at Iowa State, Atwood seriously considered establishing his own business, but there were other choices he was having to make besides those relating to his professional career. His personal life was incomplete; he wanted a family.

Between 1916 and 1920 Atwood had maintained his love and affection for Mabel Campbell. The two remained in contact even though she was teaching music in North Carolina while he was studying in Ames. It was a difficult kind of relationship they both wanted to see end happily, and it did. On June 28, 1921, the couple was married at the Saint Stephen's Episcopal Church of Petersburg, Virginia. The only person Atwood knew at the ceremony besides Mabel was his best man William Canon, a native of Atlanta, Georgia, and a former Fisk classmate. Atwood was extremely nervous about the double-ring ceremony, which was to begin at six o'clock in the evening. However, the minister's wife brought him a glass of homemade wine to settle his nerves. "I must say," recalled Atwood, "I calmed down after that. As a matter of fact, I wasn't nervous at all. . . . That homemade wine can be potent stuff." [31]

After a reception, Rufus and his bride boarded a train back to Ames, Iowa. Since music was not offered at Iowa State, Mabel enrolled at Drake University in Des Moines. While at Drake, she lived with a black family and Rufus commuted to be with her on the weekends. Meanwhile, Atwood chose not to pursue the day-old chick business. He became interested in teaching and decided to work toward a bachelor of science degree in agricultural education.

In 1923 Atwood and his wife Mabel completed their studies. That summer, Atwood accepted a position as professor of agriculture at Kansas Vocational College in Topeka, Kansas. While serving in this capacity, he was in charge of managing the school's farm and cutting and storing alfalfa as well as milking cows. The job was less than what he expected his first one to be, but at least it was a source of income. [32]

Following the 1923 summer session, Atwood was offered a job at Prairie View State Normal and Industrial College in Texas as the director of the agricultural department. The opportunity was ideal since he was interested in teaching agriculture education, but the salary must have been just as attractive. According to the school's biennial budget for 1926-27, Atwood was one of the highest paid faculty members at the school, earning a salary of $2,400.

Prairie View was a large state-supported black school located in the country about forty-five miles outside of Houston. Established in 1878, the school operated under the auspices of the all-white Texas A & M College in College Station. The president of A & M was in charge of Prairie View, thereby giving him executive authority over the school's official business. The on-campus black administrator was referred to as the principal of the school. [33]

When Atwood arrived at Prairie View, Principal J. Granville Osborne was in the process of raising the scholarly standards of the college. He was recruiting well-trained teachers in order to upgrade the institution into a full-scale college. New courses of study had been added to the departments of education, math, and English. Furthermore, Osborne had tried to bring more revenue to the school by developing a strong athletic program.

According to Ruble Woolfolk in his history of Prairie View, a "cooperative leadership" existed between Osborne and William Bizzell, president of the A & M College of Texas. Bizzell "demonstrated the most constructive type of racial cooperation," because he was "committed to broad goals of human progress and justice." While Atwood was in charge of the agricultural department, President Bizzell set aside money for its development. He even sent Atwood to Tuskegee and Hampton Institutes where there were strong agricultural departments so Atwood could observe the facilities and make improvements at Prairie View.[34]

As director of agriculture Atwood had a significant amount of responsibility. He supervised the work of seven faculty members and was in charge of the school's 1,486 acres of farmland, which included managing 300 acres of garden. The livestock belonging to the college included 500 chickens, 125 hogs, 80 dairy cows, and 24 horses and mules.[35] Furthermore, the agricultural department offered high school and college courses of study. The college course was a four-year program that led to a bachelor of science degree. It prepared students to become teachers, farmers, managers, superintendents, and extension workers. The high school course was for those students who merely wanted to become more efficient farmers.

In his 1924 annual report to President Bizzell, Osborne disclosed that there were ninety students in the agriculture department; forty-five in both the college and high school courses. Eighty students from other departments at the school were also taking classes in agriculture, thereby elevating the number of students the agriculture department taught to one hundred and seventy.

Because he held an important administrative position, Atwood was involved with several committees and activities at Prairie View. He served on the athletic and catalogue committees as well as the Council of Administration. The council was composed of the principal, the deans, the registrar, treasurer, health officer, faculty representative and heads of divisions. The council met biweekly and dealt with the school's external policies.[36]

Along with his committee work, Atwood was director of fair exhibits. He was personally responsible for supervising and arranging the exhibits Prairie View displayed at several Texas fairs. The exhibits had to be carefully planned since they informed individuals about the activities of the college. Besides chairing this activity, Atwood served as adviser to the registrar. He was responsible for recommending entrance requirements for those students interested in coming to Prairie View.

In 1927 and 1928 Atwood worked as director of the summer school session, a very demanding position. The Houston *Informer* reported that fifteen hundred students applied for admission in 1928. For ten weeks Atwood was responsible for directing the activities of the more than one thousand students admitted, who were mostly adult teachers from all parts of Texas.[37] Throughout his tenure at Prairie View Atwood was also involved with the "colored extension workers." He believed extension agents needed to participate in field trips so they could more thoroughly evaluate agricultural conditions. During his last two years at Prairie View, Atwood served as the chairman of extension centers. He organized and operated extension classes in several Texas cities, including Houston, Galveston, Beaumont, Brenham and Navosota.[38]

Atwood's administrative abilities and his numerous contributions to the school did not go unnoticed. In 1927 the *Prairie View Standard* reported on an institute Atwood had conducted for "colored teachers" in Navosota by describing him as a "ripe scholar and able educator."[39] During his administration, Principal J.G. Osborne also held high regard for Atwood's work. Osborne did not like traveling out of the state to meetings so he sent Atwood in his place.[40] The opportunity to visit other campuses enabled Atwood to examine more closely than otherwise would have been possible the inner workings of several black colleges. It also enabled him to establish working relationships with other black presidents. This experience proved invaluable to Atwood when he became president of Kentucky State College.

Atwood's years working under Osborne, however, were brief. In 1926, Osborne was succeeded by W.R. Banks, who had been president of Texas College, a private school in Tyler, Texas. There he had proved to be a successful fundraiser: he had liquidated the school's debts and constructed new buildings during his ten-year administration. The role he had at Texas College, however, was much different from that at Prairie View. While president of Texas College, Banks had complete freedom over the financial and educational activities of the school. He had supreme authority over his faculty and students. At Prairie View he treated the students as though they were his "children," but he had to answer to the white president at College Station.

It was difficult for Banks to adjust to his restrictive role at Prairie View. Despite the objections of T.O. Walton, who succeeded Bizzell as president of Texas A & M, Banks traveled outside Texas to visit schools and attend meetings. He wanted to stay abreast of the national trends in education. Though Banks did not always send Atwood on trips to represent him, he had enough confidence in Atwood to entrust him with the responsibility of running the college in his absence.[41] This opportunity, along with other experiences, further prepared Atwood for becoming an effective college administrator.

The time Atwood spent at Prairie View was good for him as well as for the college. According to Vera Edwards, a student there in the late 1920s, Atwood "did quite a lot for faculty-student relations." Unlike Principal Banks, who was "a very strict, stern, rigid kind of man," Atwood was described by Edwards as being "a warm, stimulating, motivating person." He was able to get his students involved in various activities, including those related to current events and social issues.[42]

While he was at Prairie View Atwood received and rejected several offers to teach at other colleges. After six years, though, he decided to change jobs. The climate in Texas was not beneficial to his health. Although he did not mention it, Atwood was probably also concerned about the status of extension work at the school. During his years as the director of agriculture, the extension work for blacks in Texas received inadequate financial support. Principal Banks appealed to the State Board of Education to pay teachers involved in the program, but he got little support from President Walton.[43]

In the spring of 1929 Rufus and Mabel accepted teaching positions at Virginia State College in Petersburg. Mabel left before Rufus to begin teaching music because he had to complete the school term at Prairie View. Both thought they would simply reunite after the semester and begin another stage of their lives in Virginia. But, in April 1929, their plans were significantly altered. An agent from the Jeanes-Slater Fund visited Atwood on the campus of Prairie View ostensibly to examine the agricultural program. Atwood recalled that the agent's last name was Caldwell and that he was a native of Christian County, Kentucky.

Actually, Caldwell had been sent to Prairie View by the board of trustees of the Kentucky State Industrial College for Colored Persons, which was in the process of searching for a new president. However, Atwood did not know Caldwell was at Prairie View to consider him as a possible candidate for the Kentucky State presidency. After touring the school's agricultural facilities, however, Caldwell informed Atwood about the vacancy at Kentucky State and asked if he would be interested in the position. If so, Caldwell made clear, he would recommend him to the school's board of trustees. Although he had just accepted a position at Virginia State, Atwood told Caldwell that he was interested in the idea of administering an institution.[44]

More than forty persons had applied for the position at Kentucky State, but a few days after Caldwell's visit, the Kentucky superintendent of public education, W.C. Bell, invited Atwood for an interview. In late May 1929 Atwood paid a visit to Kentucky State to be interviewed by the school's board of trustees and to inspect the school's conditions. On May 29, 1929, according to the minutes of the board's meeting, H.D. Martin offered the following resolution: "after a prolonged and searching discussion of the needs of the Kentucky State Industrial College for Colored Persons and possible solution of its problems, it is the unanimous opinion and conviction of the Board of Trustees that Mr. R.B. Atwood's training and experience, coupled with a keen insight as to the needs of the institution, evidenced by his discussion with the Board, warrant the Board in tendering the presidency to Mr. Atwood."[45]

After reading this resolution, Martin moved to offer the presidency of the school to Atwood for a year, at a salary of forty-five hundred dollars. Atwood would be housed in the school's presidential residence, which was provided with gas, light, and water. The motion was seconded by Judge W.C. Hobbs. Thereafter, the board unanimously voted to employ Atwood.[46]

Atwood's selection marked the beginning of a new era for Kentucky State Industrial College for Colored People, but before he could begin making plans for his new job, Atwood had to inform Mabel about his final decision to accept the position at Kentucky State. It was a difficult task because Mabel had looked forward to returning to her home in Petersburg. Furthermore, she had been opposed to his decision even to consider the job at Kentucky State in the first place. Consequently, Atwood knew she would be highly upset when she learned what had happened.

When Atwood called to relate the news of his appointment, Mabel replied as expected: "You shouldn't have! How can you be so foolish?" Instead of listening to her complaints, though, Atwood decided to hang up the phone and call her again after her emotions had calmed. He proceeded to inform President John Gandy of Virginia State of his decision to accept the position at Kentucky State. Gandy released Atwood from his contract, but he too tried to dissuade him from accepting the job.[47]

Atwood remained confident of his ability to administer the educational programs of Kentucky State. He had gained invaluable experience at Prairie View, had become acquainted with issues facing black education, and had learned of the peculiar problems black college presidents frequently encountered. Atwood knew that being president of Kentucky State would be a challenge, but it was too great an opportunity to ignore. As Atwood came to realize however, he was not prepared to deal with the many political, financial, and administrative problems involving the school. But, within the first decade of his administration, he would become a seasoned college president and an influential black leader in the state of Kentucky.

3
The New Administration

On July 1, 1929, Rufus and Mabel arrived on the campus of Kentucky State Industrial College for Colored Persons (KSIC). "It was a very warm day," recalled Atwood, "and the fact that I was nervous and a bit scared about the task ahead didn't make it one bit cooler." Although he would not officially begin his duties as president for another week, Atwood tried to make a positive first impression on the faculty and students. At thirty-two years of age he wanted to strike them as a mature and experienced educator. He even wore a straw hat that first day to make him look older.[1]

Atwood's concern about his youthfulness soon dissipated and his first ten years as president of KSIC proved to be the most significant of his thirty-three-year administration. He gained the trust and confidence of faculty and students, who were depressed by the leadership of the former president. President Atwood also led the improvement of the overall conditions at the school in the midst of a national depression, proving to blacks and whites alike that he was determined to establish a positive educational environment at KSIC. He took control of his new position, radiating confidence and reassurance throughout the campus. His influence was somewhat evident four months into his presidency when the school newspaper, the *Kentucky Thorobred*, printed the following statement: "A new spirit has entered into the mechanism of Kentucky State Industrial College along with the new administration—a spirit of reconstruction and standardizat'on."[2]

Although Atwood, no doubt, had control over what was printed in the school paper, there were changes taking place at KSIC. But Atwood was only one of a group of black college presidents in the South who were in the process of advancing their institutions. For much of the twentieth century black colleges had received minimal assistance. Federal and state governments placed a greater emphasis on improving the conditions of white schools, while many black institutions deteriorated. Moreover, northern missionary societies and religious denominations, which were instrumental in the funding of several black colleges, did not have the financial resources to meet the needs of these institutions adequately.[3]

Consequently, black colleges lagged far behind those erected for whites in staffing, library and classroom facilities, teachers' salaries, technical equipment, and general operating expenses. Aside from these deficiencies, black colleges were expected to offer elementary and secondary training since there were so few good schools in the South to teach black children. Thomas Jesse Jones's study noted that fewer than two thousand of the more than twelve thousand black students attending private and state institutions were enrolled in college courses while the remainder of students studied elementary and secondary subjects. Budget constraints and curriculum demands made it even more difficult for black schools to increase their college curriculum. Prior to 1930, most black institutions did not meet the requirements needed for being labeled a "college." They simply did not have the enrollment, finances, and programs necessary to be classified as a higher learning institution.[4]

By 1931 there were four so-called black colleges in Kentucky. Twenty-two miles east of Louisville in Simpsonville, Lincoln Institute was opened to blacks in 1912. Primarily an industrial school, Lincoln offered courses in agriculture, building trades, pre-nurse training, home economics, and steam and maintenance engineering. Courses in biology, economics, English, geography, and history were also given at the institute. A teacher-training program was established to prepare teachers for elementary schools.

In Paducah, a black couple, Dennis Anderson and his wife, Artelia, founded Western Kentucky Industrial College (WKIC) as a private institution in 1909. In 1918 the state legislature voted to take control of the institution, which had struggled to achieve adequate financial support. WKIC was similar to Lincoln Institute with the exception that the latter was a private enterprise.

In 1931, Louisville Municipal College (LMC) opened as a municipally supported institution supervised by administrators from the University of Louisville. As a four-year college, LMC offered instruction in several departments, including biology, English, mathematics, physics, political science, chemistry and history. Unlike Lincoln Institute and WKIC, which were eventually reduced to a high school and a vocational school, respectively, LMC and KSIC were the only two black colleges in Kentucky between 1931 and 1951.[5]

As Kentucky's only state-supported black college, KSIC shared the financial frustrations of other black schools in the South. Prior to Atwood's arrival, the school had experienced both financial and political problems. Opened to students on October 11, 1887, as the State Normal School for Colored Persons, the institution was established for "the preparation of teachers for the colored public schools of Kentucky." The legislature originally appropriated seven thousand dollars to erect a recitation building and an annual appropriation of three thousand dollars to pay the salaries of teachers. The school was constructed on the east side of Frankfort on a forty-acre hill donated by the city. The mayor, E.H. Taylor, and the city council allocated fifteen hundred dollars toward the project.[6]

During its first forty-one years, KSIC was administered by five different African-American presidents. Three of these men, John Jackson, James Hathaway, and Green P. Russell, occupied the position during two separate terms. One of Russell's terms lasted eleven years, making it the longest uninterrupted tenure served by any president prior to 1929. Russell was a graduate of Berea College, the first higher learning institution in Kentucky to admit blacks. In July 1894 Russell became supervising principal of Lexington's black schools. He held that position for eighteen years before accepting the post at Kentucky Normal and Industrial Institute in 1912.[7]

During Russell's first presidential administration (1912-23), a men's dormitory and a residence for the president were constructed. The school's annual operating budget even increased from $13,000 to $18,000 between the years 1915 and 1917. Still, conditions at the school were far from being respectable. The school operated with fifteen teachers who were expected to instruct more than eight hundred students in preparatory, normal, agriculture, trade, and manual training courses.[8] The United States Bureau of Education described the school's industrial course as "weak," an assessment based on Thomas Jesse Jones's study. The study also concluded that the board of trustees was "divided by factional controversy. Its wrangles have incited the students to revolt, developed uncertainty as to policies, and caused the school records to be lost."[9]

Mary E. Tracy Ellis, who enrolled in the school in 1921, recalled that Russell's "reign was much like that of czar. He rode a white horse on the campus, on the farm, in the school parades, etc." Students who violated dormitory rules were "locked in their rooms" until their parents came to the school to resolve the situation. "Of course," continued Ellis, "he was not popular with the students nor his faculty—his rules were iron clad."[10]

Russell was a Democrat, and his policies received even more serious criticism during the administration of Republican Governor Edwin P. Morrow (1919-23). In January 1920 Russell shared with the Kentucky Budget Commission the school's financial condition from 1918 to 1920 and outlined the institution's needs for the next year. State Financial Inspector and Examiner Henry James was concerned about the school's low production of agricultural products. Moreover, he questioned the school's need for additional funding. In March 1921, James released his study of the school's financial conditions. He reported that the school was receiving funds from the 1890 Morrill Land Grant Act, the state of Kentucky, and the 1914 Smith-Lever Act, which provided money for extension work in home economics and agriculture. Because the school received these funds, State Inspector James was suspicious of Russell's request for increased appropriations. His view toward Russell's management of the school was shared by a Hopkinsville, Kentucky, newspaper, which printed the following statement on the matter: "It is our firm belief that if a deeper probe of the affairs of the school should be made, that not only would recklessness be shown but in addition plain dishonesty. Never in in the history of the institution has it been more evident than during the administration of President G.P. Russell that the school has been considered a mere pawn in the hands of designing politicians at Frankfort who had little concern about the Negro's educational welfare but interested only in getting their hands on the money intended for the school's maintenance."[11] Two days after this criticism, Russell met with the board of trustees and defended his administration. He presented a report which revealed that the institution's debts were the lowest in its history. Despite the accusations against Russell, the board accepted his report rather than investigate the matter further, thereby vindicating him of corruption. Meanwhile, newspapers such as the Louisville *Leader* and the Pittsburgh *Courier* learned of Russell's work at Kentucky Normal and Industrial Institute and recognized his significant influence on the school's progress.[12] Nonetheless the adversity surrounding Russell's administration was not over.

On January 9, 1923, the executive committee of the board of trustees met with the institution's faculty and administrators to discuss the school's condition. The trustees expressed concern that efforts to standardize the school's work were not receiving adequate support from the administration and eventually fired the school's dean thinking he was not supporting their efforts. But this did not improve the institution's administrative leadership. The board then decided to dismiss Russell as president.

On May 5, 1923, the board of trustees hired Francis Wood to replace Russell as president of the school. This act sparked criticism from the Lexington *Herald*, which claimed Russell was removed for "political and professional reasons." According to the Lexington *Herald*, an advocate of the Democratic party, the chairman of the school's Republican-dominated board of trustees, George Colvin, had aspirations to be elected Kentucky's governor in 1923. The *Herald* claimed that black Republicans agreed to support Colvin's election for governor, providing he hire a black Republican to replace Russell, who was Democrat.[13]

Colvin, a long-time educator, had been the state superintendent of public instruction from 1919 to 1923. In a letter to the Lexington *Herald*, Colvin adamantly denied the role of "politics" in the trustees' decision to discharge President Russell. He cited the increasing indebtedness of the school as a problem with Russell's administration. Russell was replaced as president, according to Colvin, "solely for the good of the school." In a statement published in the Lexington *Herald*, Russell expressed a different viewpoint of Colvin's decision to support his removal from the office. "I knew all along that he [Colvin] was being pressed by the Reverend J.E. Wood, brother of F.M. Wood, and a few other Republican Negro politicians to remove me from office, as the price of their support of him for governor." Russell believed Francis Wood was selected as president of the school in May 1923 because of his brother's "political pull." Reverend J.E. Wood was president of the General Association of Colored Baptists and editor of the *Torch Light*, a southern black publication.[14] Russell was aware of J.E. Wood's apparent political clout but was not confident that Francis had the ability to run KSIC. Russell claimed Francis Wood did not possess "sufficient credits to make him eligible for the principalship of a rural high school." Furthermore, observed Russell, "If Mr. Colvin thinks he can ride into the office of Governor at the expense of the education of colored youths of Kentucky he will find out, if he is the Republican candidate for governor that he has reckoned without his host." Russell was confident that blacks would not support Colvin's election because they did not approve Francis Wood's educational training.[15] However, it was Russell's political contacts rather than Wood's inefficiency as an administrator that led to the latter's departure.

Wood's tenure at KSIC lasted only from May 1923 to April 1924. In the November 1923 gubernatorial election, Republican nominee George Colvin lost to Democrat William J. Fields. Because President Russell anticipated this outcome he had not left the city of Frankfort upon his removal as president in May 1923. Russell was confident that the newly elected Democrat would appoint new trustees to the school and that he would resume the position as president of the institution.

In February 1924, President Wood met with the trustees to discuss the school's conditions. In order to obtain an accurate assessment of the institution's financial situation the state inspector and examiner was called upon to review the status of the school. Although his investigation did not reveal any misappropriation of funds, the political support held by Russell as well as his efforts to reclaim the presidency proved too much for Wood. He announced his resignation in April 1924, and one month later Russell's expectations were realized when he was once again appointed president of the institution.[16]

Russell's second administration encountered even more serious problems than his first. On August 13, 1928, E.R. Burch, a public accountant, audited the financial records of the school for the fiscal years ending in June 1926, 1927, and 1928. Burch filed a report that questioned the honesty and integrity of Russell's financial management. Burch charged that Russell deposited the school's money in his personal account and revealed that Russell employed family members in unneeded capacities at the school. Burch's report also questioned some of the activities of the board of trustees. For instance, one board member, Judge W.C. Hobbs, had earlier made a motion that permitted Russell to rent several of the school's houses for personal gain.[17]

In an attempt to defend his administration, President Russell argued that the school received insufficient funding and that the state government had approved the school's accounting system. These arguments were not enough to save his job. The board of trustees asked for Russell's resignation on February 20, 1929. The dean of the school, James A. Bond, was asked to serve as acting president for the rest of the academic year.[18]

In light of the college's troubled past, Atwood was determined to correct conditions that had interfered with its advancement. However, the task would be a difficult one to achieve. As of 1929, the school was $18,000 in debt; the faculty was poorly trained; and the library, consisting of three-hundred usable books, and the domestic art and science laboratories had been closed to students. Moreover, campus facilities were in a state of neglect. The girls' dormitory was the only building that did not need repair, while the president's residence was the only building with the use of natural gas. The value of KSIC's physical plant, which included buildings, equipment, and other property, totaled a mere $317,000.00. All five of Kentucky's white institutions each had properties totaling more than a million dollars.[19]

Additionally, KSIC was ranked as a junior college, and its academic standards kept it from being recognized by college associations. Students were not guaranteed that their credit hours would transfer to other institutions. Because several states (e.g., West Virginia, Tennessee, Ohio, Missouri, Texas, North Carolina and Florida) maintained higher institutions that were accredited, the KSIC alumni were concerned about their alma mater's standing. The association requested the school's board of trustees to sponsor a program to develop KSIC into a standard four-year college with a "class A" rating. The group wanted students to have access to modern equipment and to receive instruction from competent faculty members. Moreover, they wanted the school's maintenance fund increased in order to establish better buildings on campus.[20] Atwood, who shared the alumni's concerns, began taking positive steps to improve conditions at the school early in his administration.

Two and a half weeks into his administration, Atwood submitted a brief statement to the board of trustees outlining his work since taking charge of the school. He informed the board that several facilities were being repaired with student labor; that he had invited the state financial inspector and examiner to the campus to help organize the school's system of bookkeeping, and that a budget had been prepared indicating the college's income and expenditures. Atwood had also met with Dean James Bond to develop a course of study that would meet the approval of accrediting agencies.[21]

Atwood later informed a member of the black press about his goals for KSIC. "In brief," noted Atwood, "our plan is to build an institution that will be recognized as an 'A' class college by the best agencies. . . . We intend to bring up to the proper standard our

faculty, salaries, library equipment, buildings, graduation requirements, entrance requirements and everything that goes to make a
good college."[22]

In his first year as chief administrator, Atwood initiated several
positive changes that had long-term consequences for the school's
image. He promoted a cleaning campaign for the dairy farm. All
milkers were required to bathe regularly and wear white coats and
pants as well as boots. The objective was to improve sanitation
conditions on the school's farm, but the same concern spread to
other campus facilities. The presence of vermin in the dormitories
required urgent attention. At first Atwood and a biology instructor
attempted to solve the problem by spraying the infested rooms.
When their efforts failed, an extermination company was hired and
the pests were destroyed.[23]

Atwood wanted to provide students with a comfortable academic atmosphere and solid educational opportunities. After carefully studying the school's overall condition, he presented the
trustees with a plan to reorganize the school so it could become
recognized as a "class A, four-year college." According to Atwood,
an examination of the school's offerings revealed it could not operate a broad program under the existing funds. The curriculum
would have to be limited so available funds could be used to secure
good instructors and improve library and laboratory services.

To fulfill these objectives, Atwood presented a three-part program to the board of trustees. First, he proposed a discontinuance
of the high school department, believing it would be less expensive
for black children to attend a high school in their own communities.
Parents of children attending high school at KSIC were paying fees
for transportation and room and board. If their children remained
near their homes these expenses could be avoided. Atwood's decision was based on figures furnished by the State Department of
Education, which indicated that county, city, and graded schools
were becoming increasingly available, thereby allowing the state
to concentrate its resources on the development of college work.
The increased number of four-year black high schools, Atwood
claimed, supported his suggestion that there was no longer a need
for secondary work at KSIC. Because of these changes in Kentucky's
educational system, more students could now enroll in the institution's college department. Atwood recommended that, effective
January 26, 1931, no student should be permitted to enroll in the
college unless he or she had graduated from high school. The

announcement was a significant step toward making KSIC an accredited college.

The second part of Atwood's plan of reorganization involved the temporary discontinuance of courses in plumbing, carpentry, and shoe repair. "These courses," noted Atwood, "are poorly equipped, poorly attended and necessarily poorly taught." The final part of his proposal called for the closing of the normal department. Atwood claimed this department would be useless when college work became a standard part of the institution's academic program. However, he added, students would receive teaching certificates upon the completion of state requirements.[24]

Following a discussion, the board of trustees, which had authorized Atwood and his faculty to develop a plan of reorganization, voted to implement the president's recommendations by July 1, 1931.[25] Atwood considered the passage of the plan a major step toward his objective to upgrade the work being done at the school, but he knew he needed support from influential whites if he expected to convince the state to finance improvements at KSIC. And even that would not guarantee the school larger appropriations.

In 1931, the state supervisor of Negro schools, L.N. Taylor, in a report titled "Our Colored Schools," defined the conditions of the state's black higher learning institutions. He argued that the state's black colleges, WKIC and KSIC, needed "better financial support, for more variety of courses, and for organization and administration in accordance with established professional standards." Furthermore, Taylor claimed, "it is only fair and consistent that these needs be promptly satisfied, for these colleges for the colored people have not been given appropriations comparable to the white colleges, not even in proportion to the populations they are designed to serve."[26]

Despite Taylor's sound report, there was little the state legislature was able to do considering the financial depression the nation faced during the 1930s. There were forty-two thousand Kentuckians unemployed as of 1931. Furthermore, Kentucky was a rural state that had witnessed minimal industrial development. Two of the state's most important industries, coal mining and distilling, had been in decline since the 1920s.[27] Because of the state's and nation's financial problems, Atwood began early in his administration to establish a good relationship with state legislators who might likely vote on appropriations for the school. He also familiarized himself with outside financial resources and the ways of getting access to them.

Atwood's first encounter with the legislature over state funding occurred in January 1930. Although his administration was new, Atwood realized he had to convince state officials at least to appropriate the same amount of funds allocated for the preceding administration. To better his chances, friends advised him to continue former President Russell's practice of sponsoring a banquet for members of the state legislature.

Atwood decided to expand this idea in order to include more participation from the black community. He sponsored a banquet for faculty and students and another for blacks employed in the capital. Both banquets were held prior to that of the state representatives because Atwood did not want black guests to believe "they were getting the leftovers from the white people."[28]

According to Atwood, there were two reasons for the additional banquets. The first was to assure faculty and students he was not overlooking them to win the support of the legislature. And second, he could obtain ideas from blacks on how to get the legislature to appropriate more money.[29] Over two hundred and fifty guests were entertained at the banquet given for legislators and their families. Their visit began with a tour of the campus. Afterward, the group gathered in the dining hall where they were treated to a full course meal that included roast turkey and dressing, ham, and peas with carrots.

Atwood mingled among the distinguished guests as they were being served. Though he was the host, he realized blacks and whites were not supposed to dine together. If he had used the occasion to break social barriers, whites would have identified him as a black who dishonored the rules of segregation, thereby surely eliminating his chances of receiving added funds. Instead, Atwood averted this situation by simply chatting with his guests as they dined and diplomatically lobbying for KSIC. Unfortunately, Atwood's deferential behavior toward the white legislators did not provide any substantive increase in the funding of KSIC. For the 1930-31 fiscal year the college received seventy-two thousand dollars, the lowest amount appropriated to any of Kentucky's state colleges even though student enrollments were increasing at all of them.[30]

However, the 1930 General Assembly did pass an act to appropriate eighteen thousand dollars to KSIC in order to liquidate debts accumulated by the former administration. Atwood recalled that a legislator from Paducah strongly opposed this appropriation. This particular legislator contended that the school was doing well as it was. "Those niggers," claimed the legislator, "are up there eating turkey breast and country ham and living in fine dormitories and buildings much nicer than some white folks in Kentucky have." His remark offended Atwood, who observed the discussion and decided not to try to impress the legislature with a banquet again. Instead he began attending legislative sessions and studying the actions of representatives to learn which ones had political clout. He also analyzed bills to understand the reasons why they passed or failed in the legislature.[31]

Beyond seeking the support of key legislators, Atwood worked to gain assistance from white educators in Kentucky. Early in his administration he learned from G. Ivan Barnes, state director of vocational education, that Frank McVey, president of the University of Kentucky, was interested in the advancement of KSIC. On December 20, 1930, Atwood wrote McVey and informed him he had spoken with Barnes and that he appreciated his (McVey's) "encouragement." "There is no single thing more necessary at this time for the educational advancement of the Colored people," wrote Atwood, "than a Standard Senior College for them within the boundary of the State." Atwood asked McVey to review the school's program to become a standardized college and to make suggestions as to how it could be improved. When McVey agreed to look at the school's program Atwood believed he had found an influential white leader he could perhaps call on to lobby for his interests at KSIC.[32]

On February 7, 1931, Atwood wrote Frank McVey to ascertain whether he could influence the State Association of Colleges to recognize Kentucky State as a "Class A" four-year college. "I know we may not come fully up to the exact letter of standard," noted Atwood, "but we have discontinued everything here except a small program and all our resources will be spent on the college program."[33] Exactly two months after requesting Mcvey's support, Atwood received a letter from Paul P. Boyd, chairman of the Committee on Accredited Relations with Higher Institutions of the University of Kentucky. Boyd informed Atwood that the committee had voted to recognize KSIC as a Class A four-year college. The improved ranking was granted on the condition that the school employ faculty members with advanced training and increase the library collection to eight thousand volumes. This recognition as a senior college assured graduates of Kentucky State that their credits would be accepted in out-of-state institutions if they desired to transfer.[34]

The board of trustees was especially pleased with Atwood's performance and awarded him a four-year contract.[35] While Atwood deserved credit for moving KSIC into the direction of becoming a four-year college, the school still lacked adequate facilities and course offerings. It would need significant funding in order to overcome years of neglect by the state.

Realizing the obstacles he would have to overcome to improve conditions at KSIC, Atwood saw the need to be a diplomatic leader. He studied all angles of situations involving KSIC and made sure the direction he took either directly or indirectly uplifted the school's condition. This kind of outlook demanded he be adroit, always calculating his actions to appease the expectations of whites. Because he had his own agenda, Atwood realized he had to swallow indignities forced upon him for the sake of the college he hoped to build.

Atwood was treated like a second-class educator during the 1932 budget hearing in Governor Ruby Laffoon's office. Throughout the designated week of hearings, presidents of Kentucky's regional colleges were allowed to present their budget requests to the governor and a committee of senators. Atwood arrived early in the week to make his proposal, yet, as he patiently waited to be heard, other presidents were allowed to meet with the committee and leave. Atwood was finally given a turn to speak to the committee at the close of the week.

Atwood recalled that it was not until five o'clock on Friday afternoon, as committee members put on their coats to go home, that one of the senators informed the governor that there was a "colored man" who had not met with the committee. When Atwood was granted permission to enter Laffoon's office, one of the committee members asked him: "Where're you from, boy?" Atwood proceeded to inform the committee representatives that he was from Hickman, not far from the governor's home town. Laffoon already knew Atwood and told the group how highly regarded he and his father Pomp were among the people of Hickman. Yet, Laffoon's familiarity with the Atwood family did not improve the chances of KSIC getting more money.[36]

In May 1932, Atwood recommended that the board of trustees

reduce his salary by 22.5 percent. His action was a result of budget cuts brought on by the depression, which had reduced the income of his teachers. Atwood believed the interest of the school could be "promoted" when administrative officers joined with teachers in bearing the burden of salary reductions. The board approved his suggestion and commended his altruistic concern for KSIC.[37]

Meanwhile Atwood decided to appeal to the federal government for financial aid. The Roosevelt administration had organized several agencies to aid American citizens and institutions as they struggled with the severity of the depression. An important New Deal agency was the Public Works Administration (PWA) established in June 1933. It created jobs and subsidized the construction of several different projects throughout the nation. Black hospitals, community centers and college buildings were among the works completed with government assistance.[38] As of October 1933, Federal Emergency Relief Reports revealed that blacks comprised 6.8 percent of the 472,211 Kentuckians receiving assistance. The number of Kentuckians on relief would increase to more than five hundred thousand by May 1935.[39]

The PWA sponsored six hundred projects and spent $49 million in Kentucky. Eastern Kentucky College in Richmond constructed a larger library and the University of Kentucky built a new student center with PWA funds. Sidewalks were constructed and buildings were painted at KSIC with PWA support.[40] Atwood was most concerned about constructing a new men's dormitory to relieve the overcrowding and inadequate living conditions of male students. He traveled to Washington, D.C., to request federal support since the state could not afford to grant money for the cause. With only a prayer and the need for a new dormitory, Atwood tried unsuccessfully to meet with President Roosevelt. He did manage to meet with Harold Ickes, the secretary of the interior.[41]

In 1933, Ickes ended segregation in the cafeteria and rest rooms of the Department of the Interior. He encouraged the employment of skilled and unskilled blacks on construction projects sponsored by the PWA. But most important for Atwood's purpose, Ickes believed the percentage of federal dollars granted to black facilities should correlate with the black population. Most southern officials vigorously disagreed. Less than 10 percent of PWA construction funds designated for the South went to black schools even though more than half of the black population resided in the South in 1930. Still, the collective plant value of southern black colleges increased appreciatively as $5 million went toward the construction of new campus buildings. In addition, the PWA loaned cities and states over $20 million to construct schools, auditoriums, and dormitories for blacks.[42]

Atwood was aware of the available funds and sought Icke's support to improve dormitory conditions at his school. Ickes informed Atwood that the PWA would grant 45 percent of the cost of a new dormitory, but the school would have to provide the other 55 percent. Atwood was financially unable to accept the offer. He suggested the federal government grant KSIC 45 percent and loan the other 55 percent. The secretary of the interior welcomed the idea providing Atwood get authorization to borrow money and engage in such an agreement.

Atwood returned to Frankfort and worked to get state legislative approval of his proposal. He solicited the support of John Brooker, director of school construction for the State Department of Education, and State School Superintendent James Richmond. On March 2, 1934, Representative W.L. Knuckles, Jr., from Beverly, Kentucky, introduced an act to appropriate sixty-five thousand dollars to Kentucky State if the school raised at least thirty-five thousand dollars "from outside sources."[43]

When this bill was not acted upon, another one was written and introduced by Waylon Raybourn of Calloway County that permitted the University of Kentucky and teacher-training schools to borrow PWA funds for building construction. This bill was approved by the state government. With the state legislature's approval Atwood proceeded with his plan to secure federal funding for a new dormitory. He submitted an application for a loan-grant to the federal government. The government accepted the application and loaned one hundred twenty-five thousand dollars to KSIC for the construction of a new dormitory. In 1936, the dormitory, which was named in honor of Atwood, was completed. The school repaid the loan at no cost to the state, through a self-liquidating project. The money collected from renting the rooms to students was used to repay the government.[44]

The progress of KSIC prompted State Inspector and Examiner Nathan B. Sewell to make the following observation while auditing the institution in 1935: "In the five years of President Atwood's administration the fundamental purposes of the institution have been more progressively carried out than any similar period in the past. President Atwood has proven himself a conservative and

Table 1. House Appropriations Committee Budget Recommendations to the 1936 Kentucky General Assembly

	Appropriation 1935-1936	Requested 1936-1937	Recommended 1936-1937	Recommended 1937-1938
University of Kentucky	$793,600	$935,600	$660,000	$660,000
Western State Teachers College	347,400	422,400	317,500	317,500
Eastern State Teachers College	239,400	282,000	225,000	225,000
Murray State Teachers College	194,400	407,000	200,000	200,000
Morehead State Teachers College	194,400	410,000	180,000	180,000
Kentucky State Industrial College	70,000	300,000	65,000	65,000
Western Kentucky Industrial College	45,000	86,660	35,000	35,000

SOURCE: *The State Journal*, 18 March 1936.

practical executive. The standing of the college has been materially raised and the character of the work done has been more widely and favorably recognized than ever before."[45]

Nathan Sewell's observations of the Atwood administration were not surprising. Atwood had made significant contributions to the school's improvements. Yet in comparison to Kentucky's white institutions of higher learning, KSIC and WKIC were still far behind in their educational offerings. Both schools continued to be underfunded compared to the state's white institutions.

Table 1 is the budget the House Appropriations Committee submitted to the Kentucky General Assembly in 1936. The table shows that the state's white institutions had been receiving a significantly larger amount of money than KSIC and WKIC. It also indicates that while WKIC and KSIC's budget cuts were not as severe as that of the white schools for 1936-37 and 1937-38, neither one of the black schools was receiving over one hundred thousand dollars in state funding.[46]

On April 4, 1936, Atwood wrote Governor A.B. (Happy) Chandler and asked him to allocate ten thousand dollars from his Emergency Fund to aid the school. Atwood revealed that buildings needed repair, that classrooms were overcrowded, and that the college needed more books, tables, and chairs for the students. In the closing paragraphs of his appeal, Atwood wrote: "Governor, we here would not make this plea or bother you with this matter at all if we were not really in need. We are 100 percent in harmony with your most efficient program for managing the state. We hope, therefore, that you will hear our plea with sympathy and that you will grant our request."[47] Chandler granted the requested ten thousand dollars, but this amount still increased state funds to only seventy-five thousand dollars for the 1936-37 school year.[48] In November Chandler visited KSIC and asked Atwood for a statement revealing the school's needs. Atwood sent Chandler an eight-page report highlighting in detail the repair needs of certain buildings as well as the facilities the school lacked.

Atwood also presented a strong case in justification of the school's financial needs. He claimed that between 1924 and 1937 the state had spent more than $28 million on white higher education and less than $2 million on that of blacks. He indicated that the value of KSIC's properties was $693,000, which ranked the school tenth out of fourteen southern black state colleges. According to Atwood, the Southern Association of Colleges and Secondary Schools had made clear to him that KSIC needed improved funding, among other things, before it could be given an "A" rating.[49]

A conservative increase in appropriations did follow Atwood's petition for improvements on the college. KSIC received one hundred ten thousand dollars for recurring expenses and fifty thousand dollars in capital outlay each year for the 1938-40 biennium.[50] The amount was hardly enough to meet the growing needs of the college; nevertheless, under Atwood's leadership, Kentucky State steadily improved during the 1930s.

An examination of the "Ten Year Report of Kentucky State College, 1929-1939" illustrates the able leadership Atwood brought to the school. The report was presented to the State Board of Education. Its purpose was to demonstrate the administration and faculty's desire to inform the board of the progress, trends and future needs of the college. The sixty-nine-page booklet included information on enrollment, scholarships, individual departments, finances, student services and organizations, and faculty activities.

According to the report, student enrollment increased annually throughout the decade. Table 2 is a breakdown of the school's enrollment during the 1930s. The table reveals an increase in the number of freshmen enrolling, which reflected the growing interest in the school. The larger number of scholarships awarded was a significant attraction to the college. In 1929, a one hundred dollar scholarship was awarded to one student; twenty-nine student scholarships totaling $2,485.75 were granted ten years later. Alumni chapters along with the graduate chapters of fraternities and sororities and other benevolent organizations donated to the college's scholarship fund.

Table 2. Kentucky State College Student Enrollments for the 1929-39 Regular School Terms

	Freshmen	Sophomores	Juniors	Seniors	Special or Unclassified	Total
1929-30	111	58	23	8	0	200
1930-31	134	83	34	12	4	267
1931-32	184	74	50	30	5	343
1932-33	141	133	49	35	16	374
1933-34	149	118	124	48	15	454
1934-35	180	154	114	102	28	578
1935-36	175	131	117	80	25	528
1936-37	160	160	122	84	4	530
1937-38	199	145	149	95	2	590
1938-39	197	145	102	104	13	561*

* Does not include Spring Term enrollment or new students for the second semester. All other figures found in the total column include Spring Term enrollments.

SOURCE: *Ten Year Report of Kentucky State College, 1929-1939* (Frankfort: Kentucky State College), p. 10.

In order to properly record the progress of students, a guidance and counseling program was developed upon the recommendation of the dean and registrar, J.T. Williams, with the president's approval. The program assigned instructors to work as advisors for the same students during their freshmen and sophomore years. When students reached their junior year they would be advised by the chairman of the department of their major. Developed in 1937, the student guidance and counseling program enabled the college to maintain a system of reports and records. It also provided students with individual attention on matters relating to study, curricula, probations, and dismissals. In addition to providing improved student services, the administration worked to increase the number of student organizations. In 1929, there were only seven organizations. This number had tripled by the end of the 1930s. Fraternities, sororities, dormitory clubs, and a debating society were listed as some of the new campus organizations.

Religious activities were another important part of campus life that received attention. Regular Sunday School and church services, a Wednesday prayer service and a Thursday morning chapel service contributed to faculty and student spiritual needs. In order to further develop campus religion, Atwood began a special program to train Sunday School teachers. Courses, including "the Intimate Problems of Youth," "Youth and the Bible," and "Ethics and Moral Tolerance," were offered. Students completing such courses and several others did not receive academic credit but were awarded a certificate for completing the program requirements.

As student services, organizations, and activities advanced, so did the various departments of the school. In 1931, the Department of Agriculture was organized as a "distinct collegiate unit" offering courses that led to a B.S. degree in agriculture. The Department of Education organized its curriculum to meet the requirements of the State Department of Education. Beginning in 1935, as a result of state certification laws, departmental offerings focused on elementary education rather than secondary education, which was no longer offered as a major. However, those students not majoring in elementary education were required to pursue nine hours of secondary education during their junior and senior years; and three courses in the department during their first two years of college. In so doing, all students graduating would have completed eighteen hours in the college's Department of Education.

Several other academic departments were established or reorganized in Atwood's first ten years at Kentucky State. The Department of Health and Physical Education was organized following the erection of a Bell gymnasium in 1931. The Department of Home Economics became centrally located on the second floor of the Trades Building, whereas the program had formerly operated in three small rooms of Hume Hall. The addition of sewing machines, student lockers, an electric refrigerator, and other kinds of equipment were positive changes for that department.

Obviously progressive changes had occurred throughout the college by 1939. Equipment and supplies for chemistry, physics, mathematics, and biology were valued at $1,600 in 1929. Ten years later, largely because of Atwood's success in securing funds from the General Education Board, the replacement value of science equipment was $12,000. The General Education Board and the Julius Rosenwald Fund also contributed to the library's redevelopment. In 1929 the library was housed in a small inadequately furnished room. By 1939, the library was appraised at $54,000. More than twelve thousand books, some of which were gifts from individuals, foundations, and the state and federal government, were available to students.

The departments of music, English, sociology and economics, and history and government were among those that benefitted from Atwood's leadership. The Department of Music expanded its offerings from one course on public school music to include instruction in piano, woodwind, brass, and stringed instruments. The English department offered a variety of courses in speech, composition, and literature; the Department of History and Government established connections with organizations like the Association for the Study of Negro Life and History and sponsored a program featuring an outstanding contributor to the field during black history week. The Department of Sociology and Economics was newly organized in 1931. It also worked to enhance its curriculum during the decade.

The Atwood administration did not stop with the improvement and establishment of academic departments. Having attended a prestigious black college himself, Atwood genuinely wanted to expose his students to the best possible curriculum. In September 1937 he and his staff organized the college into three divisions: the Division of Applied Sciences, the Division of Arts and Sciences, and the Division of Education. Applied Sciences included the departments of agriculture, mechanic arts, and home economics; the Division of Arts and Sciences included the departments of English language and literature, French language and literature, sociology and economics, history and government, and natural sciences and mathematics; the Division of Education was composed of the departments of elementary and secondary education, physical and health education, art education, and music education. According to the report, the arrangement was intended to: (1) encourage and facilitate the attainment of desired educational objectives; (2) make a closer correlation of the work of the departments involved; (3) make a more efficient use of administrative officers; and (4) make a more efficient use of the faculty personnel.[51]

During Atwood's first year as president there were twenty-seven teachers employed at Kentucky State, none of whom had yet earned a Ph.D. degree.[52] Because a well-trained faculty was essential to college ranking Atwood not only recruited qualified persons, but he insisted they pursue advanced degrees and publish their research. Although he did not have a doctorate, Atwood completed requirements for a masters degree from the University of Chicago in 1939. For whatever reason, Atwood chose not to pursue a Ph.D.; yet, this did not lessen his determination that his faculty pursue advanced degrees. He was a firm administrator who wanted the best results from his teaching staff.

Atwood was particularly concerned about the faculty's use of the school's library. Early in his administration he urged them to use this facility more often. He recommended all teachers become acquainted with the materials available and request the ordering of those sources not found in the library. Atwood's interest in the faculty use of the library was reflected in the frequent visits he made there to observe who was utilizing it as well as the books they placed on reserve. He believed the faculty could help establish a respected academic atmosphere when they worked in the library. In faculty meetings he made sure to commend those who did so and encouraged the others to pursue the same kind of activity.[53]

Besides teaching and research, instructors were expected to serve the college as disciplinarians. They were to make sure students abided by campus rules and regulations. They were encouraged to report violations to school authorities. Since students were prohibited from going home on Sundays and faculty members lived on campus, Atwood viewed the teacher's obligation to student development as a full-time job. "We are here seven days in the week," he once informed the faculty, "and we feel that your responsibility goes seven days in the week with these pupils."[54] Moreover, Atwood delegated to faculty the responsibility of furnishing students with "temptations upward." He urged them to encourage students to work hard and to do well in college. However, Atwood noted that "you can lead a student to college but you cannot make him think. All we can do is to furnish the temptation to think, to understand, to serve, to lead humanity and to make it as vivid and windsome [sic] as possible." Atwood wanted students at KSIC who were responsible and intelligent and who would not take advantage of the independence that existed in the college environment.[55]

During school assemblies Atwood expressed his message to students quite effectively. He encouraged students to make the most of their opportunity to pursue an education and not to squander their time on activities that would deter their intellectual development. After all, only a small minority of African-American youth were fortunate enough to be in college. In a 1933 address at the school's opening assembly, Atwood outlined principles the students should adopt and follow. He advised them to make college work their main priority, to live within their income, to budget their time, and to choose close friends carefully; he also advised them to be democratic, to cultivate their religion, and to take care of their health.

Despite the high expectations he set for faculty and students, Atwood was an approachable black college president. Charles Quillings, who attended the college in the late 1930s, remembered that students felt welcomed to talk to Atwood even as he strolled about the campus. Harrison Wilson, a 1950 graduate of the college and years later president of Norfolk State University in Virginia, said in a published history of Kentucky State: "The personal contact with faculty and administration at Kentucky State was the most important contribution for whatever success I have enjoyed. It was always that personal touch and concern for the students' welfare that made the difference."[56] Although Atwood's office was open to all members of the campus community, he still generally ran a highly paternalistic institution. Both the social and the intellectual activities of the school were closely monitored in the interest of the students.

Harvey Russell, a 1939 graduate, observed that "there were watch dogs all over." Atwood and his staff did not permit any violations of campus rules. Russell recalled that on one occasion students protested the campus food and decided to strike against the dining hall. When the students went to President Atwood with their demands, he closed the dining hall and refused to meet with them. Russell recalled that, "by the end of the second day, we were so hungry we decided we wanted to negotiate." When Atwood refused to see them they became desperate. "By the third day," said Russell, "we were in begging President Atwood. Please open up the dining room, we didn't mean it."[57]

Throughout his tenure, Atwood exhibited an interest in the total well-being of students and faculty, but he tried not to become too attached to either group. He supported the intellectual progress of his faculty and appreciated the contribution they made to the institution. Several faculty members played key roles in the development of Kentucky State during the 1930s. They included the dean and registrar, John T. Williams; Jeremy J. Marks, chairman of the Division of Applied Sciences; and H.B. Crouch, chairman of Arts and Sciences. All three men had earned doctorates and were thus prepared to give Atwood the competent and qualified assistance he needed to push Kentucky State forward.[58]

Even though Atwood worked closely with his faculty in improving the school, he maintained a purely professional association with them. "I always believed," said Atwood, "that the president had to be careful of close friendships. Some people might want to get close to him in order to receive small favors from him while others because of their closeness to the president might be denied certain rewards which they justly deserved."[59] Yet, Atwood was a youthful, sociable college president who related well with the young faculty he hired in the 1930s. He remained an amiable black educator throughout his tenure and the faculty appreciated his personality and his kind of academic leadership.

Minnie Hitch Mebane, who taught elementary education at Kentucky State under Atwood, recalled that he was a "likeable fellow." Joseph Fletcher, who began teaching English at Kentucky State in the late 1940s, remembered Atwood as "a good person to work with. He wasn't the type of man that cracked his whip on you and ran you from pillar to post." William Exxum, chairman of the physical education department and athletic director, explained that Atwood "had a degree of humbleness that you wouldn't expect in some college presidents. . . . He was a humanistic individual. . . . He was interested in what you were doing and how you felt."[60]

Clearly, Atwood was unlike some of his colleagues, who had reputations for being dictatorial and intimidating campus overseers. He and Mabel generally tried to share leisure time with all the faculty. Mabel was more reserved than Atwood when it came to socializing. When not teaching in the school's music department or giving piano recitals, Mabel relaxed by playing bridge, sewing, and reading novels. She also enjoyed working with her sorority, Alpha Kappa Alpha, and contributing her time to charitable fund-raising activities.[61] Rufus had a warm, friendly, engaging personality. As an avid sports fan, he followed closely the athletic teams of KSIC. He liked meeting new friends and reminiscing with old ones. Atwood was a good host and tried to make those who visited the campus on business or pleasure feel both welcome and comfortable. Because Rufus and Mabel never had any children, their social life centered around their activities with other African-American professionals.

Jesse O. Thomas reported on his pleasant visit to the college in the late 1930s in the Pittsburgh *Courier*. Thomas said that the Atwoods and the faculty participated in social activities once a month for two to three hours. He attended one of those gatherings and found that the group danced, played games, and enjoyed each other's company during the course of the evening.[62] In October 1957 Langston Hughes wrote Mabel a letter that included a kind observation on the hospitality he had been afforded by the Atwoods. "I have such pleasant memories of my visits to your home and campus," wrote Hughes.[63] His letter stresses his favorable assessment of Atwood's social skills.

Despite his penchant for recreation and leisure, academics was always Atwood's main focus. He challenged all of his faculty to pursue new academic heights and measures of professionalism. His objective was to gain the approval of KSIC as a "Class A" institution. Although the University of Kentucky's Committee on Accredited Relations had ranked the school as a "Class A" institution, Atwood realized that an approval by the Southern Association of Colleges and Secondary Schools (SACSS) would grant his college more prestige and respectability in black higher education.

The SACSS and other regional accrediting agencies were responsible for determining which institutions of higher education should be defined as colleges. Though schools did not have to apply for accreditation, it was to their advantage to be included among those listed as being standardized. The SACSS categorized colleges into three classes: "A" (standard), "B" (standard with deficiencies), and "C" (substandard).[64] The SACSS did not begin rating black colleges until 1928 and even then black schools could not affiliate with the association.

On April 20, 1938, Governor Chandler approved an act by the legislature to change the name of KSIC, Kentucky State Industrial College for Colored People, to Kentucky State College for Negroes.[65] The name change had resulted from a controversial decision that merged Western Kentucky Industrial College with KSIC. While the latter continued to train teachers and offer courses in liberal arts and agriculture, WKIC concentrated on vocational education. Three months after this merger, Atwood appealed to University of Kentucky president Frank McVey for assistance in getting Kentucky State recognized by the SACSS as a "Class A" school instead of a "Class B" institution. Atwood asked McVey to speak on behalf of Kentucky State to President Herman Donovan of Eastern Kentucky State College in Richmond. Donovan was president of the SACSS. "All we are asking is a sympathetic consideration," Atwood wrote McVey. McVey later informed Atwood that he hoped Kentucky State would receive favorable recognition from the SACSS and that he would write President Donovan. Meanwhile Atwood personally wrote Donovan to solicit his support. He believed Donovan's role would be a key factor in getting the school accredited since he had also served as president of the American Association of Teachers' Colleges.[66]

On December 16, 1938 Atwood informed President McVey that

the Southern Association Committee on Approval of Negro Schools had recently granted him a hearing in Tallahassee, Florida. Although the committee took an hour reviewing the school's condition, Atwood believed the session went well. His assumption proved correct as Kentucky State was recognized as a "Class A" black college by the SACSS in March 1939.[67] The following month Atwood received a letter of congratulations from President Donovan. "I talked with two members of the committee personally about your institution," wrote Donovan. "I am glad they recognized the splendid work you are doing."[68]

Although Kentucky State was short of being equal to white higher learning institutions, the school was at least offering improved educational opportunities for its students. Surprisingly, the depression had not hampered Atwood's attempt to guide the school to unprecedented growth. During his administration the faculty, curriculum, and campus facilities were improved and the student enrollment increased. Atwood had acquired valuable financial support from the General Education Board and Julius Rosenwald Fund. He had also orchestrated the programs that had been organized on the campus in order to lead the school in a new direction.

Atwood, of course, was not the only black educator to promote massive improvements on a black college campus during the 1930s. Several black colleges experienced similar progress during the decade. James Anderson wrote that black leaders and students had pressed for more collegiate programs and had rejected industrial training during the 1920s. Industrial philanthropists, southern whites, blacks, and missionaries were forced to accommodate this new demand.[69] Yet industrial philanthropists adamantly believed in supporting black leadership that was reluctant to challenge segregation. By the 1930s, northern industrial philanthropists had begun to contribute more funds toward the development of black colleges. "As black colleges became increasingly dependent on donations from northern industrial philanthropists," stated Anderson, "the missionaries and black educators found it extremely difficult, if not impossible, to accept philanthropic gifts and assert simultaneously that many of the political and economic aims of the philanthropists were at variance with the fundamental interests of the black masses."[70]

Some observers believed that increased northern white financial assistance led black students and educators to surrender their interest and responsibility to improve the conditions of the black population. W.E.B. Du Bois and Carter G. Woodson expressed profound resentment at the growing selfishness among black students. Langston Hughes lashed out against the "meek professors and well-paid presidents" who were reluctant to speak out against racism. Critics of the era did not always grasp the complexity of problems black college presidents faced. It was a tremendous challenge for them to promote their school and maintain their dignity and fortitude in the midst of white opposition.[71]

Black college presidents in the era of segregation had a difficult leadership role to play. They were supposed to represent power and influence in the black community and yet not allow it to consume their personal identity. They were expected to educate properly black youth despite receiving insufficient state and federal funds. They were to serve as outspoken advocates of civil rights at the risk of being fired by racist whites. The magnitude of the responsibilities they faced was endless and the circumstances in which they worked created a tightrope black college presidents were forced to walk.

4
Walking a Tightrope

As president of Kentucky State, Rufus Atwood had to be mindful of the school's development and yet guard the tenure of his administration. He did not want financial mismanagement or political interference to lead to his dismissal. While working at Prairie View, Atwood learned how political patronage influenced the tenure of college presidents. There, the appointment of the school's principals was controlled by the Democratic party.[1] Aware of Kentucky State's political history, Atwood was concerned about the longevity of his administration. He knew he would have to walk a tightrope as he tried to dodge the political challenges of dealing with Kentucky's white politicians. He knew that if he made one false move they would not hesitate to dismiss him as president.

Atwood was not alone in heading a black college institution controlled by politics and insensitive white state and local officials. Black presidents of private institutions experienced difficulties avoiding political squabbles and gaining financial support for their schools. On August 5, 1944, the Washington *Afro-American* reported that "politically minded" bishops were attempting to oust Charles Wesley as president of Wilberforce University in Ohio. Opposition to Wesley's administration emerged as he sought state financial and administrative assistance for his school. Benjamin Mays, esteemed president of Morehouse College, noted in his memoir that his "greatest disappointment was in fund raising. I must admit," wrote Mays, "that I was hurt many times during twenty-seven years because I was never able to get white Atlanta to accept Morehouse College as an integral part of the higher educational structure of Atlanta and therefore entitled to significant support."[2]

Most presidents of black public colleges faced similar and even greater challenges. Black college presidents at Langston University in Oklahoma and Lincoln University in Missouri were trapped in the sticky web of political patronage. In his memoirs President Joseph W. Holley of Georgia Agricultural Industrial and Normal

School (later named Albany State College) related how he tried to adjust to the political demands of his job. Holley claimed that his association with the state's governors began before they were even elected. "It was my policy," wrote Holley, "to make friends with the two leading candidates, so whoever won I would not lose. I didn't put all my eggs in one basket." According to one witness to his administration, Holley "wore a number of different badges—Republican, Democrat, liberal, conservative—it would depend on the situation." But, during the 1930s and early 1940s, Holley made a serious mistake when he maintained close ties with Democratic Governor Eugene Talmadge, a staunch segregationist. In 1942 Talmadge lost the gubernatorial election and shortly thereafter Holley was terminated from a position he had held since 1905.[3]

President John Robert Lee of Florida A & M College in Tallahassee encountered financial pressures and demands from the black and white communities after he took over the school in 1924. Yet, one contemporary observer noted that Lee "met and mastered the traditional problem of the school's presidents—how to walk the tightrope between the extremist elements in their own race and between the white officeholders who held the purse strings."[4]

Similarly, President John W. Davis of West Virginia State College in Institute managed successfully to walk the tightrope. When Davis became president in 1919 he inherited a school suffering depressed academic and physical conditions very similar to those Atwood found at Kentucky State a decade later. Davis presided over the school for thirty-four years. Under his leadership, the school was accredited by the North Central Association of Colleges and Schools in 1927. In his report for that school year, Davis proudly boasted that the school was "the first ever to be fully accredited in America with a Negro man as president on one hand, and a full Negro faculty on the other."[5]

By 1930, Davis was one of the leading African-American educators in the nation. Born in 1888 in Milledgeville, Georgia, Davis had graduated from Morehouse College with honors in 1911. Upon the encouragement of the school's eminent president, John Hope, Davis pursued graduate work in chemistry and physics at the University of Chicago. He returned to Morehouse to teach before deciding to accept a position in Washington, D.C., as the executive secretary of the Twelfth Street branch of the YMCA in 1917. There Davis established a cadre of friends, including a close association with the distinguished black historian, Carter G. Woodson.[6]

Davis was successful in preventing the presidency from being used as a political plum even though his school was less than ten miles from the state capital. His politics were succinctly clarified as he spoke to his faculty during a meeting on November 9, 1944. "I have never felt it my duty to go and dabble in partisan politics. I hold the position that I have a unique place in the life of the state. You and I are to cooperate in guiding this school, that whatever party is in power, the success of the institution can be a credit to that party."[7]

Although Davis expressed disinterest in partisan politics, he was an excellent politician. He wrote letters to legislators soliciting their support on matters involving the advancement of the college. He used his faculty as a reliable resource for obliging the requests of influential white state officials in need of some kind of expert assistance. For instance, when a West Virginia senator expressed an interest in finding someone to translate German papers, Davis recommended one of his faculty members for the task. He assured the senator that the professor would remain "quiet" about his involvement with the project. Davis believed the favors he did for influential leaders would be returned when it was time to vote on appropriations for the school.[8]

President Davis's style of leadership, especially his ability to utilize political contacts, influenced Atwood's role in administering Kentucky State. Atwood utilized Davis's strategy not only in orchestrating Kentucky State's early development but also in preventing the presidency from being used as a "political payoff." Years later, Atwood even admitted that it was "Davis [who] took it upon himself to guide me" through political problems.[9] With Davis as his mentor, Atwood decided on the means to safeguard his administration at Kentucky State and eliminate the school's role in state politics.

First, Atwood realized that it would be unwise to continue to publicize his political party preference. This was no easy task since his father was a well-known black Republican in Hickman, a predominately Democratic community. Pomp had told Rufus when he was a boy never to vote for the Democrats since it was the party of Lincoln that freed slaves.[10] For several years Rufus followed his father's advice. Like most African-Americans of his generation he pledged his allegiance to the Republican party. The 1928-29 edition of *Who's Who in Colored America* listed Atwood as a Republican. Ten years later this same biographical dictionary made no mention of

Atwood's political affiliation.[11] He probably made a special request to have his party preference deleted from the publication.

Atwood also took further precautions to remove himself from mainstream Kentucky politics. Instead of registering as Democrats or Republicans, he and his wife registered as Independents. Their decision involved a marital compromise. He agreed to join Mabel's religious denomination, which was Episcopalian, and in return, she voted as an Independent. This compromise helped reduce speculation about Atwood's political preference, but it did not erase his chances of facing political pressures.

In order to assure further the secrecy of his political persuasion, Atwood placed the pictures of a distinguished Democrat, Franklin Roosevelt, and Republican Abraham Lincoln side by side in his office.[12] He worked diligently to avoid creating political enemies. Yet, despite his ingenious efforts to stay clear of partisan politics, avoiding political squabbles in Kentucky was difficult. As Neal Peirce wrote, "Kentuckians like politics so much they have elections every year, choosing national officials in even years, state and local officials in the odd. In this nonstop political theater, there is never a dark night—and scarcely enough respite between elections for Kentucky officeholders to get down to the serious business of governing." Kentucky's political climate compelled Atwood to be "very careful" in association with the state's governors.[13]

The 1920s were an especially significant and theatrical period in Kentucky politics. Factionalism and personality conflicts disrupted the power and unity of the Democratic party, allowing Republican governors to be elected in 1919 and 1927. Furthermore, politicians in both parties continued the practice of offering jobs as a form of patronage to campaign supporters. Atwood was adjusting to his role as a college president while struggles for control raged in Kentucky's political arena. But his responsibilities became more onerous when politics threatened the early years of his administration. Yet Atwood withstood the challenge with his own set of political maneuvers. That he went on to serve under eight different governors during his thirty-three-year career reflects highly on his ability to mix well with people regardless of their political agenda.

Republican governor Flem Sampson was in office when Atwood came to Kentucky State in 1929. Elected two years earlier, Sampson had served as the chief justice of the State Supreme Court before being elected governor. Sampson wanted to improve the state's school system and provide free textbooks to children.[14] He did not pressure Atwood to do any direct campaigning on behalf of the Republican party. Instead Sampson spent much of his term busily embroiled in a struggle for political power with Ben Johnson, a Democrat, who was chairman of the state highway commission. The position guaranteed Johnson power, patronage, and a source for campaign funds. Both Johnson and Sampson realized the political importance of this state committee. In 1930 Johnson and the Democrats successfully passed a "ripper bill" in the state legislature, which made it possible for their party rather than the governor to control appointments to the commission. The bill effectively eliminated Sampson's effort to organize a strong Republican machine in state government.[15]

Atwood's impressions of Sampson were not based on the governor's political failings. "Governor Sampson impressed me as a sincere Christian gentleman," wrote Atwood in his autobiography. "I heard him on several occasions apologize to Negro audiences for the harsh treatment accorded them by whites. This may have been a trick on his part to let the Negroes think he was on their side, but I don't think so. I truly believe he was sincere."

According to Atwood, his "main trouble" with Sampson was that the governor would call him at seven o'clock in the morning and ask him to meet with him in his office as soon as possible.[16] Atwood's most serious entanglement with Kentucky politics followed the election of Ruby Laffoon and involved former Kentucky State president, Green P. Russell. While Atwood was teaching at Prairie View he met Russell for the first time at a meeting of the Conference of Presidents of Negro Land Grant Colleges. Following his second removal as head of the institution, Russell relocated his family near the school's campus because he was confident he would be reappointed president of Kentucky State following the election of a Democratic governor in 1931.[17]

A staunch Democrat, Russell had the support of William "Billy" Klair, a Lexington political boss. According to "Happy" Chandler, Klair was "a tough operator" who "did politics while other people slept." From 1899 to 1909 Klair served as a representative from Lexington in the state legislature. He also served several terms on the Democratic State Central and Executive Committee. On March 29, 1912, he and businessman Tom Scott incorporated the Klair-Scott Insurance Agency. Because of Klair's political connections their company handled much of the state's insurance contracts. Most likely Klair and Russell met while the latter was the supervising principal of Lexington's black schools. Their political connection probably was strengthened during Russell's presidency of Kentucky State since Klair had contracts to insure several of the school's buildings during that time.[18]

No doubt the political relationship Klair and Russell maintained over the years offered a troublesome threat to the Atwood administration. By 1930 Klair was among the "Big Six" political bosses who controlled power in Kentucky. The others were Democrats Ben Johnson of Nelson County; Michael J. "Mickey" Brennan from Louisville; Allie Young from Morehead; political organizer Percy Haly; and Republican Maurice Galvin of Covington. Together these men were influential in determining who would be elected Kentucky's governor in 1931.[19]

With powerful boss Ben Johnson leading the way, Ruby Laffoon, a sixty-two-year-old judge from Madisonville, gained the Democratic party's nomination. According to Atwood it was rumored that Russell contributed a thousand dollars toward Laffoon's campaign. Some blacks who supported Atwood's administration suggested that he too campaign for Laffoon in an effort to better his chances of remaining president. Atwood remembered that one acquaintance was so confident of Russell's reappointment with Laffoon's election, he told him, "R.B., you won't last very long after Laffoon's election. You'd better get in on the thieving as rapidly as possible, so you'll have something to show for your two years here."[20] Atwood did not consider misappropriating school funds or the suggestion to campaign for Laffoon. Instead Atwood believed his progressive administration would convince Laffoon, if he was elected, to retain him as president of Kentucky State.

The Republicans, of course, were campaigning for a member of their party to succeed Governor Flem Sampson. Success appeared highly unlikely as the state and the nation spun into a financial depression. The Republicans, however, nominated Louisville mayor William B. Harrison for governor. Harrison had strong support in the local black community. Moreover, the Colored Republican Campaign Committee, with state headquarters in Louisville, urged black voters to support Harrison. The Louisville *Leader*, a black publication, reminded voters that Harrison had appointed several blacks to serve as juvenile court officers, detectives, and uniformed police officers. The Democrats, observed the *Leader*, had attempted to disfranchise Kentucky's black voters and were responsible for passing a statewide jim crow railroad law. Furthermore, the Democrats did not entirely welcome black political participation. During a "Laffoon for governor" rally at Mercer Park in Hopkinsville, black participants were initially told to leave, but authorities eventually relented and permitted them to stay and share the leftover barbecue and festivities that had first been enjoyed by the all-white crowd. Despite opposition from the Louisville *Leader* and the Republican's best efforts, Laffoon, "a balding, limping, but amazingly resilient politician," easily won the election.[21]

It appeared that Atwood's administration was destined to be terminated. With this thought in mind, the *American Baptist*, a black religious publication out of Louisville, vehemently denounced the possibility of changing the administration at Kentucky State. In its November 27, 1931, edition the *American Baptist* noted that "this paper has always opposed the injection of politics into the management of the public school system and we see no reason for it being done now. All of the colleges established by the state for white students are not being troubled in that way." Consequently, the paper observed, "our people . . . should vigorously protest against the KNIC [Kentucky State] being disrupted by any change for political reasons in that institution."[22] Yet Russell remained so confident that he would soon be reappointed president of Kentucky State that he began having his mail addressed to president Atwood's office. He even served as one of the marshals in the governor's inaugural parade, leading the Frankfort Negro Democratic supporters.[23]

Despite Atwood's claim to eschew politics, he proved that he too had a few political strings to pull. On December 1, 1931, he wrote presidents McVey and Donovan for assistance in solving his problem with G.P. Russell. In both letters Atwood included the following paragraph:

My predecessor, Prof. G.P. Russell, entered the recent state campaign and made speeches for the winning ticket. It is not known to me what he plans to ask for as a reward, but as I have carefully avoided implicating in any way this educational institution in politics and as our record here has served to carry the school further forward in two years than my predecessor did in 18, I am requesting you to join us in taking steps to see that our administration here is not upset. I do not know what will be the attitude in this matter of the incoming state administration, but since rumors, reported as originating with Prof. Russell, are to the effect that we will be disturbed, I am requesting a few of our friends to intercede in our behalf. This intercession, in my judgement, should be with the new Governor and the new state superintendent.[24]

A week after receiving this letter, President McVey informed Atwood that he would do all he could to help resolve the problem in Atwood's favor. However, wrote McVey, "I shall have to deal with the matter in my own way."[25] Exactly what action McVey decided upon is unknown, but, as president of the state's largest white higher learning institution, any favorable action from him was definitely a plus for Atwood.

Donovan responded more directly to Atwood's letter. He informed Atwood he would discuss the matter with James Richmond, superintendent of public instruction. Donovan optimistically believed that Richmond would support Atwood "enthusiastically." After complimenting Atwood's performance at Kentucky State, Donovan added: "Politics should not be a consideration in the appointment of the President or anyone connected with your school. I will render you all the support I can, for I believe you are doing good work in the position you occupy."[26]

As the Laffoon administration settled down to business, Atwood found himself facing more serious challenges, obviously emanating from the Russell camp. Ben Johnson, chairman of the state highway commission and friend of Billy Klair, sent a letter to his son-in-law, newly elected state auditor, J. Dan Talbott, claiming that he had learned from an unnamed source that there was a duplication of salaries at Kentucky State and excessive expenditures of state funds. Johnson accused several Kentucky State faculty members of getting their salaries plus additional monies for teaching extension courses and summer school. Moreover, claimed Johnson, Atwood's wife was receiving a salary for teaching music at the college, which was against the school's nepotism policies. Atwood vehemently denied the charges. He argued that Johnson's information was "incorrect and incomplete."

Atwood strongly defended his faculty and the integrity of his administration in a letter to Talbott. The extension courses were started, noted Atwood, "in order to help colored teachers in public schools improve themselves and their teaching." State funds were not used to pay those who taught extension classes, declared Atwood. Instead their salaries came from the students who attended the extension classes. Atwood also explained that the salaries his teachers earned for teaching summer school, with the exception of agriculture and home economics, came from the fees collected from students attending the summer session rather than from tax dollars.

In defense of his wife, Atwood politely informed Talbott that she received no salary for teaching in the music department. She was a trained musician who wanted to continue polishing her skills. Since the school lacked funds to hire sufficient music teachers, she voluntarily offered trained assistance. "We do not know what we would have done in this department," wrote Atwood, "without the excellent service she has rendered the institution free of charge." Atwood also responded to Johnson's claims that members of the faculty were receiving the extravagant salaries of $150 to $275 a month. In defense of his teachers Atwood claimed that "even though our salaries may seem high they are not high enough to get the best rating possible from the Southern Association of Colleges. . . . There are a number of schools for colored people in the south that pay their colored teachers better salaries than we do," Atwood added.

Atwood refused to be intimidated by the political machinations that threatened his administration. He even invited the state auditor, J. Dan Talbott, to examine the school's records.[27] Despite his apparent confidence in his management, Atwood was not politically naive. He knew very well that he needed to expand his support among influential white leaders. He visited his family in Hickman to share his problem with his father. Although Pomp was a Republican, he had important connections in the white community. He contacted a few of the influential white Democrats in Fulton County and informed them of his son's burdensome situation.[28]

That western Kentucky was the stronghold of the Democratic party assured Pomp and Rufus reasonable white support in this political tug of war between two black men. Fulton County Circuit Court Judge W.J. McMurry and county attorney Elvis J. Stahr, Sr., knew Governor Laffoon and had attended his inauguration in December 1931. However, it was Judge McMurry, Sheriff Goalder Johnson, and an unidentified representative from Hickman who scheduled a meeting with the newly elected governor early in his administration. Tall, red-headed, and weighing close to two hundred and fifty pounds, Johnson was particularly well-known throughout Fulton County and western Kentucky. In 1910 he became the youngest man elected Fulton County sheriff. After serving four years in this capacity, Johnson was elected postmaster, a position he held for several years. In 1929 he was reelected sheriff of Fulton County, becoming the only man elected to two four-year terms to this office.[29]

The Hickman delegation strongly urged Laffoon to retain Atwood as the chief administrator of the Frankfort school. Cognizant of the support he had received in Hickman and the surrounding counties, Laffoon realized his visitors wielded legitimate political power, hence their concern could not be easily overlooked. Atwood attended the meeting between Laffoon and the three representatives from Hickman. He recalled that they insisted the governor retain him as president. According to Atwood's recollection, Sheriff Johnson exclaimed: "We don't know this Russell, but we do know R.B. He's Pomp Atwood's son, and they are Hickman people. There are no better colored people in the world than Hickman colored people." The meeting was successful, as Laffoon adhered to the request of the Hickman delegation.[30]

To be sure, Atwood endured this political storm because of the backing he received from black and white Kentuckians. Black Republicans abhorred Russell's leanings toward the Democratic party. The white delegation from Hickman supported him because he and his family were blacks who knew their place in relation to whites. Presidents Donovan and McVey probably supported Atwood because of the satisfactory work he was doing at Kentucky State and his willingness to acknowledge their influence on education in Kentucky.

After overcoming this political challenge and securing his position at Kentucky State for at least another four years, Atwood then concentrated on getting individuals appointed to the board of trustees who took their position seriously. Since the school's founding, the governor had reserved the right to appoint the three members to the board of trustees, who in turn selected the college's president. In May 1893 the General Assembly voted that board members had to be residents of Franklin County. This act allowed local politicians and businessmen to utilize their connection to the school as a means of fulfilling personal ambitions.[31]

In 1914, Clarence Timberlake, a graduate of the Kentucky Normal and Industrial Institute (Kentucky State) agricultural department and a messenger in the Department of Education, expressed vehement opposition to the 1893 act in a brief publication titled, "Politics and the Schools." Timberlake, who later became principal of several schools in western Kentucky, argued for a statewide board of regents rather than a board composed of local residents. "It is to be hoped that the State of Kentucky will open its eyes, shake off its lethargy and without further delay, expunge from the statutes this most childish and unprogressive law," wrote Timberlake.[32]

In March 1918 the General Assembly revised the law regarding the school's appointment of trustees to read that "no two appoint-ive members of said board shall be resident of any one county."[33] While Timberlake had led the struggle to achieve this statutory victory, the new act still did not prevent the school from being exploited by unscrupulous board members. Atwood recalled that very early in his administration there were board members who took advantage of the school and their position on the board. For instance, one board member, whom he did not name, operated a hardware store that sold the school outdated equipment. Another, Judge W.C. Hobbs of Lexington, submitted false expense accounts claiming he had spent the night before and after board meetings at the Capital Hotel in Frankfort, but he actually drove to the meet-ings on the day they were scheduled and returned to Lexington immediately afterward.[34] Atwood believed that in order to estab-lish Kentucky State as a viable higher learning institution he would need honest, dependable, trustworthy individuals serving on the board. He initially did not realize, however, that this objective would require him to venture further into the political circles he wanted to avoid.

When Governor Laffoon asked Atwood and Superintendent Richmond to recommend persons to serve on the board, Atwood submitted the names of Allen Prewitt, a Frankfort attorney, and Patrick Callahan, president of the Louisville Oil and Varnish Com-pany. Both men were Democrats, but Laffoon was skeptical about appointing Callahan to the board.

Callahan was Catholic and had been an active supporter of prohibition. During the 1928 presidential election, he had even campaigned against the Democratic candidate, Alfred Smith, who was also Catholic but an opponent of prohibition. Callahan's posi-tion on this issue had differed from that held by Billy Klair, who had supported the liquor interest during the 1920s. Klair had used his political power to get Laffoon elected in 1931; consequently, Laffoon was sensitive to their political expectations.[35]

Laffoon informed Atwood he would accept Callahan's appoint-ment on the approval of Michael "Mickey" Brennan, a saloon owner and political boss in Louisville. Atwood met Brennan and informed him that he would like to have Callahan appointed to the board of trustees. Brennan agreed to approve the appointment on the condition that Atwood give Chandler Morris, one of his "good colored men" who was out of work because of prohibition, a job at Kentucky State. That Callahan had served as vice-president of the

Kentucky Commission on Interracial Cooperation, supported the creation of the Louisville Urban League, and recommended the Catholic Press vehemently oppose lynching must have weighed heavily on Atwood's decision to agree to such an arrangement. Yet, as Callahan's biographer clearly argues, he "never advocated a complete end to segregation. His views of blacks were paternalistic but contrasted with the blatant racism of many other leaders in Louisville."[36]

On May 4, 1932, the Louisville *Courier Journal* casually reported that Governor Laffoon had appointed P.H. Callahan and Allen Prewitt to the Kentucky State board of trustees to replace Harry Martin and J.M. Perkins. Two days later, the board authorized Atwood and Chairman Richmond to employ a night watchman at the school, and subsequently Chancellor Morris was hired. Needless to say, few persons at that time knew of the political dealings that took place behind the scenes to make Callahan's appointment final and Morris' employment possible.[37] Yet the whole process had made Atwood more adept in his understanding of Kentucky politics. He came to realize that it was essential for him to utilize his connections with influential whites as well as blacks to protect his job and promote the growth of his school.

In 1936 blacks in large numbers switched their political allegiance from the Republican to the Democratic party. Nancy J. Weiss in her study, *Farewell to the Party of Lincoln*, notes that "blacks became Democrat in response to the economic benefits of the New Deal and that they voted for Franklin Roosevelt in spite of the New Deal's lack of a substantive record on race."[38]

As the depression worsened in Kentucky, blacks took advantage of the available New Deal programs. They participated in the Civilian Conservation Corps (CCC) and the National Youth Administration (NYA). The CCC established segregated camps in Morganfield and Russellville, while the NYA operated a program for unemployed black teenagers out of the Louisville Municipal College. Whereas the Works Progress Administration provided additional jobs, the Public Works Administration aided the physical improvements of black schools and other facilities. Gradually, black Kentuckians were among those who began to increase their support for the Democratic party.[39]

On February 12, 1935, close to three hundred black Democrats responded to a call by John T. Merrit of Frankfort to meet at the state capital. Black Democratic organizations from throughout the state sent at least one delegate to the meeting. According to an article in the Louisville *Leader*, the participants "declared themselves politically emancipated."[40] As Kentucky readied for another gubernatorial election the black vote was given serious consideration. During the 1935 campaign Lt. Governor "Happy" Chandler introduced the sound truck in order to promote his platform. His campaign promoters eventually asked Atwood to ride the truck into black neighborhoods to urge residents to vote for Chandler. Atwood was "tempted" to campaign for Chandler. Although he and Mabel were registered as Independents, it was during this period that they too began to align with the Democratic party. Still, Atwood, in trying to keep the school as free from politics as possible, side-stepped the chance to work for the party.

Realizing the possible ramifications if he firmly rejected Chandler, Atwood made up an excuse to explain why he could not participate. He informed Chandler's supporters that he had an "educational appointment" at Tuskegee Institute in Alabama on the date they needed him to campaign. He then called his former classmate at Iowa State, Fred Patterson, the president of Tuskegee, and told him he was coming for a visit and to verify his appointment if someone asked about it. The excuse worked, and it seemed Atwood had emerged politically unscathed.[41]

But, on June 3, 1936, Edward Oden, head of the Department of General Repair Work at Kentucky State, wrote a letter to Chandler claiming Atwood had endorsed Tom Rhea during the 1935 run-off election between the two men for the Democratic nomination. "President Atwood," wrote Oden, "bought five tickets to go on the train to Mr. Rhea's Campaign Opening." The tickets were distributed to members of Atwood's administrative staff. Oden noted that he, on the other hand, had always supported the governor and "hauled over a hundred and fifty people to vote for Chandler" during the main election. Oden said he was fired on December 13, 1935, shortly after the general election, and replaced by Langley A. Spurlock, whom he identified as one of the persons receiving a ticket from Atwood. Although Oden did not request that Chandler assist him in getting rehired, he did want the governor to know who his supporters were as well as the circumstances behind Spurlock's appointment.[42]

Despite Oden's apparent contention that he was fired for his political activities, his argument was weak. Had Atwood wanted to fire Oden because of his political preferences, he would most likely have done so immediately after the run-off election rather than wait until Chandler had won the general gubernatorial race. On December 18, 1935, Atwood informed the State Board of Education that Oden "drinks intoxicants while on the job and becomes almost violently aggressive at times in attempting to start trouble. On three occasions," reported Atwood, "he has been both disrespectful and insubordinate to my office and on two occasions, I have forgiven him."[43] For some unexplained reason Oden waited six months to register his complaint with the governor.

It is also worth noting that Kentucky State was being reorganized during the mid 1930s. Spurlock, who had formerly served as Atwood's secretary, was given the title superintendent of buildings and grounds. He had a B.S. degree in business administration, making him qualified to professionalize the maintenance department.

While Oden's accusation that he was fired for his politics is questionable, his discussion of Atwood's political interest in the Rhea campagn is believable. Rhea had the support of Ruby Laffoon while Chandler had the endorsement of Ben Johnson.[44] Given Atwood's disagreement with Johnson and the relationship he had established with Laffoon, Atwood most likely saw Rhea as the more favorable candidate. Whether Chandler ever discussed Oden's letter with Atwood is unknown, but if he did, Atwood no doubt explained to the governor that Oden was a disgruntled former employee seeking Chandler's influence in getting his job back.

For several years after the 1935 gubernatorial election, Atwood was successful in keeping Kentucky State clear of political campaigns, but he remained cautious all the while. In 1943, following the election of Republican governor Simeon Willis, Atwood wrote John W. Davis a brief memo which in the closing statements suggested that he was uneasy about his job. He wrote: "P.S. Have a complete new state administration down here—all is ok, so far."[45] Persumably, Willis exerted no political pressure on Atwood during his term as governor. However, during the state elections of 1947, W.H. Childress, a black Democratic candidate from Louisville seeking election as state representative from the 42nd Legislative District, claimed Atwood had allowed the black Republicans to hold a Lincoln Day dinner at Kentucky State. In a political speech in Louisville, Childress proclaimed: "We do not want President Atwood or the institution to sponsor any dinners for the Democrats or

Atwood at work in his office in 1948. Courtesy of Kentucky State
University Photographic Archives.

the Republicans. . . . Let the institution be absolutely free of politics."

O.M. Travis, a black member of the Republican State Central
Committee, along with G.F. Spencer, Jr., and J. Todd Simpson,
denounced Childress's charges. In a signed letter to the Louisville
Defender, the three men claimed: "President Atwood nor his institution sponsored or promoted no [*sic*] dinner whatsoever. He did
permit the use of the college dining hall by a group of citizens who
desired to celebrate the birthday of Abraham Lincoln. We attended
the dinner and we know that those invited and those present were
of both major political parties."[46] Atwood was particularly concerned that representatives of both parties attend the dinner. He
had probably agreed to schedule the dinner at the school since
segregation limited the public eating places in the state where
blacks could gather in significant number. Still, the controversy
presented no serious threat to his administration. The whole matter
subsided immediately after the state elections.

By the end of the 1940s, Atwood had less cause to worry about losing his job as a result of political interference. He was providing the school with stable, honest, and efficient leadership. With the exception of the period 1943-47, the Democrats controlled the governor's office during Atwood's tenure at Kentucky State. Consequently, he rarely faced having to confront a vengeful administration. That Atwood was from the western part of Kentucky, as were several of the governors he served under, assuredly worked in his favor. Newly elected governors realized the political clout Atwood had and did not want to risk losing it by removing him from office. Furthermore, in 1948 the General Assembly voted to repeal the state's 1934 Ouster Act, which had formerly allowed the governor to displace regents, professors, and state college presidents. The new law read that the "governor may remove officers, appointed by him, without cause, except in case of boards of state university and colleges."[47] Because Kentucky State was supervised by the State Board of Education during that time, the revised Act did not protect Atwood from being removed by the governor, but at least it established a less politically hostile climate for college presidents in Kentucky.

When Atwood retired as president he claimed he never made a speech or wrote a letter in favor of a political candidate during his presidency. This is not entirely true. Atwood had a subtle way of campaigning for his agenda for Kentucky State. As former governor Lawrence Wetherby recalled, Atwood was not a politician "as we recognize politicians," but "he was a great mixer with politicians. . . . He knew who to talk to and who to visit with to get something done."[48]

It was no secret that Atwood held significant influence in the black community. Adron Doran served in the General Assembly in the 1940s and early 1950s and observed that, politically, Atwood "had a pretty good underground railroad" as a result of his association with black leaders in Kentucky. "They were always sitting by to watch his motions and his signals." Moreover, recalled Doran, Atwood "was pretty adroit in getting the word out to his people as to how Kentucky State was [doing] and whether or not . . . candidates were taking a fair look at Kentucky State to support it." That a number of black professionals had graduated from Kentucky State worked in Atwood's favor; thus Atwood had an effective "network" to influence.[49]

Wetherby noted that Atwood "influence[d] several black people in Franklin County" to support his campaign for governor in 1951. Atwood simply suggested that black leaders meet with the then acting governor in order to get better acquainted with him. One of the persons who met with Wetherby upon Atwood's suggestion was Clarence Timberlake, then president of West Kentucky Industrial College. Timberlake was a very active Democrat in west Kentucky and no stranger to the governor's mansion since he had been a close acquaintance of Wetherby's Democratic predecessor, Earle Clements.[50]

By secretly endorsing politicians, Atwood eliminated the political hostilities that were sure to occur had he campaigned otherwise. However his efforts to get elected to the legislature whites who supported the social and economic interests of blacks as well as the financial well-being of Kentucky State were not as successful as he would have liked. For there were some white elected officials who used Atwood's ties to the black community to promote their own political agenda.

For example, on one occasion Governor Flem Sampson, while preparing his address to the state legislature, asked Atwood to write the paragraph relating to the status of black Kentuckians. Unsure of what to say himself, Atwood depended largely on the advice of several of his faculty in preparing the governor's request, a delegation of power that he had no doubt learned from his mentor, John W. Davis.

Atwood recalled that Lt. Governor Keen Johnson used his name when he announced his candidacy for governor to the state convention of black women's clubs in Richmond. Johnson informed the group that early in his administration he would seek to improve equal educational opportunities for blacks and that he would call in Atwood, with whom he was "very well acquainted," to advise him on his program for blacks. Atwood, however, had never even met Johnson.

Governor Earle Clements was another state official who at least once depended on Atwood's services. Clements was invited to speak to a national conference of the African Methodist Episcopal Zion Church in Louisville. He called Atwood for assistance in preparing his manuscript. Atwood called upon experts from his faculty to write the entire speech. According to Atwood, Clement's talk was so well received that one of the bishops even complimented him on his intimate knowledge of the AME Zion Church.

Governor "Happy" Chandler, who twice served as governor of

Kentucky during the Atwood administration, claimed to have respected Atwood, but he actually considered him, as well as all blacks, inferior. Like his contemporaries, Chandler endorsed segregated education during the 1930s. In 1938 the Louisville branch of the NAACP criticized the governor for informing Louisiana senator Allen J. Ellender that "there [was] no agitation amongst colored people of Kentucky for the anti-lynching bill."[51]

Despite their unbalanced relationship, Atwood established his closest ties to Chandler out of political expediency. Chandler was a skilled politician. Thus, both men developed a convenient partnership that served each's needs relatively well for that period. That their wives were both from Virginia sealed a long relationship between the two families. As late as May 1984, former governor Chandler wrote Mabel recalling Atwood's work at Kentucky State. "I deeply appreciate the tremendous contribution he made to Kentucky State University during the period of his presidency," said Chandler. "Mama Chandler and I always enjoyed your visits with us at the mansion."[52]

During Chandler's first administration from 1935 to 1939, Atwood considered him to be somewhat supportive of the needs of Kentucky State. On an occasion when the school needed emergency funds to meet expenses, Chandler responded favorably. Beginning in 1938, Kentucky State received the largest appropriation thus far in the school's history, one hundred ten thousand dollars, in addition to fifty thousand dollars in capital construction. The following year a women's dormitory was built on the campus and named for Mildred Chandler. According to Atwood, Mildred was also generous to the college. In fact, she once made available linen and silver from the governor's mansion to be used for a dinner party welcoming Alpha Kappa Alpha sorority to the campus.[53]

Atwood was a consummate politician and manipulator. He stroked the egos of white politicians by saying things they wanted to hear. In an April 8, 1938, letter to Chandler, Atwood wrote: "We want you to know, Governor, that we here are genuinely thankful for such a man as you as the chief executive of our state, and we think that such men as you are rare, and should be continued in the service of the people in whatever capacity to which you may aspire." Cognizant that Chandler held significant political power in Kentucky, Atwood believed he could improve Kentucky State with Chandler's financial backing.

Likewise, Chandler did not hesitate to call on Atwood for his cooperation when he deemed it necessary. When Chandler recommended black students for employment on the Kentucky State campus Atwood tried to fulfill his requests. During his second administration as governor in the late 1950s, Chandler met the national black leaders Atwood invited to the campus for speaking engagements, with intentions of securing political support from them. When civil rights attorney Thurgood Marshall spoke at commencement in 1959, Chandler was unable to attend, so he asked Atwood to bring Marshall to the governor's mansion so he could solicit the political friendship of the man who had argued the famous 1954 Brown decision.[54]

As Atwood fulfilled favors for influential whites such as Chandler, Johnson, Clements, and others, he gained their confidence and trust. Some of the governors even relied on his recommendations when appointing blacks to state offices. Although Atwood apparently never utilized his power enough to be considered a political boss, he was definitely plugged into the powers that be. Rather than exploit his position solely for political gain, Atwood preferred to spend his energy building Kentucky State. The educational organizations he joined and the various important leaders he met enhanced Atwood's vision for improving Kentucky State while simultaneously expanding the school's visibility in black higher education.

5
Beyond the Campus

"I have always operated on the philosophy," proclaimed President Atwood to the Kentucky State freshman class of 1945, "that the real reason for the existence of schools and colleges is the welfare of boys and girls so that they in turn will be enabled to serve the welfare of society."[1] Yet, while Atwood promoted this philosophy, he was cognizant of the barriers black students would face upon graduation. Their skills would have to be exceptionally polished in order for them to contribute to society at large. Because of this reality, Atwood was disturbed about the preferential treatment given to white schools. He wanted black students to have an equal chance of receiving a quality education.

During the course of his career, Atwood wrote more than a dozen articles on issues relating to black education and equal treatment for blacks in general. One third of his publications dealt with the black land grant college, which Atwood believed had been a major force in education. "They emphasized vocational education, provided instruction in the liberal arts, and extended academic opportunities to the masses instead of the classes," stated Atwood in one of his many speeches.[2]

Atwood's promotion of black land grant colleges is not surprising since he specialized in agricultural education and was the president of a black land grant institution. He believed black land grant colleges needed to develop programs to meet the changing needs of American society, especially following World War II. In a July 1942 article published in the *Journal of Negro Education*, Atwood suggested that black land grant insititutions teach black farmers how to operate and maintain farm machinery and encourage them to organize cooperatives for purchasing and using such equipment. He also noted these colleges should establish courses that prepared students for modern industrial work in communications and transportation. Corporations and the government, according to Atwood, would need qualified individuals to fill these kinds of jobs.[3]

While his advice had merit, Atwood's faith in the agricultural industry was not shared by most blacks. During the 1930s and 1940s thousands of blacks abandoned farming and the rural South and migrated to urban communities. According to historian Harvard Sitkoff, "the AAA [Agricultural Adjustment Act] did nothing to lift the Afro-American from the lowest rungs on the agricultural ladder or to insist that black farmers be treated equally with whites." In Kentucky the number of black male and female farmers declined significantly within a ten-year period. According to the U.S. Census, there were 22,598 black farmers in the state in 1930 and less than half this number by 1940. Moreover, the percentage of the state's black population had dropped from 8.6 to 7.5 percent.[4] Atwood simply overlooked this change because of his appreciation of farm life and his ties to Kentucky, a rural state. He did not relinquish his interest in agricultural education until enrollments in the program at Kentucky State began to decline after World War II.

Atwood did indicate that schools like the one he headed needed to offer a broad curriculum. He observed that "the Negro land grant colleges must not concern themselves solely with vocational pursuits. Occupational competence, as important as it is, should not be the only function of education." In particular, Atwood observed that business courses that addressed the needs of the African-American community were important because they would teach African-Americans how to avoid operational and financial mistakes. "When the Negro concerns grow sufficiently large and numerous to give employment to large numbers of Negroes," proclaimed Atwood, "much of the fear that blackens Negro life will disappear. More and more Negroes will have employment at work in which they can take pride and find happiness."[5]

The task of promoting the education of African-Americans on his campus and beyond was difficult, but Atwood met the challenge and did what he thought was right for African-Americans in Kentucky and the nation. He became involved with African-American state and national educational organizations immediately after he took over as president of Kentucky State. As an active participant in these groups, Atwood remained steadfast in pressing state and federal officials to improve the curriculum, quality of instruction, and facilities available in African-American learning institutions. His commitment to advance black education is unquestionable, considering the influential positions he held in several leading African-American educational organizations.

During his presidency, Atwood promoted black education by providing distinguished service to several educational committees and organizations. He was president of the Association of Colleges and Secondary Schools for Negroes in 1940-41. He was one of the founders of the all-black Mid-Western Athletic Association, an organization he presided over for nine years (1940-49).[6] Atwood gave the Conference of Presidents of Negro Land Grant Colleges and the Kentucky Negro Education Association the most significant attention, however.

The Conference of Presidents of Negro Land Grant Colleges was an organization that included the chief administrators of the seventeen black land grant institutions. These men represented black land grant colleges from Alabama, Arkansas, Delaware, Florida, Georgia, Kentucky, Louisiana, Maryland, Mississippi, Missouri, North Carolina, Oklahoma, South Carolina, Tennessee, Texas, West Virginia, and Virgina. Seven black higher institutions were awarded associate memberships: Atlanta University, Atlanta, Georgia; Central State College, Wilberforce, Ohio; Hampton Institute, Hampton, Virginia; Howard University, Washington, D.C.; Savannah State College, Savannah, Georgia; Texas Southern University, Houston, Texas; and Tuskegee Institute, Tuskegee, Alabama.[7]

The conference was an invaluable organization to black educators. It gave them an opportunity to address educational problems affecting black private colleges and state land grant colleges and also advanced collegiality among black college presidents, who shared common objectives and experiences in their role as leaders of the nation's African-American higher learning institutions. At conference meetings they could exchange ideas and solutions to similar problems. They could analyze and evaluate the work at their respective schools by listening to presentations on activities being initiated on other campuses. The mere existence of this type of organization was a major contribution to African-American education.[8] The positive actions that emerged because of it simply accentuated its effectiveness.

The founding of the conference began with informal meetings of presidents of black land grant colleges. These meetings were at times scheduled in the same city as those of the Association of Land Grant Colleges and State Universities, a group that was all white. Though some of the black land grant college presidents were invited to selected sessions of the white association's meetings, black presidents as a group were not allowed full membership until the mid-1950s.

In January 1923, black land grant college presidents had formed a permanent organization while meeting at Tuskegee Institute for the Southern Conference on Education in Negro Land Grant Colleges. At this gathering, the Committee on Organization and Policy recommended establishing an Association of Negro Land Grant Colleges. This Association was to include the chief administrators of black land grant colleges and the officials or representatives from departments of the federal government. In 1924 the Association of Negro Land Grant Colleges changed its name to the Conference of Presidents of Negro Land Grant Colleges. The group agreed to meet annually and hence began working toward definite plans of action.[9]

Atwood's association with the conference began while he was director of agriculture at Prairie View State College. In April 1925, the president of the college, W.R. Banks, was unable to attend the conference meeting and sent Atwood to represent the school. Being twenty-eight years of age, the young Atwood was impressed with the gentlemen he became acquainted with at the meeting. The feelings must have been mutual as Atwood was appointed secretary of the Committee on Resolutions. When the committee met and failed to make any definite suggestions, the chairman delegated Atwood the responsibility of writing the report. After spending several hours in a quiet room, Atwood returned to the committee with a report that met with the satisfaction of the members.[10]

In November 1929, the Conference of Presidents met at the Wabash Avenue YMCA in Chicago, Illinois. Here Atwood began his long and distinguished affiliation with the group. He became one of its most influential leaders, serving as president for one year (1938-39) and secretary for more than twenty years (1931-55). Atwood also served on various committees including the Executive Committee, Committee on Findings, Nomination Committee, Investigation of Federal Funds Committee, and the Committee on Agricultural Extension Services among Negroes. On occasion he made presentations at conference meetings that suggested ways land grant colleges could improve their contribution to black education.

At the 1935 meeting Atwood spoke on "Agriculture in the Negro Land Grant College." Atwood suggested that students, regardless of their discipline, should receive a well-rounded education. Early in his paper he made clear that training should encourage students to appreciate racial heritage; to develop a

Christian philosophy of life, to achieve scholastic excellence, and to maintain good personal health, among other things. Beyond these observations, Atwood made several suggestions for black land grant colleges. He recommended they provide a general course that dealt briefly with field crops, dairying, plant diseases, rural sociology, farm economics, and animal husbandry while concentrating on the practical skills associated with farming. To satisfy students interested in teaching agriculture, he favored adding professional courses to the curriculum.[11]

Yet Atwood was concerned with improving other conditions associated within the black land grant college. During the 1937 conference meeting, Atwood discussed the inadequate financial attention being given to the cooperative extension programs in black land grant institutions. In his "Report of Study on the Organization and Administration of Creative Extension Work among Negroes with a Recommendation," Atwood found, not suprisingly, that the extension program was administered by whites with little input from blacks. He discovered in his research that in states with segregated institutions the legislature would delegate the responsibility of administering the cooperative extension program to the white land grant colleges. Consequently, white schools, with a few exceptions, were awarded a greater amount of state and federal funds than those designated for blacks. This situation allowed white educators to control the agricultural curriculum of black schools and impede their ability to progress, and it kept blacks dependent on whites for financial assistance and leadership in the field.

Because of the disparity of funds between black and white schools, Atwood believed black land grant colleges should be permitted to administer the cooperative extension program for blacks. He added that this could be done in cooperation with a white land grant college and under the supervision of the federal government. To reach this objective, Atwood urged the conference to submit ideas to the United States secretary of agriculture, who supervised the extension program, in order to get black schools more involved in this educational arrangement. Atwood further proposed that the secretary of agriculture make participation of black schools in these programs a prerequisite for states with segregated schools. "In offering this recommendation," Atwood claimed, "it is believed, it is not done in a spirit of discontentment and fault-finding criticism, but rather a calm, sober analysis of the actual situation."[12]

Conference members expressed significant interest in Atwood's findings and recommendations.[13] They recognized the need to provide extension funds proportionately to black schools and appointed Atwood to explore ways of eliminating the financial disparities they faced. As chairman of the conference's Committee on Federal Funds, Atwood met with the Executive Committee of the Negro Newspaper Publications Association in an effort to begin solving this problem.

On January 18, 1946, the group met in St. Louis, Missouri. There Atwood discussed the uneven distribution of funds allocated to black land grant colleges for agricultural experiment stations and cooperative agricultural extension work. Cooperative agricultural extension work would allow faculties in agriculture to conduct research in order to develop their skills. Following that meeting, Atwood disclosed in "A Confidential Report" addressed to the Committee on Federal Funds that the black publishers agreed to study the situation in more detail and to use their organization to "press" for improvement. Atwood added that he and the black publishers believed however that the conference was "not in a position to press this matter as virulently as theirs." Thus, continued Atwood, "they will take the 'front' in the matter with our moral and research support in the background."[14]

Atwood joined the executive committee of black publishers when they later met with the United States secretary of agriculture, Clinton P. Anderson, to discuss the inequitable distribution of federal funds to black land grant colleges. Although the meeting did not improve the handling of funds for extension service and experiment stations, Atwood regarded the group's effort as a success. Because of this meeting, he claimed later that land grant colleges and universities in the South administering the funds were "more careful in the distribution of them, and how they were expended, and how the services were carried on as among white and negro farmers."[15] However the difference in treatment Atwood witnessed was likely the result of increased pressure from the Supreme Court mandating that southern states grant black higher learning institutions equal facilities and the increasing importance of the black vote in national elections.

President Truman came to realize how important the black vote was during his first term in office. Upon becoming president in 1945, Truman favored the abolition of the poll tax and supported the existence of the Fair Employment Practices Commission. He appointed the President's Committee On Civil Rights in December

1946. The following October the committee's report, titled *To Secure These Rights*, was published recommending the government work to end racial discrimination.[16]

During the late 1940s the conference members took advantage of the federal government's maturing interest in civil rights legislation and presented their concerns to President Truman. The executive committee, which included Atwood, chairman John W. Davis, and conference president Sherman Shruggs, prepared a statement for the president to consider. It highlighted the aspects of black land grant colleges that needed improvement in order to offer a better education to future black generations. Their statement suggested the government assist black land grant institutions by organizing research and making experiment stations more accessible, by extending greater support for their physical expansion, by activating more ROTC units, and by fostering adult education programs that increased the personnel and support given to cooperative agricultural and home economics work.

On October 22, 1946, the executive committee and members of the conference met with President Truman at the White House to present him with the statement regarding their interests.[17] Truman assured the delegation he was concerned about the institutions they represented and would consider their suggestions. The most important aspect of this meeting was probably the national exposure it provided black college presidents. These men had long been involved in the effort to promote black education, yet they had not as a group received much national attention for their efforts until the meeting with Truman.

While equitable distribution of federal funds to black schools was a major concern of the conference, it was not the only concern the black educators addressed. Throughout its existence the conference conducted various programs to benefit members and their schools. Several activities were devoted to vocational opportunities, yet on one occasion the conference sponsored a three-day program with the National Negro Business League on developing black businesses. Additional early activities of the conference were revealed in the Committee on Findings reports during the late 1930s. Based on results of surveys conducted by subcommittees, the Committee on Findings promoted the need to establish programs that addressed health problems and consumer education and the need to provide information on government services such as agricultural cooperatives and farm credit associations.[18]

During the 1940s the conference sponsored a Social Studies Project organized to uplift the general conditions of African-Americans. The project was conceived and launched by the black scholar W.E.B. Du Bois and later coordinated at Howard University through sociologist E. Franklin Frazier. The study involved a cooperative effort among the faculty of black colleges to study the social and economic conditions of African-Americans during and after World War II. The project struggled to yield significant information because most of those who taught social science courses at black land grant institutions did not have the experience needed to carry out the proper investigations.[19] The Social Studies Project, however, was one of the largest programs sponsored by the conference during its existence.

Although the conference offered various programs, members wanted eventually to merge with the all-white Association of Land Grant Colleges and State Universities. Conference members believed they would have to become a part of that organization in order to receive equal treatment. On November 8-9, 1953, the Executive Committee of the conference was invited to Columbus, Ohio, to meet with the association's Committee on Cooperation with Negro Land Grant Institutions. Prior to this meeting the conference's Executive Committee agreed that if the association wanted to establish cooperation between black and white land grant colleges, they should invite black schools to become members of their organization. Members believed they had a right to be affiliated with the all-white group since they also headed land grant colleges. Atwood was appointed by the Executive Committee to serve as its spokesman during the meeting.

The exact date Atwood and two other members from the conference met with the association's Committee on Cooperation with Negro Land Grant Institutions was not made clear in the conference minutes, but following that meeting Atwood and representatives of the conference were invited to meet with the association's Senate so he could make a statement to that official committee. During this meeting on November 10, 1953, Atwood made a presentation that highlighted the advantages of merging the two groups. He claimed it would improve programs in black land grant colleges, promote democratic ideals, contribute to professional growth, strengthen education, create opportunities to develop intercultural values, and eliminate the need to duplicate the promotion of land grant programs. Furthermore, Atwood noted, "the Association of

Land Grant Colleges and Universities [was] the only national educational organization of its class and status which [did] not have Negro Membership."[20]

Following Atwood's remarks the Senate voted to refer the conference's request to the association's Executive Committee. On November 16, 1954, the Executive Committee recommended to the Senate that black land grant colleges be invited to join their organization. Within the next year all seventeen black land grant colleges accepted the invitation, and the conference members agreed to dissolve their organization as of December 31, 1955.[21]

Although the merger of the conference and the association was inevitable because of the Supreme Court's 1954 decision to outlaw segregation in education, Atwood was praised highly for the role he played in integrating the two groups. Fellow conference president E.B. Evans of Prairie View sent Atwood a complimentary letter on the matter. Evans wrote:

I always believe in giving credit to those persons who deserve it. I believe further that the statement which resulted in our being accepted was made by you at the opening session of the two committees that met in the basement of the hotel in Columbus when you said we did not come to discuss cooperation between the two organizations but we came seeking membership. Your statement struck at the very heart of the situation and was the turning point in the whole affair. Then when you went back to the executive meeting to make a final statement, that clinched our situation. I want to commend you and shall see that you are given due credit whenever and wherever I can.[22]

Clearly, Atwood contributed greatly to the Conference of Presidents of Negro Land Grant Colleges in all respects. He had served as one of the group's most dependable and hardworking members. John W. Davis claimed that Atwood was an effective leader because of his "training, character, acceptability to people; ability to think, plan and execute; travel; keen understanding of people; and common sense."[23] His work with the conference was significant in promoting the concern of black land grant colleges, but while Atwood contributed much to the conference he received even more in return as a result of his association with it.

His relationship with the other black heads of colleges enabled him to enhance his reputation as a respected college administrator. As a member of the conference, Atwood was situated in a social and professional atmosphere where he could learn from his contemporaries such as Davis. Atwood's association with President John H. Clark of Southern University in Louisiana taught him that governors were at times more responsive to black schools in private than in public. According to President Clark, Governor Huey Long approved all of Southern's budget requests and suggested that he disregard the racist talk he heard. "This helped me," noted Atwood, "in later dealings with men of high positions. . . . For I learned that what a man says in public can be very different from what he will do in private."

The most significant lesson Atwood learned through his work with the conference was the "power of patience." According to Atwood, "this was the technique used by the men of that day. . . . To do what you could, when you could, and wait for better things." Over the years this was the strategy Atwood depended on to improve black education in Kentucky.[24] Yet, ironically, the "technique" served to advance Atwood's stature in the white community more rapidly than it did the progress of black education. Whites were attracted to Atwood's style of leadership because it was not forceful. He accepted their slow and inadequate response to racial issues; meanwhile the education of black children received scant attention.

Despite Atwood's questionable style of leadership, his effort to promote black education in Kentucky was just as earnest as it was on the national level. Upon assuming the presidency of Kentucky State he joined the Kentucky Negro Education Association (KNEA) and shared his ideas and experiences with that organization. He participated in its programs and wrote articles in the KNEA Journal, worked on the legislative committee, and served two years as the organization's president. Each of these activities carried much responsiblity considering the influence the KNEA had in directing black education in the state.

Similar to that of other southern states, Kentucky's general association of black teachers had been organized during the last quarter of the nineteenth century. The KNEA was originally founded as the State Association of Colored Teachers in 1877. Besides launching the movement to establish what became Kentucky State College, the body held annual meetings and discussed various topics related to education. Corporal punishment, industrial training, and ways of creating educational enthusiasm were a few of the topics discussed in the early meetings.[25]

During the early twentieth century the association was reorgan-

Members of the Kentucky Negro Education Association in 1949.
Courtesy of Kentucky State University Photographic Archives.

ized and its name changed to KNEA. The organization sponsored a range of activities for students, including essay writing and spelling contests and industrial and fine arts exhibits as well as musicals, art exhibits, and presentations focusing on educational issues. The KNEA's influence was best reflected, however, in its total membership, which was almost fifteen hundred by 1930.[26] As the representative body of Kentucky's black teachers it was an important lobbying group for education issues.

Rufus Atwood was first introduced to members of the KNEA during their general session on April 16, 1930. The following day, "the KNEA by a special vote, pledged loyalty and cooperation to the educational policies" advocated by the new Kentucky State president.[27] This early expression of support was not surprising considering Kentucky State's depressed condition when Atwood arrived at the school in 1929. Many of the KNEA members were graduates of the college and desired improvements for their alma mater. They liked Atwood—a young, experienced, hardworking administrator, who appeared to have the necessary qualifications to lead the school on a productive path.

Atwood's credibility as an able black educator increased as Kentucky State began to make noticeable progressive changes. By 1933 he had garnered enough support to be considered for the presidency of the KNEA. This was a position he, along with many others, wanted badly. In past presidential elections, supporters of particular candidates for the office had actually paid membership fees to individuals in order to secure their vote. That the president of the KNEA provided leadership on matters pertaining to all levels of education was alluring to potential candidates. Being president of the KNEA was one of the few influential statewide positions available to black Kentuckians. "It meant prestige and status to be its head," recalled Atwood. "I wanted it and my faculty wanted to help me get elected."[28]

Atwood easily won the election, defeating his opponent, W.J. Callery, a principal from Bourbon County, by a vote of 353 to 151. According to the Louisville *Independent News*, four factors worked to Atwood's advantage. He demonstrated an understanding of rural problems; a number of rural teachers were unable to attend the meeting and vote because their salaries had been cut; some of Callery's supporters switched alliances and supported Atwood; and, finally, nominating speeches were disallowed on the eve of the election. More important, the reporter made clear, Atwood's previous educational work convinced skeptics of his "common sense, manliness and sympathy, the capacity and character, the prestige and standing to guide the educational destinies of Kentucky Negroes."[29]

Atwood did not leave a lasting impression on the history and educational contributions of the KNEA. He did not create any new programs or sucessfully spearhead a movement to bring about the equality of black education in Kentucky. He did, however, during his presidency (1933-35), "vigorously" pursue the duties of the KNEA. His administration was devoted to providing school transportation for students residing in isolated areas, extending agricultural services to black farmers, coordinating the curriculum of the state's higher institutions, adopting a state minimum salary schedule, and equalizing opportunities available in graded school districts.

During his presidency of the KNEA Atwood also chaired the Special Committee on Negro Schools in Kentucky. Based on recommendations from this committee and from Governor Ruby Laffoon's Education Commission, the state legislature passed a school code in 1934. This school code gave legal recognition to two kinds of districts, independent and county, thus eliminating board systems for blacks and whites; it provided that each school district pay

Former presidents of the Kentucky Negro Education Association, photographed in 1940. Courtesy of Kentucky State University Photographic Archives.

teachers on a salary schedule that considered experience and training; and it created a new state board of education that had control over Kentucky State and Western Kentucky Industrial College (WKIC). These measures generated optimism among the state's black educators. In a letter to Kentucky's black teachers Atwood wrote: "The 1934 General Assembly has written into the organic laws of the state a code that is progressive and that furnishes the foundation upon which the state can build a public educational system. Prepared by men of the teaching profession, and other citizens interested in the schools, the new school code is fair to all groups and is destined to lift education in Kentucky out of the lowly rank of 42nd place and place her among the leading states of the Union."[30]

Despite Atwood's optimism over the school code, blacks continued to receive inadequate funding. Differences in salaries paid black and white teachers remained a problem in Kentucky for the remainder of the 1930s. Meanwhile Atwood's influence in the KNEA continued to increase. According to Lyman Johnson, "Atwood was a key figure in managing the KNEA. . . . The fact that he was president of Kentucky State College gave him quite a bit of influence over the graduates from his school, and many of the graduates from his school became teachers throughout the state and so therefore the alumni went along with their president. They were practically his emissaries all over the state."[31]

While Atwood had his share of supporters in the KNEA, a significant number of persons disagreed with his proposals. For instance in late 1937 and early 1938 the KNEA became involved in the controversial statewide issue of closing Western Kentucky Industrial College and merging it with Kentucky State. Governor Chandler, in an effort to reorganize state government and revamp Kentucky's fiscal standing, decided that it would be in the best interest of black higher education to merge the two schools. Atwood supported the governor but the proposal was a volatile issue among members of the KNEA, many of whom opposed Atwood's position on the matter.

Chandler's plan to close WKIC was not the first time the state had considered the idea. The Efficiency Commission of Kentucky, organized by the 1922 General Assembly to examine the cost, function, and structure of state government, had made a similar proposal. In a 1924 report, the commission cited poor facilities, inadequate instruction, and the large number of blacks living in central Kentucky as reasons to reconsider whether WKIC should remain open. The commission recommended that Kentucky State "be strengthened and enlarged, and that Western Kentucky Industrial be abandoned."[32] No action was taken on the commission's suggestions. Meanwhile conditions at WKIC did not improve.

In 1932, Dennis Anderson, president of WKIC, was removed by the state as manager of the school's financial affairs. Warren Vanhoose, assistant inspector and examiner for Kentucky, reported that the school had outstanding debts several years old. He also disclosed that Anderson had not been keeping the school's funds in the bank, but instead had commingled his personal money with that of the college. In 1936 Anderson experienced additional problems when students of WKIC went on strike because he resided in the girls dormitory. The strike was just another indication that definite changes were needed at WKIC.[33]

In 1937, Harvey Clarence Russell, Sr., replaced Anderson as president of WKIC. A graduate of Simmons University in Louisville and the University of Cincinnati, Russell had served as dean at Kentucky State. His experience there enabled him to launch significant administrative reforms at WKIC.[34] But, as Russell worked to build WKIC, the school's future was once again reconsidered.

On October 27, 1937, Atwood wrote a "confidential" letter to Governor Chandler informing him that "confidential information" on his decision to merge WKIC and Kentucky State had been obtained through J. Howard Henderson, a reporter with the Louisville *Courier-Journal*. He proceeded to inform the governor that he believed the merger would be in the best interest of black higher education in Kentucky. Atwood said that WKIC had a smaller student enrollment yet it received twice as much money per student as Kentucky State. According to Atwood, "One state institution, if given the annual support now given to the two colleges, and additional buildings, can adequately serve the needs of the Negro population with less cost, and less waste."[35]

One month later Atwood reiterated his argument to Chandler in a detailed discussion of black higher education in Kentucky. In this seven-and-a-half-page paper, Atwood reminded the governor that the Efficiency Commission had suggested the Paducah school (WKIC) be closed in the 1920s. He used statistical tables to show that more than half of the black population lived closer to Frankfort than Paducah; and the former was centrally located to more black high schools thus it was more accessible to students.[36]

Being the politician that he was, Atwood offered Chandler sound arguments to justify the decision to close WKIC before his contemporaries knew anything about the matter. Atwood pursued this matter so aggressively because he was worried about improving the standing of Kentucky State. In 1936, Louisville Municipal College (LMC), supervised by the University of Louisville's administrators, received an "A" rating from the SACSS. Kentucky State then became the only college in the state, black or white, besides WKIC, that did not hold a similar rating. Consequently, Atwood feared he might lose potential students to the Louisville school. Atwood, therefore, desperately needed more funds in order to maintain the growth and development of Kentucky State.[37]

Governor Chandler was aware of Atwood's concern for more funds and evidently did not want to see the state's black institution (Kentucky State) outranked by the city-sponsored LMC. During the 1937 academic year Chandler had allocated ten thousand dollars from his emergency fund to Kentucky State. He had also received a request from Atwood that this amount be increased to twenty-five thousand dollars for the fiscal year ending June 30, 1938. It would take fifteen thousand dollars of this money to raise Kentucky State to an "A" rating, according to Atwood in an earlier letter to the governor. Hence long before Chandler's announcement to merge WKIC and Kentucky State, Atwood was also prodding the governor to do more financially for his school.[38]

Not until December 1937 did Governor Chandler meet with a group of Kentucky's black civic and educational leaders. The black delegation included Atwood, M.J. Sleet, E.E. Underwood, J.B. Caulder, Luther Stewart, Earl Pruit, and J.A.C. Lattimore. Originally they had intended to ask for larger appropriations for the state's two black institutions of higher learning. However, during their discussions with Chandler, the governor mentioned that he was contemplating the idea of merging WKIC's liberal arts program with that of Kentucky State. Not surprisingly, Sleet, who was the business manager at WKIC, was the only member of the group meeting with Chandler who disapproved the idea.[39] Shortly after meeting with the black delegation Chandler received a letter from representatives of the KNEA urging him to develop WKIC into an industrial school rather than close it down.[40]

The decision as to whether to merge WKIC with Kentucky State erupted into a serious debate among members of the KNEA. On December 18, 1937, the KNEA board of directors held a lengthy discussion on the subject. KNEA president, W.H. Fouse, invited Atwood to attend this meeting. Atwood met with the group and informed them of his support for the merger. He received strong opposition from the chairman of the KNEA's Legislative Committee, A.E. Meyzeek, who believed the merger would reduce educational opportunities for blacks living in western Kentucky. The board of directors decided to obtain the opinions of other members of the association before making a decision. A questionnaire was mailed to members in order to provide them with an opportunity to express their views.[41]

Sharing the KNEA's concern over this issue was Representative Charles W. Anderson, Jr., a Republican and the first black to be elected to the Kentucky legislature. A representative of the 58th District in Louisville, Anderson had been asked by Chandler to submit the bill to merge the schools in the General Assembly. Cognizant of the controversial debate which surrounded this issue, Anderson decided to hold a public forum on the proposed merger in Louisville on January 2, 1938. Those who attended the meeting voted overwhelmingly against the merger.[42]

In response to the Louisville meeting, Atwood wrote Governor Chandler criticizing the gathering. Atwood claimed that he was "reliably informed that the Louisville meeting of Negroes opposing the merger was packed with Paducah people and disgruntled Republicans who oppose any worthwhile thing being done for Negroes by a Democratic administration. D.H. Anderson attended the meeting," continued Atwood, "and was paying 'key people' to oppose the merger." Atwood claimed he "refrained from such procedure" even though supporters of the merger suggested he do likewise. Atwood concluded his letter to Chandler by encouraging him to merge the schools. "I hope you will go right ahead, as I know Negroes and in a year's time they will be in favor of the one strong school."[43] Whether Atwood was reporting the truth to the governor about the events in Louisville is unknown since he had a vested interest in the outcome of the issue.

The January-February 1938 edition of the KNEA *Journal* printed the views of Atwood, Fouse, and Meyzeek. In his article President Fouse stated that WKIC's new president, Harvey Russell, should be given an opportunity to institute his program before the state merged it with Kentucky State. He also argued that the merger would deny students in western Kentucky an opportunity to experience the spiritual, cultural, and social values of college life. Furthermore, Fouse highlighted the indefinite terms of the proposed merger. Would Kentucky State have departments of journalism, dentistry, and law? Like Fouse, Meyzeek was also concerned about the educational opportunities available to black students in western Kentucky. He argued that other southern states such as Alabama, North Carolina, and Louisiana provided funds to more than one institution; Kentucky could likewise support two black institutions.

Atwood, for his part, continued to argue that merging the institutions was best for black higher education in the state. "I am convinced," wrote Atwood, "that two good colleges cannot be operated on the amount of money which the Negro race has a just right to expect the state legislature to appropriate." According to Atwood, blacks had a right to expect appropriations for higher education in proportion to their population. Kentucky's black population was declining, and that would mean fewer dollars for their schools. According to Atwood, black institutions in the 1937-38 school year should have received $154,000, yet the state legislature allotted them only $135,000. In clarifying his argument Atwood stated: "Colleges are good institutions to have. I wish we could have one in every community but we must take into consideration the numbers to serve and the amount of support to be expected."

Atwood firmly believed that consolidating the schools would enable Kentucky State to develop more rapidly since it would receive the funds otherwise allocated to WKIC.[44]

As blacks expressed disagreement over Chandler's idea to close WKIC, Charles Anderson and legislators from west Kentucky worked to compromise the matter. In accordance with the governor's proposal, they introduced a bill to close WKIC on June 30, 1938, but it would reopen the following day as a vocational school for blacks. The liberal arts program of WKIC would be merged with that of Kentucky State. On April 20, 1938, Governor Chandler approved the bill and the controversy surrounding WKIC and Kentucky State was finally resolved.[45]

Atwood assumed that the results of the controversy would assure Kentucky State of a significant increase in funding. But it did not. Atwood continued to face financial difficulties in his effort to build a quality institution. But, in spite of the challenges he confronted, Atwood handled each problem with the same unwavering persistence he demonstrated while promoting black education outside the state of Kentucky.

6
Difficult Days

"To be president of a college and white is no bed of roses. To be president of a college and black is almost a bed of thorns," wrote Benjamin Mays.[1] Mays's testimony described Atwood's presidency. For thirty-three years Atwood struggled to better conditions at Kentucky State College. He faced racism, politics, and insufficient financial support. As each year passed, the burdens of the job became heavier and more frustrating to overcome.

In 1940 the General Assembly granted Kentucky State $110,000 for annual "ordinary recurring expenses for operation." This amount was less than half of what was given to each of the five white state higher learning institutions. This situation was made worse by news that revealed the school had in the past overspent its appropriation by $18,895. According to state auditor David Logan, the problem resulted from the "carelessness" of the school's bookkeeper, Ben Finch. Finch had failed to pay bills incurred between the fiscal years 1937 and 1940. Logan's report to Democratic governor Keen Johnson did not suggest that someone at the institution had stolen funds from the school's account. Instead Logan found that the bills resulted from "emergency purchases" made by the college that were not reported to the State Finance Department.

Rather than "censure" Atwood and the State Board of Education, Logan applauded their efforts to make Kentucky State an accredited institution. He did note, however, that it was imperative for the school to have an experienced business manager in order to avoid future problems. Atwood did not accept the incident lightly. As soon as the problem was known Atwood fired Finch as the college's bookkeeper. In addition, he met with Governor Johnson to discuss the situation and to offer his resignation. Johnson investigated the incident and decided Atwood's resignation was unnecessary. In referring to the ordeal Johnson stated: "It's a condition that used to be common some years ago in a number of state agencies." Moreover, Johnson suggested that those with unsettled accounts sue the bondsmen of the individuals linked to the problem.[2]

Atwood's decision to submit his resignation was surprising considering his laborious effort to build up Kentucky State. But Atwood did not want to encounter any political pressure from whites who might have tried to use the situation to threaten his position as president. Thus, instead of allowing the governor or other state officials to use him for their own political objectives, Atwood wisely made the first move, an action designed to offset the agenda of those who may have opposed his administration. Fortunately for Atwood, it paid off, and he was not forced to leave office. But, being the shrewd politician that he was, Atwood had figured the situation would be resolved in his favor anyway.

However, Atwood remained concerned about the college's financial reputation and paid the bills from the school's account. A new business manager was hired and all the school's purchases were conducted through the state purchasing division. The new arrangement improved the financial record of Kentucky State. In September 1941, State Auditor David Logan reported that the college had a $17,611 cash balance on hand at the close of the June 30 fiscal year.[3] Although the 1940 deficit problem was resolved with little difficulty, it was just the beginning of several other problems Atwood encountered while trying to expand the offerings at Kentucky State.

During the Second World War the college was unable to obtain the federal government's support in gaining permission to establish courses that would prepare students for wartime jobs. The government did not support the college's request for permission to organize an Army Reserve Officer Training Corps Program (ROTC), and when the administration submitted applications to establish welding courses the government claimed such courses were unnecessary since industrialists did not hire blacks.

Although the government did not support the college in these requests, it did select the institution as one of the country's one hundred eight War Information Centers charged with disseminating information on civilian defense. Still, Atwood wanted to establish a program of civilian defense at the college. He organized the Committee on the College and National Defense in order to adjust the services of the school to meet the problems of national defense. Like other Kentucky colleges, the administrators at Kentucky State made it possible for students to complete a standard four-year curriculum in two and two-thirds years. The plan was intended to allow students to go to college as well as to use their education in the interest of the war effort. In spite of the federal government's conclusion that industries would not hire blacks, Atwood was convinced that the country needed a "reservoir" of skilled workers. Classes in first aid, nutrition, and homemaking were offered to students and nonstudents. The University of Kentucky assisted Kentucky State in developing an Engineering, Science and Management War Training program which was sponsored by the federal government. With the University's assistance, a course in radio operations was formed as well as an engineering drawing course. According to Atwood, "when our country went to war, we attempted too, to take our institution into war."

Yet World War II was responsible for the decreasing enrollments that Kentucky State suffered during the early 1940s. As of 1939 there were 682 students on the campus, but this number had dropped to 310 by 1944. A large number of students took advantage of job openings that resulted from the war. Others were either drafted or volunteered for the armed services. The decline in the student population was most apparent in the number of males attending the college. In 1941 Kentucky State had 203 male students compared to 31 by 1943.[4]

Atwood's concern about student enrollment was an issue of equal importance among the white presidents of Kentucky's state teachers colleges. As early as the fall of 1941, Morehead reported that its student enrollment had decreased 25 percent; Western's had dropped 20 percent; Eastern's had fallen 15 percent; and Murray's had declined by 9.3 percent. Because of lower student enrollments, colleges looked for additional financial assistance from the state government in order to run their institutions.[5] The loss of students was especially detrimental to Kentucky State since it had never received funds equal to the white colleges. But Atwood was not reluctant to inform whites about the needs of Kentucky State during the nation's military crisis.

On June 20, 1941, Atwood solicited advice from the State Board of Education when reporting on the "needs" of the college. He revealed that the school needed repairs and renovation on several campus buildings, a new building for classrooms and administration, a building for the elementary training school, housing facilities for teachers, departments of industrial arts and business administration, and a larger gymnasium. Furthermore, he stated that the annual appropriation should be increased by ten thousand dollars because the college still had not fully met the requirements of the Southern Association of Colleges and Secondary Schools.[6]

Atwood's original estimate for the above repairs and renovation was under $300,000, but he knew that for the school to secure what it needed from the state legislature it was necessary to request an extremely high appropriation. In his letter to the State Finance Department, Atwood requested $761,600 for expansion and an increase in the biennial budget from $220,000 to $357,629. In making this request Atwood argued that the salaries paid to Kentucky State's teachers were not equal to those of other southern black colleges and they were "far below those of other state colleges in Kentucky." Despite his strong plea for greater financial support, the legislature increased the school's annual appropriation to only $130,000 for the 1942-44 biennium. The 1944-46 biennium was not much better; the school's funds were increased to $150,000 a year.[7]

The frustrations Atwood felt in his effort to acquire adequate funding for Kentucky State was no different from that of other black educators in the south. Atwood and his contemporaries did what they could to convince whites that their schools were worthy of state money. Black college presidents even utilized unconventional means to get funding for their schools, and often these efforts were not enough. Lawrence Davis, president of Arkansas A & M College in Pine Bluff, often paid a prominent state senator five hundred dollars so that he would vote in favor of appropriations for the college. Davis also sought to impress white lawmakers by taking the school's choir to the state capital to present a concert of Negro spirituals and opera selections so they could witness the versatility of the students attending his college.[8] Exactly how many black presidents bribed legislators is unknown but the number was probably small given their limited access to financial resources. However, black presidents routinely entertained white officials with "annual side shows."[9] The event was their way of assuring southern whites that black education had not discouraged students from singing the slave spirituals whites romanticized about.

Florida A & M University's John Robert Lee was another black president who periodically held special singing programs for white state officials as a means of lobbying their support. William Jasper Hale, president of Tennessee A & I, went all out to welcome legislators to banquets at the school, "lining up as many as fifty-nine locally black-owned automobiles to transport the guests to the campus."[10] Horace Bond, a distinguished black educator with family ties to Kentucky, recalled that when he taught at Langston University in Oklahoma the administrators also humbled themselves to the expectations of visiting white legislators. "On the day of the visit," stated Bond, "the entire teaching staff was marshalled by order of the president of the school to a nearby pea patch where enrobed in blue jeans and calico, our scholarly faculty waited the arrival of these patrons of the arts. The eyes of the visitors sparkled with enthusiasm when they were informed by the president that what they saw was no unusual occurrence in this state college, dedicated as it was to the great ideals of honest labor and toil." The legislators' visit ended, Bond recalled, with a dinner on the campus and a student musical program devoted to "plantation melodies."[11]

While Rufus Atwood ended the practice of holding banquets for legislators after his first year in office, he too utilized various practices for acquiring money for the school. For instance, Atwood on one occasion sent a case of "Old Pepper 20 year old Kentucky Whiskey" to a senator in order to get his support on a proposal involving Kentucky State. At other times Atwood wrote to white and black leaders explaining the financial needs of the college. He made personal appeals to legislators in the halls of the state capitol. He made personal visits to the governor's office late at night to request additional funds, which led the state's white college presidents facetiously to call Atwood after the biblical figure Nicodemus.[12]

Atwood also allowed Kentucky State students to perform on occasion for white state officials. Young Harvey Russell recalled the choral society being invited to perform at a sesquicentennial event sponsored by Governor "Happy" Chandler on the lawn of the governor's mansion in Frankfort when Russell was a student at Kentucky State. Choir members were told to sing spirituals, wear bandannas, and pretend they were picking cotton during their performance. Several students refused to follow these requests, which they rightfully considered to be racially demeaning. "This really put President Atwood in a bind," remembered Russell; "he didn't know what to do. He almost threatened to put us out of school." Eventually Atwood and the students reached a compromise; they agreed to sing but not to wear bandannas and pretend to pick cotton. Russell recalled that on other occasions the choir performed at dinner parties hosted by Chandler. The governor enjoyed hearing the students sing spirituals, and after their performance he invited them into the kitchen for fried chicken. At that time the students did not understand why Atwood subjected them to this kind of treatment from the governor. They believed he was too obliging to the state's highest office holder; yet the reality of Atwood's situation was that he did not want to jeopardize the school's chances of receiving funds, so he and his contemporaries felt compelled to accompany their students in degrading exhibitions to acquire even the lowest of state funds.[13] It was a demeaning personal experience for them, but their situation reflected the society in which they lived and worked rather than their moral character. Still, even this excuse cannot be used to completely exonerate Atwood and others like him whose obessive financial worries contributed to the stereotypical images whites had of African-Americans. Clearly, as the above illustration proves, Atwood was not forthright in proclaiming the dignity and integrity of his race in the presence of whites.

The personal humiliations Atwood and his students and faculty endured over the years were not measured in the two reports that revealed the school's deficiencies as of 1945. The first report was issued in October by a committee from the University of Kentucky upon the request of President Atwood. Atwood had earlier asked Herman C. Donovan, then president of the university, to appoint a committee from his faculty to study conditions at Kentucky State.

Donovan complied with Atwood's request because he thought such a study would not only help Atwood with his administrative duties but would also support the continuation of black higher education. He selected five members from various departments throughout the university to serve on the committee, which proceeded to study specific aspects of the college, including the organization, physical plant and equipment, curricular offerings, financial support, faculty, enrollment, general, and departmental needs.

Following a review, the committee reported on the instructional units of Kentucky State. The committee suggested combining economics and business administration and establishing a Department of Social Studies to include history, government, and sociology. It also recommended that courses in secondary education and a professional course for teachers become part of the Division of Education. The committee also discussed the possibility of establishing a graduate program at Kentucky State. This was, no doubt, partly in response to the increasing judicial pressure exerted on southern states to provide equal graduate and professional training facilities for blacks and whites. Since Kentucky State was the only black public college in the state, it was considered to be the most suitable institution in which to establish graduate education for Kentucky African-Americans. Atwood was concerned about the ability of his institution to carry out an advanced program. Yet the committee claimed in its report that an initial graduate program could be developed at Kentucky State by allowing white University of Kentucky instructors to teach courses at the school.

The committee recommended that the school's graduate program begin with instruction for teachers during its summer session, but, if administrators desired, a few graduate courses for certain departments could be offered during the regular school term.[14] The committee's conclusion on this issue was no surprise. Had it disapproved of graduate instruction at Kentucky State it would have weakened white efforts to maintain segregation. The committee's report then served to foster the retention of separate but equal higher education in Kentucky.

The committee's most valuable contribution was to reveal the weaknesses of the college. The committee found that the college was in "serious" need of financial assistance in order adequately to upgrade its standards. It pointed out the need for new buildings on campus to provide adequate classroom and laboratory facilities. Expanding library facilities would also be necessary to assist students with their academic requirements. The committee further suggested that faculty salaries be increased and that teachers be allowed the opportunity to pursue advanced education. This was necessary to enable the college to retain its good teachers in the face of competition from other schools.

In conclusion, the report claimed that Kentucky State had constructively utilized appropriations from the Kentucky General Assembly and that it was offering "excellent service to the Negroes of Kentucky." The committee recommended an increase in the college's budget in order to accommodate the student's academic needs.[15] This kind of report must have pleased Atwood; it complimented his administration as well as supported his petition for additional funding.

In November 1945, Atwood's effort to gain financial support for Kentucky State was augmented by the report of the Kentucky Commission on Negro Affairs. The commission had been established through an executive order issued by Governor Simeon Willis in September 1944. The purpose of the Kentucky Commission on Negro Affairs was "to obtain and to study all the facts and conditions relating to the economic, educational, housing, health, and other needs for the betterment of Negro citizens of Kentucky." In cooperation with the commission's report, Atwood, who served as advisor to the Commissioners on Education,[16] used this opportunity further to highlight the shortcomings at Kentucky State and the need for greater financial assistance from the state. His concerns were strongly represented in the commission's report.

In many ways the commissioners' report replicated that of the University of Kentucky. It stated that Kentucky State was "doing a good job with limited facilities and finances." It found that increasing faculty salaries, expanding the physical plant, strengthening departments of the college as well as broadening the curriculum were necessary improvements. In making these recommendations the commission realized that appropriations to Kentucky State would have to be increased. According to a table included in the report, Kentucky spent $150,000 on black higher education and lagged far behind Oklahoma, Tennessee, Virginia, and West Virginia in its appropriations during the year 1944-45.

In order to correct the deficiencies of Kentucky State, the commission recommended that appropriations to the college be increased to five hundred thousand dollars for the 1946-48 biennium. According to the commission, the additional funding could be distributed by appropriating two hundred thousand dollars for capital outlay and sixty thousand dollars for increasing the equipment in departments, and by supplying books and furniture for the library. The commission also recommended that fifteen thousand dollars be used to hire additional faculty and the remaining seventy-five thousand dollars be allocated to bring the salaries of Kentucky State faculty in line with those in other state colleges. "Clearly," stated the commission's report, "considerable increases in the appropriations for Kentucky State is [sic] essential to its operation on an adequate basis, and imperative, if even reasonable progress toward desirable standards is to be made."[17]

The improvements the commission recommended were necessary in order for the college to meet the demands of an increased student enrollment. With the end of World War II, black veterans would be returning to Kentucky to take advantage of the G.I. Bill. Since the Louisville Municipal College was the only other black higher institution in Kentucky, the student enrollment at Kentucky State was likely to increase. In addition, the number of out-of-state students attending the college was also expected to be high. Students from twenty of the nation's forty-eight states had attended the college during the 1939-40 school year, and even though the war had caused decreased enrollments, students from sixteen different states were attracted to the institution in 1944-45.[18] The state would have to address the school's financial needs in order to maintain and expand the number of out-of-state students attending the college.

In 1946, it appeared that the reports of the University of Kentucky and the Kentucky Commission on Negro Affairs had had a positive impact on the amount of money allocated to Kentucky State. The Kentucky General Assembly increased allocations to $225,000 in annual appropriations and to $200,000 in capital outlay. These amounts were the largest that had been appropriated in the college's history. Republican Governor Willis observed in his "State Of the Commonwealth" address that Kentucky State was receiving more money "because its enrollment and the work it is expected to accomplish could not be done without it." He added: "In view of the importance of that school, it must be more strongly supported to enable it to meet the demands the state is putting upon it."[19]

Willis's statements implied that the legislature was attempting to answer the recommendations presented in the reports issued on Kentucky State in 1945. But the state government was actually trying to avoid opening the doors of the University of Kentucky to blacks. Atwood and Representative Charles Anderson knew this was the reason for the increased funding for Kentucky State, and they became especially aggressive in seeking even greater funding for the school.

Here, Atwood was clearly working in the best interest of his race. Had he not pressed for more funds he would have been doing a disservice to Kentucky State and would have discredited his leadership role in education. Thus Atwood adroitly put pressure on the government either to make Kentucky State equal to colleges for whites or to open all state colleges to blacks. Whenever Kentucky could not afford to pay for segregation and subsequently had to desegregate its schools, Atwood figured Kentucky State would remain open because by then the state would have invested too much money in the college. Consequently, in Atwood's mind, by requesting an increase in funds he could possibly upgrade Kentucky State, retain his position, and eventually force the state to desegregate its public colleges.

In 1948 Atwood asked the Kentucky General Assembly to appropriate $450,000 a year to his school in order to finance the construction of new buildings and to remodel the existing ones. The legislature refused to support his request, however. The college's annual appropriation was increased to a little more than three hundred and fifty thousand dollars with less than ten thousand dollars for capital outlay.

While it seemed apparent Atwood's crusade to get adequate funds for Kentucky State was hopeless, he remained steadfast. In 1950 the state granted the school five hundred thousand dollars in capital outlay.[20] As the decade progressed Atwood continued to face the financial problems of the past. For years he had to make personal appeals to the governors or meet individually with certain state legislators to secure their votes on appropriations for Kentucky State.

By the late 1950s, all of Kentucky's state college presidents were meeting in a room among themselves to decide on the budget they wanted for their respective schools before the governor presented it to the legislature. Adron Doran, president of Morehead State College, recalled the room where the presidents met being referred to as "the room of the big knives." "Everybody was cutting his part of the budget," stated Doran. Although a formula was developed to make the process less difficult, Atwood still did not secure the necessary funds to adequately operate Kentucky State. For the 1960-61 term the General Assembly granted Kentucky State $697,600, but, with the exception of Morehead, the other state colleges received more than double that amount.[21] The new budget was indicative of the kind of burden Atwood had to shoulder throughout his administration; yet lobbying for adequate funds was just another one of several obstacles Atwood faced over the years.

Atwood desperately wanted Kentucky State to have an ROTC Unit. In 1948 Governor Earle Clements buttressed Atwood's effort by writing a letter to Lieutenant General L.T. Gerow on the college's behalf. Despite Clements's support, the request for an ROTC program was denied. According to Gerow, budget restrictions only allowed for the establishment of three ROTC units. The Department of the Army decided to give priority to the institutions with the largest number of male students who were not veterans. Since Kentucky State had a large number of veterans, it was disqualified by the army's standards.[22]

Despite the rejection, Atwood was persistent in trying to establish ROTC at Kentucky State. He believed that since Kentucky State was a land grant college and federal law required such institutions to teach military science, the school should have an ROTC program. However, H.A. Houser, a rear admiral in the Navy, disagreed. He claimed the act did not require ROTC units to be established at civilian educational institutions.[23]

In February 1953, Atwood went to the Pentagon to seek the government's support for an ROTC program. Atwood disclosed in his conferences with officials that, of the fifteen states that had black colleges, four did not have ROTC units for blacks. Among those states without such units were Kentucky, Georgia, Arkansas, and Mississippi. While meeting with Major General William Persons, President Dwight Eisenhower's liaison between the White House and Congress, Atwood noted that only 2.3 percent of the army's 10 to 12 percent black enlistment were officers. He believed there was a need to increase the number of black officers proportionately to the number of men enlisted. The chances of fulfilling this need would be greater if the army permitted additional black colleges to establish ROTC curriculums. Atwood believed Kentucky State was qualified to establish an ROTC unit. It had more than three hundred male students, and the government's minimum requirement was one hundred males to establish an ROTC program.[24]

As a black veteran and a war hero himself, Atwood may have thought the government would make exceptions and support his proposal, but it did not. An ROTC program was not established at the college during his presidency. The inability to establish a unit must have been disheartening for Atwood. He wanted his students to have the chance to acquire some of the future financial benefits and educational rewards that he had obtained while a young soldier in the army, but, since he was not able to establish this kind of program, Atwood focused on other activities relating to the college both directly and indirectly. His goal was to create a positive and progressive educational environment that would serve the well-being of Kentucky State students long after they had graduated from the institution. He learned, however, that even this would be a difficult task.

In November 1948, Atwood led a protest against Clarence Harrod's attempt to establish a package liquor store near the campus of Kentucky State College. Harrod, a resident of suburban Franklin Heights, filed an application with the State Alcoholic Beverage

Control Board to establish a liquor store on U.S. 60, east of the college campus. At a hearing before the State Alcoholic Beverage Control Board, Atwood testified against Harrod's application, stating that the liquor store would serve as a temptation to the students of Kentucky State. Although Harrod claimed the distance between the college and the liquor store was more than twelve hundred feet walking distance, Atwood revealed that one of his faculty members conducted measurements and found the distance to be near five hundred feet.

With legal counsel at his side, Atwood noted that he was not opposed to the sale of alcohol or to Harrod's petition for a liquor license. "I am," stated Atwood, "opposed to his getting one so close to the school." Because the college had rules against the purchase of liquor by students and since students had been dismissed from the college each year for breaking such rules, Atwood argued that a liquor store near the campus would worsen this problem. Before making a decision in the case, the State Alcoholic Beverage Board decided to hold another hearing in December 1948. At that time, Atwood presented 270 signatures opposing a store near the campus. Harrod introduced a petition of 240 names favoring the establishment of the liquor store. However, the college's attorney, Philip Ardery, found an error in one of Harrod's affidavits, and the case was still not resolved. During a third hearing the board approved Harrod's petition to establish a liquor store six hundred feet from Kentucky State. According to Thomas J. Hennessy, distilled spirits administrator, the board decided in Harrod's favor because most of the students at Kentucky State were not old enough to purchase liquor and were thus protected by the law.

After the board's decision, Atwood told reporters that he had done his best and that he would accept the decision. Actually, the issue was not settled. Less than a month after the board's decision, Theodore R. Daley, a member of the Kentucky State faculty, filed a suit in Franklin Circuit Court against Harrod's liquor license. Daley, who owned property near the liquor store, was represented by Ardery. In the suit Ardery charged that the State Alcoholic Beverage Control Board had exceeded its quota for the number of package liquor licenses that could be established in Franklin County and thus was not qualified to issue a permit to Harrod. The board's decision was reversed when the circuit judge decided on Daley's behalf. Exactly how much influence Atwood had in Daley's decision to file another suit against Harrod is unclear, but, considering Daley's ties to Kentucky State and how vigorously Atwood had initially pursued the matter, it is likely that Atwood had a significant role in initiating this suit.[25]

In June 1950, Harrod launched another campaign to establish a liquor store near Kentucky State. But this time the State Alcoholic Beverage Control Board ruled in the college's favor. The board decided that the liquor store would not be in the best interest of the community.[26] The decision was indeed a gratifying victory for Atwood. He had pursued this problem with the same vigor as he did all others relating to the college, but this time he won.

Atwood's successful effort to protect the college from negative influences symbolized the beginning of other advancements the institution would make during the 1950s. In 1951, the United States Office of Education conducted a study of public higher education in Kentucky. The study was done for the Committee on Functions and Resources of State Government. The committee recommended that Kentucky State have its own separate board of regents. It observed that there was no reason for the State Board of Education to continue controlling the affairs of Kentucky State College. "The primary interests of the State Board," the committee noted, "are in the public system at the elementary and secondary levels."[27]

In 1952, as a result of the United States Office of Education's survey and the recommendation by the Committee on Functions and Resources of State Government, the legislature passed a bill to create a board of regents for Kentucky State, and on September 26, 1952, they held their first meeting.[28] This was an important occasion in the history of Kentucky State and in Atwood's administration. The school's governing affairs would now be handled in a manner similar to those at Kentucky's other state colleges, giving Atwood a board of regents that would maintain an undivided interest in the school's future.

Although Atwood and the faculty were excited about the new arrangement, they had trouble with the student body in the spring of 1953. The ordeal began after two students were expelled because they had stolen a typewriter and money from a pay telephone and a coin-operated washing machine on campus. A third student, Elvin Eady, who was a freshman scholarship basketball player, was suspended after he was identified by the accused as having been a participant in the affair. Four hundred students were outraged by his dismissal and participated in a brief class walkout. The administrators immediately responded to the situation. A faculty-student committee chaired by Dean David Bradford was appointed to reinvestigate Eady's expulsion, and he was reinstated.[29] The final outcome of the student strike was an indication of Atwood's attempt to maintain a positive relationship between students and faculty members. Although he was a stern disciplinarian and paternalistic in his role as president of the college, Atwood realized tensions between students and faculty were another problem the school did not need. He simply preferred that the faculty continue furnishing students with "temptations upward" rather than engage in bitter controversies with them.[30] He wanted students and faculty to represent Kentucky State with distinction.

Archie Surrat, who taught science at Kentucky State, remembered that Atwood believed in "creating a good image as far as Kentucky State was concerned to both the black community and white community." On one occasion some faculty members were photographed at a social event by the black press while sitting at a table that had liquor bottles on it. Atwood later suggested that faculty take liquor bottles off their tables before being photographed because he did not want students' parents to believe that the college had faculty who condoned that kind of public socializing.[31] Atwood wanted his students and faculty to serve as an inspiration and a source of support for other blacks throughout the state and nation. Moreover, he wanted them to extend their best effort in order to make the college more productive.

In March 1957, however, this image was seriously tarnished when Mahatma White, a twenty-three-year-old senior at the college, was arrested for abducting and raping a six-year-old white girl alongside highways 35 and 151 (Main Street). The incident enraged the white community in Frankfort and neigboring Lawrenceburg. Minnie Hitch Mebane recalled hearing a rumor that some white men from Lawrenceburg planned to drive to Frankfort and randomly attack black men. Upon observing several cars of white men circling the campus, Atwood phoned the city police department and asked for a more frequent patrol of the school. Atwood advised all faculty, staff, and students to avoid the downtown area until the situation had calmed.

According to Mebane, Atwood called Governor Chandler and asked him to intervene to help settle the anger of whites. Mebane remembers Chandler asking the community to remain peaceful and not to attack black male students at the college; however, one black man not associated with the school was attacked by four whites and pistol whipped. White was convicted four months after the crime and was sentenced to life imprisonment despite his plea that he was innocent.[32]

In the midst of these troubling events the Kentucky State College campus was expanding. In 1957, the board of regents approved a $410,000 program to construct a library, an alumni guest house, and a student union building.[33] During the same year, Atwood suggested to Governor Chandler that a portion of the college's 268.53 acres of farm land be sold for industrial and residential development. Specifically, Atwood wanted to sell 221 acres and retain the other 47.53 acres for the college's athletics field and elementary laboratory. Since the agriculture department was experiencing declining enrollments, there was a surplus of farm land. Furthermore, the federal government was proposing a slum clearance housing project and the available land would give the displaced an alternative site to relocate.

Atwood's primary concern was providing a location and opportunities for his faculty to build and buy their own homes. His objective was strongly endorsed by blacks since it would establish the first black residential subdivision in Frankfort since 1911. Ten black faculty members from Kentucky State joined in the organization of the College Park Development Corporation. In December 1958, the board of regents sold 32.82 acres of the college's farm land to the corporation for $16,410. The corporation then subdivided the land into seventy lots and resold it to blacks interested in building new homes.[34]

The arrangement enabled the faculty to gain a stronger sense of appreciation for Atwood's administrative skills. Joseph Fletcher was one of the faculty members who moved into the subdivision, and according to him, "it was Atwood who had backbone enough to make the whites give him permission to set up residences. . . . I have always appreciated that in him." Although "there were whites who didn't want him to do it," Fletcher continued, "he fought for his black teachers to have decent residences."[35] In this struggle, as in others, Atwood could not have succeeded without the support he received from his black faculty and influential whites. Each succeeding year of his administration, the two groups became increasingly important in determining the growth of the college.

In the September 1957 edition of the *Kentucky Thorobred*, Atwood highlighted the progress Kentucky State College had made in recent years. For instance, in 1955 and 1956 student enrollment increased 10 and 11 percent respectively. The much increased student population represented several foreign lands, including Pakistan and Japan as well as the continents of Africa and South America. More important, the college had begun to desegregate with three new white instructors and staff members and several whites from the Frankfort community enrolled part-time at the institution.[36] Yet Atwood remained most concerned about the college being accredited by the Southern Association of Colleges and Secondary Schools.

In 1956, at its meeting in Dallas, Texas, the SACSS voted for the first time to admit qualified black colleges to full membership. The decision was prompted by the 1954 Supreme Court ruling prohibiting racial segregation in public schools. Like other black colleges, Kentucky State had formerly been a member of the Association of Colleges and Secondary Schools for Negroes. The Southern Association's decision to integrate its organization gave blacks an opportunity to become affiliated with the region's most prestigious accrediting agency; however, the association specified that blacks schools would have to meet the organization's standards by 1961. After that year there would be only one list of accredited colleges and any schools that had not qualified would be considered unaccredited.

In 1957, the Southern Association admitted fifteen black colleges and three black junior colleges to membership. Kentucky State College filed an application but did not obtain the association's approval for membership. According to Donald Agnew, executive secretary of the Southern Association, the college was weak in some areas of training and needed more faculty members with Ph.D. degrees in order to qualify for membership.[37]

As he was in handling other business of the college, Atwood was relentless in his efforts to get the school accredited. This was imperative since the college was forced to compete with other schools as a result of school desegregation. A 1958 study of Kentucky State emphasized the school's weaknesses. This study was compiled by W. Scott Hall, director of counseling and professor of economics and sociology at Transylvania College in Lexington. Hall was asked to serve as a curriculum consultant while Kentucky State prepared for desegregation. He listed the college's courses that "adequately" prepared students in several professions and vocations and made several observations and recommendations regarding elementary education, secondary education, liberal arts,

business administration, social work, agriculture, and a professional curriculum that met the entrance requirements for law, medicine,
dental, and veterinary schools. Hall recommended that agriculture
be discontinued since only a small number of students were enrolled in the program. He also noted weaknesses in course offerings for political science, public administration, psychology, and
library science, but he added that they could be strengthened with
additional courses.

Hall recommended that the college add more Ph.Ds to the
faculty, attract community interest in the college, accept more
qualified students, establish a placement office, reduce the job
responsibilities of the dean, and place less emphasis on teacher
education. Hall predicted that interest in teaching would decline
since blacks would find it difficult to obtain jobs because of more
rapid integration of black students into formerly white schools,
which would reduce the need for black teachers.[38]

Hall's recommendations were taken seriously by the board of
regents. In the spring of 1958, the board of regents discontinued the
agriculture department, reorganized the business administration
and education departments, and voted that a faculty member with
a doctorate chair the English and psychology departments. These
changes worked to the college's advantage. The SACSS approved
Kentucky State for full membership on December 4, 1958.[39] The
announcement represented a significant achievement for Atwood
and the faculty. In spite of racism and discrimination the college
appeared to be making some important progress in the wake of the
early years of desegregation.

Atwood was primarily responsible for successfully guiding
the institution. He had implemented ideas and solutions he had
learned from his participation in educational organizations and
conferences. He made the necessary political and educational contacts with those in positions to influence positive changes for his
school. He did not hesitate to convey the school's problems to the
state's governors and other white politicians.

Atwood's calm approach to solving the institution's problems
was acceptable to whites. As one newspaper writer observed:
"Atwood has the neat ability to stay in the background and yet
make his presence felt." He was a frequent spectator at legislative sessions,[40] always looking for opportunities to promote the
needs of Kentucky State. He worked closely with the state's white
colleges in order to obtain their support for improving condi-

David H. Bradford, professor and head of the Department of History and
Government in 1935 and later dean and registrar of Kentucky State
College. Courtesy of Kentucky State University Photographic Archives.

tions. Their reports virtually mirrored Atwood's own objectives a
Kentucky State.

Atwood could not have achieved his success as an administrato
without the support he received from the faculty. During much o
his administration, Dean David H. Bradford was a valuable as
sistant. Born in Abbeville, South Carolina, Bradford had a bach
elors and masters degree from the University of Michigan. Atwoo
hired him at age twenty-seven as professor and head of the Depart
ment of History and Government in 1935. When he later receivec
his Ph.D from the University of Chicago, Atwood appointed hin
dean and registrar of the college. Bradford presided over facult
meetings when Atwood was out of town, and he provided in
sightful recommendations for the faculty to consider in their at
tempt to offer academic excellence. Had it not been for Bradforc
and other dependable faculty members like him, Atwood woulc
not have been able to accomplish what he did.

Whereas the educational achievements Atwood won at Ken

tucky State were the result of a concerted effort, the racial pressures he faced as president were personal. This pressure created a dilemma that only Atwood could resolve. As the civil rights movement began to attack racial discrimination in the South, Atwood became a lonely warrior trying to carve out a safe place for him and Kentucky State to survive the struggle. He was concerned about protecting his personal gains and the future of the school, which made his situation even more challenging.

7

School Desegregation

During the 1930s and 1940s, as Atwood tried to better conditions at Kentucky State, the National Association for the Advancement of Colored People (NAACP) was leading a movement to guarantee equal educational opportunities for African-Americans. On May 17, 1939, the executive secetary of the NAACP, Walter White, wrote Atwood congratulating him on completing ten years as president of Kentucky State. "Ahead of us lie days not only of grave difficulties," wrote White, "but of great opportunity as well. . . . It is good to know that a man of your vision, character, and courage is at the helm of a great institution like the Kentucky State College at a time like this."[1]

At the time, White did not realize Atwood's attitude toward school desegregation was not that progressive. Although Atwood wanted equal treatment for blacks in all phases of life, his "vision" and "courage" were not as broad as that of the NAACP's executive secretary. Atwood had to be more selective, cautious, and conciliatory when articulating black inequalities and promoting racial integration. But at least he tried to do something.

In 1935 the Kentucky State administration, faculty, and students joined the NAACP and other civic groups in threatening to boycott the Capitol Theatre in Frankfort. The controversy evolved when the Frankfort Amusement Company, owners and operators of the Capitol Theatre, attempted to have the Grievance Board of the National Recovery Administration close the campus theater. The Frankfort Amusement Company charged that the campus theater paid no taxes and presented unfair competition to local establishments. The black community in Frankfort organized and planned to boycott the segregated Capitol Theatre until the complaint was withdrawn and accommodations were improved at that establishment. According to a report in the Louisville *Leader*, the Kentucky State administration informed the Cincinnati Grievance Board that the campus theater was nonprofit and that the segregated accommodations in the Capitol consisted of dirty floors and bug-infested seats. These arguments and the boycott threat were effective. Upon learning of the black community's position the management of the Capitol Theatre rescinded the complaint and assured blacks its facilities would be improved.[2]

In 1936, Atwood and the dean of LMC, Rufus Clement, organized the Negro State Coordinating Committee. Working as a "statewide, non-partisan body" for "equality of opportunity for the Negro," the committee presented Governor Chandler several recommendations for improving the status of blacks. According to the committee, the state should: employ more blacks in health services and road construction, allow blacks to participate in the operation of federal agencies, appoint a black to the State Board of Education, provide equal wages for work, establish a Negro history curriculum in the public school system, and provide greater support for the Kentucky State and Western Kentucky Industrial colleges.[3] Despite the committee's valid concern about the low status of blacks in Kentucky, the situation remained unchanged.

Unlike the generation of civil rights activists of the 1950s and 1960s, Atwood was a gradualist who preferred to compromise with whites on racial issues rather than to engage in a risky confrontation with them. Atwood was more concerned with protecting the existence of Kentucky State than with getting black students into the University of Kentucky. He wanted equality within the context of segregation first, before pressing for school desegregation. This position eventually placed Atwood at odds with the NAACP and other black leaders in Kentucky who favored an immediate end to school segregation.

The NAACP began its campaign by initiating lawsuits against public graduate and professional schools in the South that denied African-Americans the right to enroll. Attorneys for the NAACP believed that graduate and professional schools would have to desegregate because it would be financially difficult for southern states to offer blacks and whites equal facilities for this kind of education.[4]

Believing that resistance would be less difficult in the border states, the NAACP took on the case of Donald Murray at the University of Maryland. In 1935, Murray, a resident of Baltimore, was denied admission to the University of Maryland's Law School. When Murray took his case to court the University of Maryland maintained that it provided out-of-state scholarships for blacks seeking professional education; therefore, even though blacks could not attend white state universities, they could enroll in institutions out of state that would accept them. Murray's attorneys, furnished by the NAACP, countered the defense by arguing that such scholarships could not provide equal education for blacks. They revealed that the scholarships covered only tuition, and they could not exceed two hundred and fifty dollars. In addition, Murray's attorneys disclosed that no provisions were made in the tuition grants to cover the difference in living and travel expenses between Maryland and the other states. The NAACP's argument proved successful, and the Maryland circuit court of appeals ruled in support of Murray's application.[5]

Following Murray's admission to the University of Maryland, another prospective law student filed a similar suit. In 1936 Lloyd Gaines's application was rejected by the University of Missouri's School of Law. Two years later, the Supreme Court rendered a major decision in favor of Gaines and all blacks seeking equal opportunities for graduate and professional training. The Court ruled that out-of-state scholarships did not meet requirements under the "separate but equal" education doctrine and that the state had the responsibility of making provisions in education for all its residents within the state. Despite this mandate, southern states remained adamant in their refusal to equalize advanced education for blacks and whites. They either appropriated more money for black state colleges in order to establish makeshift advanced educational programs for blacks, increased allocations for out-of-state scholarships, or totally ignored the Gaines decision.

Segregated education in Kentucky had been legalized as a result of the passage of the 1904 Day Law. The law stipulated that private and public schools be segregated and that persons or institutions found violating it be fined.[6] That Kentucky was a border state with one poorly financed black public higher learning institution increased the chances of the University of Kentucky becoming involved in a lawsuit to admit blacks. Because the academic program of Kentucky State College was not as broad as that of the University of Kentucky, blacks had to enroll in out-of-state institutions to pursue graduate school or to do undergraduate work in areas of interest not provided at the state's black college.

Similar to Maryland, Missouri, Tennessee, and Oklahoma, Kentucky made legal provisions to offer scholarships to black residents. With Representative Charles Anderson leading the campaign in the House of Representatives and Stanley Mayer in the Senate, Kentucky passed the Anderson-Mayer Act in 1936. The Act appropriated $5,000 annually toward funding education for blacks who had to go elsewhere for their training. Each student requesting assistance was given $175 per academic year, and the amount was hardly enough to satisfy the requests of all qualified applicants. Between 1936 and 1938 the governor had to allocate more than two thousand dollars from the emergency fund to support the tuition payment plan.[7]

In January 1939, Alfred Carroll, a Louisville resident, graduate of Wilberforce University, and a law student at Howard University, applied to the University of Kentucky's College of Law. He did so because the funds under the tuition payment plan were depleted. Although Representative Anderson had attempted to secure additional funds, it was only after Carroll's application that Governor Chandler allocated more money. Familiar with Carroll's case, Atwood commented to the press that he believed Carroll would withdraw his application to the university providing a scholarship was made available for out-of-state study. Carroll publicly disagreed with Atwood's assumption. He claimed Atwood was "not authorized" to make the statement and that he had never communicated with him. In explaining his comment to the press, Atwood noted that Carroll had written a letter that "implied" he would remain at Howard with receipt of a scholarship. While publicly the matter appeared to be a misunderstanding of Caroll's intentions, Atwood was actually trying to steer him away from filing a lawsuit against the university.

Carroll did not bring suit against the University of Kentucky, but some black leaders did consider the possibility of using his application to challenge school segregation in the state. On February 4, 1939, representatives from the KNEA, the Negro Business and Civic League, and the Louisville branches of the Urban League and the NAACP met to discuss Carroll's case as well as the recent Gaines decision.[8] Four days after this meeting, Atwood, who was a member of the legislative committee of the KNEA, wrote Governor Chandler to share with him the group's plans. Atwood believed he could increase the chances of Kentucky State gaining accreditation and funding by doing what he could to reduce racial tensions in the state. Rather than operating as a civil rights leader, Atwood preferred to conduct himself as an interracial diplomat. In doing so, he could show moderate support for civil rights causes, maintain his alliances with whites, and protect his image and influence in the black community.

Atwood informed Chandler that the legislative committee of the

KNEA voted to have Chairman A.E. Meyzeek write him a letter requesting that the governor consider equal educational opportunities for blacks in Kentucky as a result of the Gaines decision. The committee also wanted to schedule a conference with Chandler, the superintendent of public instruction, and whomever the governor wanted to invite in order to learn about the state's proposed course of action on this issue. Atwood told Chandler that he believed the conference would be a better approach than "rushing into the courts at this time." Yet Atwood made clear to the governor that he wanted the state to establish equal facilities for the races. "Naturally," observed Atwood, "we are anxious to secure equality of opportunity for our race; we are also anxious to avoid unnecessary irritation, and evasion of what we believe to be the law." Atwood continued his letter by assuring Chandler that blacks had not organized in support of Carroll's application to the university. "As a matter of fact," Atwood wrote, "Anderson assured the committee verbally that no suit would be filed at this time."[9]

Despite what Charles Anderson may have told the committee, he had not totally given up the idea of using the Carroll case as a test suit against the University of Kentucky. He wrote the legal office of the NAACP to ascertain whether Carroll's undergraduate training at Wilberforce, an unaccredited school, would have any bearing on the success of a possible lawsuit. The national office replied that it would, yet Thurgood Marshall, special counsel for the NAACP, wrote: "We would like very much to see a case started in Kentucky for two reasons. In the first place we have you [Anderson] there to act as local counsel, and in the second place Kentucky is more or less civilized."[10] While Marshall's latter statement may have been considered a compliment, it did not hold true. The battle to desegregate the University of Kentucky would be won only after a long and unfortunate struggle.

Between the years 1939 and 1949 black educators and community activists in Kentucky pressed for equal education in higher learning institutions. Meanwhile, white officials exhausted various attempts to keep black and white graduate and professional students from attending the same schools. In March 1939, upon the request of the legislative committee of the KNEA, Chandler met with black and white educational leaders of the state. Chandler reminded the group that the state's constitution prohibited blacks from attending white schools. He also advised blacks against demanding admission to white schools. "If you insist on going to the University of

Kentucky now," noted Chandler, "you are making a mistake because there are barriers which we did not make and for which we are not responsible to prevent you from going to the university." While having the audacity to boast that his administration was the first in Kentucky to provide out-of-state scholarships for blacks, his attitude toward equal education was not encouraging. "I see no immediate prospects," observed Chandler, "for completely equalizing opportunities for higher education at the present time."[11]

David Lane, dean of Louisville Municipal College, strongly disagreed. "The right thing to do," stated Lane, "is admit Negroes to the University of Kentucky." Lane's response was no surprise since he could afford to speak out. At the time of the meeting Lane was still a relatively new black educator in Kentucky. He had a masters degree from Harvard University and had served as the dean of West Virginia State College for fifteen years before accepting the position in Louisville in 1937. Although the Southern Association of Colleges and Secondary Schools had recognized LMC before Kentucky State, it was still a small school compared to the latter. During Lane's tenure (1937-42), there were only twelve full-time faculty and fewer than ten staff members.[12] He did not have Atwood's level of influence and prestige throughout the state. Moreover, Lane presided over a municipally sponsored school that was not connected to the state college system, and he had less to lose by speaking out. In contrast, Atwood did not want to challenge Chandler's opinion and risk losing his job and funding for the school.

At the March 1939 meeting Chandler decided that "the best thing to do" would be to appoint a committee to investigate inequalities in education. He immediately appointed President Frank McVey of the University of Kentucky, President Raymond Kent of the University of Louisville, and the State Superintendent of Public Instruction Harry Peters to represent whites.[13]

Soon after the conference was held Atwood wrote to the secretary of the national branch of the NAACP, Walter White, discussing Kentucky's situation relative to the Supreme Court's decision in the Gaines case. According to Atwood, the two-hour conference with Governor Chandler was held in a "pleasant atmosphere," but none of the white representatives supported at that time the admission of blacks to either the University of Kentucky or the University of Louisville. Atwood noted that "the white people in the state may be expected to resist vigorously *immediate* attendance by Negroes in the University of Kentucky or the University of Louisville. Many of the leaders express themselves as approving such attendance personally, but not officially as they do not believe the "state is ready for it."[14]

Atwood further explained to Secretary White that white leaders were "willing to attempt to work out a program for full equalization of educational opportunity for Negroes" on the elementary, secondary, and college levels and to promote equal salaries. The University of Louisville had agreed to make some of its courses available at the Louisville Municipal College, and the University of Kentucky had agreed to do the same at Kentucky State College, while not duplicating the courses in Louisville. "It is believed by some Negroes and some of the whites," wrote Atwood, "that [this] plan . . . might gradually work Negroes into the two universities, inasmuch as it might prove inconvenient and expensive to set up complete equipment, etc., at the Negro institution, but rather the professor would gradually begin to have the students come where the equipment already was." "In other words," continued Atwood, "we would hope that Negroes may eventually get into the universities by method of the 'inclined plane' rather than by the perpendicular." Atwood gave no indication in his letter to White that black leaders were interested in filing a suit against the universities of Kentucky and Louisville to gain black equality in education. Instead Atwood believed each state should handle the issue independently, and his comments to the secretary of the NAACP indicated that he believed Kentucky blacks should first consider other options before supporting a legal case.[15]

Atwood's strategy for desegregating Kentucky's higher institutions was passive and weak and lacked the aggressiveness of other African-American leaders in the state. At that time, Atwood, who was still early in his career, was concerned with maintaining his job as president of Kentucky State and building on the improvements that had been made at the college since his administration began.

His motivations were selfish but not thoughtless. He was human and simply wanted an equal chance for himself and the school he represented to have an opportunity to contribute to the well-being of society. Atwood was willing to work with whites on their schedule for desegregating the University of Kentucky instead of pressuring them to immediately abide by the Gaines decision. Being the black president of a public institution restricted the level of civil rights leadership Atwood could provide black Kentuckians. If he was overly aggressive in his demands on whites, he would be fired as president of Kentucky State. This kind of situation created a dilemma that Atwood shared with other black educators throughout the South.

Following the success of the Gaines case, most southern black college presidents simply believed that participating in a "militant movement" would not only jeopardize their jobs but would instigate a "retaliation" from their state legislators, which would ultimately mean a reduction of funding. This legitimate concern could not be overlooked. Consequently, Atwood was not the only black southern college president who accommodated whites in the face of black opposition. Miller F. Whitaker, president of South Carolina State College in Orangeburg, even accepted an offer from Governor J. Strom Thurmond to serve as a consultant for the Regional Educational Council to study the prospects of establishing a segregated regional graduate and professional school in the South for blacks. In 1933, President James Shepard of North Carolina College for Negroes in Durham, simply refused to cooperate with the NAACP's legal efforts to desegregate the University of North Carolina. When Thomas Raymond Holcutt, a graduate of North Carolina College for Negroes in Durham, applied to the all-white University of North Carolina in Chapel Hill to attend pharmacy school, Shepard refused to send his transcript to the university's admissions office. Shepard's reluctance to cooperate with Holcutt's application prevented the NAACP from successfully challenging segregation in graduate and professional schools in North Carolina.[16]

Shepard did, however, exploit the situation by using it to expand course facilities and increase his school's appropriations. He wrote the director of the Division of Negro Education in North Carolina and orchestrated a letter-writing campaign to the governor in request of larger appropriations. His efforts proved worthwhile as state approriations significantly increased during the 1930s and 1940s.[17]

While Atwood did not directly interfere with the NAACP's legal efforts to desegregate the University of Kentucky, he did tacitly endorse the programs developed by whites to keep blacks out of the university. Thus Atwood should not be recognized as an early leader in the struggle to desegregate higher education in the state. Atwood wished white officials in Kentucky would respond to the Gaines decision by favorably supporting his school, and he surely did not want to do anything that might discourage whites from supporting Kentucky State less than they were already.

During the struggle to desegregate schools in Kentucky, Atwood operated as an interracial diplomat rather than an Uncle Tom. He did not blindly accommodate the segregationists. He thoughtfully positioned himself with whites to fulfill his objectives during the freedom struggle. Moreover, he met with blacks and whites individually and collectively in an effort to promote racial equality. Being a racial diplomat became increasingly difficult for Atwood as blacks and whites in Kentucky debated further solutions for equalizing higher education in the state. On November 24, 1939, Governor Chandler's advisory committee on black education convened in the chamber of the House of Representatives. Because Frank McVey, the chairman Chandler had selected, was ill, Raymond Kent was elected to the position. The other members present at the first meeting were Harry Peters, state superintendent of public instruction; Paul Garrett, president of Western State Teachers College; R.E. Jaggers, State Department of Education; A.E. Meyzeek, principal of Jackson Junior High School in Louisville; David Lane, dean of Louisville Municipal College; J.A. Thomas, executive secretary of the Louisville Urban League; W.H. Fouse, principal of Dunbar High School in Lexington; S.L. Baker, president of KNEA; L.N. Taylor, supervisor of Negro schools, State Department of Education; Alvin E. Evans, dean at the University of Kentucky; and Atwood, who was elected secretary of the committee. Those members not present at the first meeting were H.L. Donovan, president of Eastern State Teachers College; Frank Peters, state comptroller; W.H. Humphrey, principal of John G. Fee High School, Maysville; and attorney Charles Anderson, Jr. Despite their absence, the committee was still composed of a cross-section of black and white state leaders.

Prior to the advisory commission meeting, McVey had requested that each member issue statements concerning the governor's assignment to them. Thus, Evans suggested the group begin their meeting by commenting on the letters they had submitted. He suggested that Atwood begin with his written statement. Atwood observed that it was necessary for the committee first to decide whether its work would focus on higher education or on all levels of black education. Next he observed that black inequalities in education could actually be solved by allowing blacks into white schools. However, rather than push this issue, Atwood agreed with white leaders who claimed Kentucky was not ready to desegregate; he suggested that the committee work to equalize facilities between black and white schools. Atwood believed this alternative could be realized by offering blacks a "university opportunity" through combined curriculums at Kentucky State College and Louisville Municipal College with assistance from the universities of Kentucky and Louisville. Atwood also believed state scholarships should not only be continued but that they should be increased to include the difference for the cost of out-of-state study.

Atwood's measures for educational equality did not satisfy the concerns of fellow committee member A.E. Meyzeek. Meyzeek believed the committee should consider the option of admitting blacks into the state's white colleges and universities. More important, Meyzeek also argued that blacks should be given "full equality" in educational opportunities offered in the state. Despite Meyzeek's objections, the committee voted to limit its work to providing equal treatment for blacks in higher education.

A subcommittee was then organized to ascertain information concerning inequalities in education and to make recommendations for improvement. To provide the larger body with complete details, the subcommittee was asked to report on the courses offered at the state's white institutions that were not available at Kentucky State College, thereby disclosing the services and facilities needed to establish them there; to report on the courses offered at white schools that could be duplicated at Kentucky State, including the cost to establish them; to report on the courses that could not be duplicated at Kentucky State; to report on the percentage of black undergraduate and graduate students willing to take courses not available at Kentucky State at the University of Kentucky; and to ascertain the funds needed to offer each student an out-of-state scholarship. Finally, the subcommittee was asked to report on the kind of legislation or court action that would comply with the Supreme Court's decision in the Gaines case.

Because the state had not assumed equal provisions for higher education, the governor's committee recognized that blacks had a legal right to enter the University of Kentucky. Thus, the subcommittee had an important task since it was responsible for finding ways to meet the mandate of the Court. To make sure the problem of solving inequality in higher education was completely reviewed, the subcommittee was assigned to study ways in which the University of Louisville might cooperate with the state in establishing a program of higher education for African-Americans. It was also ordered to maintain a close association with the United States Office of Education and its study on black higher education. Atwood suggested the group complete their report in time for it to be discussed at the 1940 legislative session.

Upon this recommendation another meeting on black higher education was adjourned. Several black members, however, were not satisfied with the results. They believed Atwood had relinquished a significant opportunity to desegregate the University of Kentucky when he compromised with whites on the issue of integration. Instead of creating a subcommittee to investigate the means of providing equal education for blacks and whites, Meyzeek, Lane, and W.H. Fouse wanted the committee to work toward admitting blacks into white institutions.[18] They firmly believed that integration was essential for blacks to achieve full equality.

Atwood's patient attitude toward desegregating the University of Kentucky was critically appraised by Walter White, who learned about the meeting from Lizzie Fouse, whose husband served on the governor's advisory committee. On December 14, 1939, in a letter to Mrs. Fouse, White commented on Atwood's role, writing, "I am shocked at President Atwood's introduction of a motion to exclude from consideration the admission of Negroes to the University of Kentucky, but I am thankful that Mr. Fouse and Mr. Meyzeek disagreed with him. What are we going to do to stiffen the backbones and broaden the vision of our people . . . A little more courage could speed up the process of getting what rightfully is ours if only we could inject some of that courage into some of those who need it."[19]

To be sure, Atwood had a vested interest in segregation, as did other black educators, businessmen, and professionals who comprised the black middle class of that period. The black middle class, which had achieved its successes by assimilating into white America, was concerned about a white backlash if it forcefully attacked racial discrimination.[20] Had whites perceived Atwood as an agitator, he would have, no doubt, sacrificed personal and professional gains. As the chief administrator of an all-black institution, he held an important, highly visible position in the community and state in which he worked. He was in a strategic position to work with whites in recommending jobs for black teachers throughout Kentucky. He feared desegregation would eliminate the need for his kind of leadership since Kentucky State, the smallest college, faced a higher probability of being closed. Atwood risked losing more personally and professionally than did Meyzeek, Fouse, and Lane. So, rather than press whites into admitting black students to their schools, Atwood wished to use the meetings on black higher education as an opportunity to lift Kentucky State to a level equal to the state's white colleges.

Yet Atwood truly believed in the intangible advantages black education provided, even in the realm of segregation. He thought black schools offered students and faculty a supportive network and social and educational opportunities that would be lost with desegregation. Atwood placated whites who preferred upgrading Kentucky State to desegregating the University of Kentucky not only because his stand on the matter was constricted by whites but because their proposals paralleled his personal views and his plans for the growth of Kentucky State.

Regardless of the opposition toward desegregation, Atwood made sure that white members on the committee knew he appreciated the support given to his administration. For example, following the November 24 meeting of the governor's advisory committee, Atwood wrote President Garrett of Western State Teachers College to thank him for serving on the committee, but he also included a note that said, "Just this additional word to let you know how grateful I am for your sympathetic attitude toward our problems. I believe I express the feelings of Negro people generally. Thank you."[21]

On January 30, 1940, at the follow-up advisory committee meeting, the subcommittee presented a report that recommended establishing graduate courses at Kentucky State. David Lane objected, explaining that offering advanced courses at Kentucky State would not solve black inequality and that the amount of money suggested for the program was insufficient. W.C. Buford, a vice-president with the black-owned Mamouth Life Insurance Company in Louisville, strongly supported Lane. Buford represented Meyzeek at the meeting.

Charles Anderson also believed desegregating the University of Kentucky was the best action for the committee to take. He countered arguments that black students enrolled at the University of Kentucky would be isolated on campus. He did not believe admitting blacks would discourage whites from attending the university. Anderson said he found law students at the University of Kentucky to be friendly, and he maintained that some members of the governor's advisory committee were afraid of "something that is not there." According to Anderson, the state, if given a chance, was actually more prepared for the desegregation of its graduate facilities than leaders realized.

Atwood believed that forcing whites to accept an integrated

policy would result in the establishment of inadequate courses and departments at Kentucky State College. He also believed that whites were closer to accepting the integration of graduate and professional schools than some members of the committee recognized. Meanwhile, Atwood saw the proposal to promote graduate work at Kentucky State College as an opportunity for his school to advance its standing in academic circles. The college needed to offer graduate work, explained Atwood, in vocational agriculture, home economics, and trades and industries to teachers who could only take courses during summer months.[22]

The final report of the governor's advisory committee appeared to offer Kentucky State a chance to grow. For instance, it proposed expanding programs at Kentucky State to include more training in agriculture, business administration, industrial arts, teacher education at the undergraduate level and one year at the graduate level. However, the committee's report also included other alternatives for equalizing higher education between the races. It suggested expanding Louisville Municipal College to offer preparation in nursing, public health, and social service administration, exchanging faculty personnel, and continuing out-of-state scholarships with the possibility of modifying the Day Law for blacks students who sought to enroll in courses at white schools because they were not offered at the state's black institutions.[23] These suggestions did not solve the problem of providing equal higher education for blacks. Instead they served as temporary measures until whites could find other ways to continue segregation in education.

NAACP secretary Walter White was highly disappointed with the recommendations of the advisory committee. On March 20, 1940, he wrote to Chairman Frank McVey and reiterated his opinion that the committee should take a stand. According to White, "A careful study of the Supreme Court's decision makes it clear that equal educational opportunities within the State must be furnished all citizens. If Kentucky is to follow this decision it must either admit qualified Negroes to its graduate and professional schools or establish a separate and *equal* facilities for Negroes. It seems that the Committee is unwilling to take an an affirmative stand on whether it will recommend one or the other. Scholarships for Negroes to out-of-state institutions do not furnish equality."[24] In the last paragraph of the two-page letter, White argued that blacks should be admitted to the state institutions in Kentucky. "The question of attempting to establish a separate university for Negroes would be a distinct step backward for the State of Kentucky." Despite White's scathing attack on the committee's solutions for equalizing higher education in Kentucky, the committee refused to support desegregating the University of Kentucky. Several days after receiving White's letter, McVey replied: "We shall be glad to give it careful consideration if the question comes up in the immediate future."[25]

Although White was frustrated and disappointed with Atwood's role in the struggle to desegregate schools in Kentucky, he soon found that President Frederick Patterson of Tuskegee University, a private black institution, endorsed a philosophy similar to that of Atwood. In 1940 when President Franklin Roosevelt decided to allow the army to train blacks to become aviators, Patterson lobbied to get the base established at Tuskegee, even though he knew it would be segregated. In doing so, he contradicted the interest of NAACP officials who were struggling to get the War Department to offer an integrated aviation training program. Patterson's eagerness and eventual success in getting the airfield constructed at Tuskegee brought strong criticism from the NAACP. Walter White was angry that blacks comprised less than 1 percent of the fifty thousand aviators being trained as of July 1941. "This is what comes about because a Negro asked for segregation," lamented White. Civil rights attorney William Hastie described Patterson's efforts as "an object lesson of selfish and short-sighted scheming for immediate personal advantage with cynical disregard for the larger interests of the Negro and the nation." Yet Patterson figured the airfield would create new jobs for the black community of Tuskegee and promote the image of his school.[26]

Atwood, too, exploited the pressure the NAACP placed on white institutions to advance conditions at Kentucky State whenever possible, however, Atwood's partly noble intention was the result of a failing strategy that slowed down the progress of desegregation. Ironically, had Atwood been less vehement in his attempts to better his school, the NAACP might have been successful in its initial attack against segregation in Kentucky. Instead, Atwood's crusade to upgrade the college gave white officials an excuse to delay school desegregation even further.

White willingness to overlook the inequalities in higher education encouraged black activists in Kentucky further to improve problems in black education. In 1941 blacks in Louisville eliminated the 15 percent pay difference between black and white teachers in the city.[27] While the issue of salary differentials was being challenged, several blacks were making efforts to challenge segregation at the University of Kentucky. Prentice Thomas, a Louisville attorney and local NAACP legal advisor, wrote national NAACP legal advisor Charles Houston to inform him that he was a member of a committee of four trying to get a black student to apply to the university. Between 1940 and 1941 Thomas corresponded with Houston concerning the possibilities of attacking the Day Law. Initially, Thomas, upon advice from Houston, had considered getting a black student to apply to Berea College for a course not offered at the state's black schools. Despite having support from a couple of the white faculty members at Berea, Thomas decided to forgo this idea since the college only admitted students from the mountain areas, and he did not have the funds to go there and find a suitable applicant.[28]

Meanwhile, Atwood, in his own way, was diligently advocating black equality. In February 1941 he joined more than seventy black and white civic and religious leaders from throughout the state to form the Kentucky Council on Interracial Cooperation. The council was formed to suggest ways for improving the educational and economic opportunities available to blacks. As vice-chairman of the council, Atwood attempted to build support among whites who favored equal education. While the council did not endorse the desegregation of public schools or colleges through the masters level, it did consider the statewide economic advantage of allowing blacks to pursue their doctoral studies and other advanced professional training in white schools. According to the council's executive committee, it would be too expensive for the state to establish a separate but equal education in advanced graduate and professional academic levels. However, the committee, not surprisingly, did favor expanding Kentucky State so it could offer science and liberal arts training up to the masters level. Quite naturally, this suggestion was strongly endorsed by Atwood, who wanted Kentucky State to offer advanced study.[29] Indeed, Atwood had everything to gain if the state established quality advanced training for blacks attending Kentucky State, and, to be sure, the prestige of the college and Atwood's influence as a black educator would be enhanced by the progress of the institution he represented. Yet the academic programs established at Kentucky State supposedly to equalize education would never parallel those at the University of Kentucky.

In August 1941, Charles Lamont Eubanks, a black honors graduate from Central High School in Louisville, applied to the University of Kentucky's College of Engineering. Despite having a 91 percent grade average, Eubanks was denied admission because of the Day Law. Originally, neither the KNEA, the Louisville NAACP, nor the Education Equalization Committee backed Eubanks's application; however, attorney Prentice Thomas considered Eubanks's case as an opportunity to challenge the Day Law. He wrote Howard University Law School professor Leon Ransom, who was a colleague of Houston's, and informed him that "Eubank [sic] has nothing to lose nor does his family have any position as city employees or such that would cause him to be 'on the spot.'"[30]

Thomas was genuinely impressed with Eubanks's character. He considered Eubanks "an unusual fellow with magnetic and impressive personality." Soon after Eubanks's application to the university was rejected, Thomas filed a suit on his behalf. The initial brief, filed in Fayette Chancery Court, was not well organized and failed to include significant legal demands. On October 17, 1941, Thomas and Thurgood Marshall withdrew the initial suit and filed a new complaint in United States District Court that called for $3,000 in damages against the registrar, Leo Chamberlain, and an injunction to force the university to admit blacks.[31]

The lawsuit generated serious concern among white officials in Kentucky, who had successfully sidestepped the issue of equal education since the Gaines decision of 1938. On November 5, 1941, the executive committee of the State Board of Education established a two-year curriculum in civil engineering at Kentucky State College. The board also announced its "desire" to see the curriculum "comparable" to that of the University of Kentucky. However, Thomas had doubts about the board's resolution. "No matter how good the intentions of the Board of Education," said Thomas, "I don't believe they will be able to secure the money to establish absolutely equal opportunities in the engineering course. It would require an enormous outlay of buildings and equipment and an increase in faculty."[32]

Atwood also doubted that the state could provide the necessary funds to support the engineering program, but all he could do was continue to challenge the General Assembly to appropriate more funds to Kentucky State. Thomas informed Thurgood Marshall that Atwood claimed he had to abide by the orders of the board if he wanted to keep his job. Furthermore, wrote Thomas, Atwood had been told by the dean of the Engineering School at the University of

Kentucky that students would not need equipment during their first two years in the program.[33]

Essentially, Atwood was a political pawn of whites who looked to him to cooperate in their plans for maintaining segregation. He realized this and tried to use his connections with influential whites as a means to advance Kentucky State. His dependence on whites for political and financial support, though, confined him to endorsing their solutions for remedying unequal education. The best he could offer blacks was an aggressive effort to secure more money for the Kentucky State engineering program and the tuition-payment plan.

Neither the engineering course nor the tuition-payment plan received adequate financial support from the General Assembly. Kentucky State received a twenty thousand dollar annual increase for the 1942-44 biennium. The tuition payment plan remained at $175 per student each academic year. In November 1943, NAACP legal advisor Charles Houston traveled to Lexington and Frankfort to compile a report on the "Eubanks Case." He found that in April 1943 the State Board of Education had added courses in general and civil engineering at Kentucky State and that the curriculum in civil engineering had been expanded to train students in their junior and senior years. Yet, as of the fall 1943 semester, only two students had enrolled in the engineering program, and they were both first-year students. Houston also had inspected the engineering college at the University of Kentucky and compared it to the program at Kentucky State. The latter had "insufficient" equipment in its physics lab and a poorly qualified instructor.[34]

The Eubanks case had problems from the start that hindered its chances of success. For instance, Thomas and Marshall had incorrectly listed the defendants in their complaint and had to amend it to name the defendants as the "University of Kentucky" instead of the "Board of Trustees." The case was delayed further when summonses were not properly served on all the defendants. Thomas's decision to accept a position as an assistant special counsel in the NAACP legal office in New York did not help the case either. After having invested considerable time in the Eubanks case, Thomas was compelled to secure resident counsel. Also, Eubanks had experienced personal problems that had interfered with his interest in the suit. He received little support from the Louisville black community, which did not ease the situation. According to Thomas in a letter to Louisville attorney S.A. Burnley, "'the first families of

Louisville' are not interested in this young man and some of them are even antagonistic toward him."[35]

In 1945, Federal District Court Judge H. Church Ford dismissed the suit because Eubanks's attorneys neglected to prosecute during two consecutive terms of the court. It was a court rule to remove from the docket all cases that had not been prosecuted within two years. Charles Anderson blamed the court's final ruling on Atwood, who he believed should not have allowed an engineering program to be established at the school. Anderson charged that Atwood's willingness to administer the engineering school at Kentucky State enabled attorneys for the University of Kentucky and the state to argue that equal education was available to blacks.[36]

But Atwood was a victim of circumstances. As the state's highest ranking black employee, he was torn between representing blacks as an educator and representing them as a civil rights leader. He wanted to do the right thing but found it virtually impossible to work in one arena. Any decisions he made as an educator influenced his contribution to the civil rights struggle, and whatever he did to boost civil rights restrained his efforts to advance Kentucky State. It was an unfortunate dilemma that Atwood found difficult and burdensome.

Atwood's situation was complicated even more by the unwillingness of black leaders to focus on one solution to resolving inequality in education. Instead of just working to get blacks admitted to white graduate and professional schools, black leaders were concerned with increasing the funds of out-of-state scholarships as well as increasing available services at Kentucky State College. As Atwood observed, all of these proposals were "contradictory." Out-of-state aid would not be necessary if the University of Kentucky accepted blacks, but neither the Day Law nor the scholarship program would have to be amended if Kentucky State were given adequate financial support. Furthermore, noted Atwood, if the University of Kentucky admitted black students, there would be less need for Kentucky State.[37]

Black leaders struggled with these concerns as they sought to guarantee black equality in education. On February 4, 1944, State Representative Charles Anderson submitted House Bill 245 to the Kentucky General Assembly. The bill was written to modify the Day Law by opening white graduate and professional schools to black students. Originally the bill was part of a strategy by Anderson and Atwood to advance conditions at Kentucky State. During previous legislative sessions the two men had worked out a plan in which Anderson would sponsor a bill to repeal the Day Law with intentions of urging lawmakers to extend more financial support for Kentucky State. The objective was to remind white politicians of the unequal conditions in education and to motivate them to lend support to the black college.[38]

Four days after the Anderson bill was introduced, James Dorman, a Lexington Democrat, submitted H.B. 265, which he claimed would provide Kentucky State with the plant equipment and faculty equivalent to that of the University of Kentucky. The Dorman bill launched a controversy among the state's black leaders. William Warley, black publisher of the Louisville *News* and a member of the Louisville chapter of the NAACP, strongly supported the Dorman bill. He wrote, "If this bill should become law Kentucky State College would become a million dollar university giving to Colored youth law, medicine, and everything the 'white' universities would give." When Anderson's bill was voted on by the executive committee of the Louisville NAACP, Warley and Stephen A. Burnley were the only two members who cast dissenting votes.[39]

In spite of the division among NAACP members regarding his bill, Anderson remained firmly in support of the measure. In campaigning for the bill on the House floor, Anderson told his colleagues that the state's tuition payment plan was "unfair and inadequate." Anderson emphasized that his bill would save the state from having to spend the $1 million it would take to establish a duplicate black university. To the surprise of Anderson and Atwood, the House chose to support the Anderson bill by a vote of 41 to 38.[40]

Although Atwood wanted improvements for Kentucky State, he chose to support the Anderson bill. In a letter to the editor of the *Courier-Journal*, Atwood urged the Senate to pass the bill. Similar to Anderson's arguments, Atwood expressed concern over the state's financial ability and its commitment to provide equal education for the races. He believed either inadequately run courses or "unjustifiably expensive" courses would be established at Kentucky State because few students would be enrolled in them as a result of the state's small black population. The Anderson bill, Atwood explained, was "the sanest and most practical approach to solve the problem of inequality in higher education in the state." Furthermore, noted Atwood, Anderson's bill would allow "the state to concentrate its funds upon making the Kentucky State College for Negroes the strong undergraduate college it ought to be."[41] After

the Anderson bill passed in the House neither Anderson nor Atwood sought other progressive changes in black higher education.
Thus, when the bill failed to pass in the Senate, the effort to gain a
significant increase in funds for Kentucky State was also lost.
Anderson conveyed his disappointment in a letter to NAACP leaders
Thurgood Marshall and Roy Wilkins. He wrote, "I am certain that
we missed victory and a great fight by reason of our own group."
Anderson blamed the bill's defeat on "a small group of Negroes"
who had asked senators to oppose the bill. He mentioned in his
letter, however, that Atwood was for his bill,[42] but this was of little
value to Atwood, who had chosen to support the Anderson bill
over the possibility of obtaining a major increase in funds for
Kentucky State.

Atwood was frustrated and disappointed with the modest increase in funding his school received during the 1944 legislative
session. That summer he met with Anderson in his Louisville office
to discuss the lack of progress they had made in equalizing education. Atwood told Anderson that he was "going to stand for the
development of Kentucky State College first, and after this was
done, [he] would join him [Anderson] and others seeking to open
the doors of several institutions for those things which KSC could
not justify establishing."

Representative Anderson did not agree with Atwood's position,
and, although he and Atwood were friends and black leaders who
respected each other, he challenged Atwood's objective. In a
speech before a forum at the Lexington, Kentucky, YWCA, Anderson criticized Atwood for encouraging support for Kentucky State
College rather than an end to the Day Law. According to a newspaper report, Anderson said that "when a college president thinks
in such terms, then his thinking is warped and selfish and his
usefulness as an educational leader is questionable."[43]

Atwood's reply to Anderson's charges was published in the
Louisville *Leader* and the Louisville *Defender*. Atwood summarized
the unsuccessful attempt to advance equal education for black
Kentuckians during the 1944 legislative session. He also reiterated
his argument for developing Kentucky State College first before
pushing for the admission of blacks into the University of Kentucky. In clarifying this position Atwood wrote:

I am for providing full equality of educational opportunity for the members
of our social group at the earliest possible moment. To provide that equal-

ity I believe the Kentucky State College should be given the necessary funds to expand in every area that the number of anticipated students will justify. In time the doors of the University of Kentucky and other similar institutions will be opened to Negro students in those fields of study in which the demand is not sufficient to warrant the creation of separate departments at KSC, but we should first develop our own institution as far as the number of anticipated students will justify.[44]

Despite his public statements, Atwood knew that the graduate and professional programs at the University of Kentucky would have to be desegregated if there was any chance of Kentucky State becoming a good higher learning institution. Experience had taught him that the empire he was hoping to build in Frankfort had limitations. It was a remote possibility that Kentucky State could offer quality advanced education even in some phases of science and liberal arts. Whites had never supported the development of Kentucky State as an undergraduate institution, thus there was no reason to assume they would establish strong graduate and professional programs at the school. But, in the early 1940s, Atwood could not express this view to white officials and expect to remain president; he had to accept the plans whites presented to him regardless of whether they were in the best interest of the school.

As Anderson and Atwood offered opposing solutions for equalizing education, the KNEA took a neutral position. In April 1945, the legislative committee of the KNEA reported that educational equality could be achieved by expanding Kentucky State and/or by modifying the Day Law in order to allow the integration of some courses. "The KNEA does not wish to say which method should be pushed first," stated the committee, "or whether both should be pushed simultaneously. This is a question of strategy which the Association can not decide, but must rely upon its leaders to decide and effect for the best interest of the minority group." The KNEA did, however, "demand that something tangible be done by those in authority" to establish equal educational opportunties between the races.[45]

Atwood had a valid reason for being concerned about the creation of makeshift graduate programs at Kentucky State for the sake of maintaining the Day Law. While he was anxious to establish some graduate programs at the school, he was also concerned about the quality of instruction and the availability of facilities to support such programs. As his administration progressed, Atwood realized that building up the college and opening the graduate and

professional schools of the University of Kentucky were inseparable issues. Kentucky State could possibly acquire more funding
and create a solid academic program if the University of Kentucky
offered blacks graduate and professional education.

The disagreement between Atwood and Anderson resurfaced
following the dismissal of the Eubanks case. The two men clarified
their positions on expanding the educational opportunities of
blacks in a public forum held at the Plymouth Congregational
Church in Louisville. Atwood made clear that he wanted a "top-
notch" black undergraduate college and not a black university.
While recalling his disagreement with Anderson in his autobiography, Atwood wrote, "I had been appointed to the college presidency to do my best to make Kentucky State a first-class institution.
This was my job second to none. Charlie was a state legislature [sic];
his job was not confined to one particular issue. Therefore, though
he was concerned about Kentucky State, he could not devote all his
time to that one area." [46]

During the 1940s, however, Atwood's solutions for expanding
the educational opportunities of blacks appeared to be more self-
indulgent than a reflection of his role of leadership. His focus on
building Kentucky State gave the overwhelming impression that he
was narrow-minded, timid, and conservative on race issues. Although he was constrained in his civil rights activities, he was not
as willing to be silent about black inequality as were some black
college presidents. Atwood did get involved in the movement to
equalize black education.

In October 1945, Atwood issued a prepared statement to the
state's legislative council outlining a program for desegregating
education. He requested the General Assembly pass legislation
admitting blacks to white colleges for graduate and professional
courses not offered at Kentucky State. He also suggested increasing
the tuition payment plan from $175 to $350 a year with the stipula-
tion that the program be gradually eliminated until the state offered
blacks equal education. Atwood was especially concerned with the
need to expand facilities at Kentucky State. According to Atwood,
the college needed a total of five hundred thousand dollars annually for the next biennium. Each year, two hundred thousand
dollars of this appropriation would be used for capital outlay while
the remainder would go toward general expenses. The assertive-
ness of Atwood's statement to the council came through clearly
when he wrote: "The time has come when we must build up the

state college for Negroes in a substantial way and make provision for their equal education. Nearly seven years have now passed since the United States Supreme Court decreed that equality of higher education must be provided within each state. Negro Kentuckians are growing restive over the fact that thus far our state has done so little for them and so much less than many other southern states."[47] To further his plans for equal education, Atwood was active in organizations that shared his basic objectives. In 1945, he was elected treasurer of the Southern Negro Conference for the Equalization of Educational Opportunities. The conference, which met in Jackson, Mississippi, was composed of newspaper publishers and educators from thirteen states who opposed "the principle of a dual school system." The group wanted full educational opportunities for blacks.[48]

The conference's efforts were augmented by the NAACP, which had been advocating equal education for several years. Following the end of World War II, the NAACP increased its efforts to equalize graduate and professional training for blacks. In 1946, the organization filed lawsuits on behalf of Ada Sipuel and Heman Sweatt. Both were seeking professional training in their respective states. Sipuel, a graduate of the State College for Negroes in Langston, Oklahoma, was denied admission to the University of Oklahoma's Law School despite having an impressive undergraduate background. Sweatt, a letter carrier and graduate of Prairie View University, which held this standing in name only, had his application rejected to the University of Texas's Law School.[49]

In response to the NAACP's legal attack, white officials in Oklahoma and Texas quickly established makeshift law schools. The Oklahoma Board of Regents hired three law instructors and quartered off a section of the state capital to serve as a separate law school for Sipuel, who refused to attend this kind of facility. Heman Sweatt encountered similar circumstances at the University of Texas, which hired part-time faculty members to teach him. Three basement rooms in a downtown office building in Austin were converted to qualify as the separate law school for Sweatt and other black residents in Texas. Makeshift programs such as these only temporarily stalled the NAACP's legal campaign. The organization pressed onward in its efforts to prove that such conditions perpetuated unequal education.[50]

In 1948, the NAACP filed a law suit for sixty-eight-year-old George McLaurin, who had his application rejected by the graduate school of the University of Oklahoma. The District Court ruled that Oklahoma had to provide McLaurin equal education in the state. White officials decided to admit him to the university on a "segregated basis." Instead of being free to mingle with the other students socially and academically, McLaurin was assigned specific places to sit in the cafeteria, library, and classroom.[51] Although the NAACP's objective had not been fully reached, it was making progress in attacking the existence of jim crow in higher education.

Throughout the South, white state officials searched for a workable solution to overcome the Gaines decision. In February 1948 members of the Southern Governors Conference signed a compact to create segregated regional colleges in the South for blacks and whites. The governors believed this arrangement would enable each southern state to offer a range of expensive programs to black as well as white students. The colleges were intended to provide equal advanced education. Although the Southern Governors Conference failed to get congressional support for regional schools, the plan was endorsed by the Regional Council for Education. The council called upon black and white educators to serve on study committees in order to assist with the development of regional schools.[52]

Both the Conference of Presidents of Negro Land Grant Colleges and the Association of Colleges and Secondary Schools for Negroes opposed the regional schools. Most black educators did not believe it was possible to establish separate but equal facilities. They were concerned about adequate funding and staffing for regional institutions. Atwood strongly opposed the idea of establishing regional schools. In a letter to John Ivey, director of the Regional Council for Education, Atwood declined an invitation to work with the council. He explained to Ivey that he opposed establishing segregated schools personally and as a member of the Conference of Presidents of Negro Land Colleges. Atwood believed segregated schools would perpetuate segregation. He wrote: "all of this is contrary to my notion of true democracy, which looks forward to eliminating rather than perpetuating segregation."[53]

Atwood was not pressured by state officials to cooperate with the regional program, which made it easier for him adamantly to refuse the project. Governor Earle Clements, a Democrat, met with Kentucky's black leaders including Clarence Timberlake, active black supporter of the Democratic party, Atwood, Meyzeek, and Frank Stanley, editor of the *Defender*, who offered suggestions for equalizing black education.⁵⁴ Because he depended largely on support from white voters, Clements had to be tactful in the approach he used in dealing with racial issues. Although Clements was not a fierce opponent of segregation, he was not a staunch advocate of the system either. Instead, he was a shrewd politician who looked for ways of eliminating school desegregation gradually. But, as the national movement to desegregate graduate and professional schools gathered momentum, Clements keenly recognized Kentucky would have to amend the Day Law soon.

On March 15, 1948, Lyman T. Johnson, a black teacher from Louisville's Central High School, applied to the University of Kentucky's graduate school to pursue a doctorate degree in history. He was denied admission because of the Day Law. Johnson filed a suit against the university declaring that the school's adherence to the Day Law violated the Fourteenth Amendment to the Constitution.⁵⁵

Initially, Atwood was not pleased with Johnson's decision to bring suit against the University of Kentucky. He believed Johnson should have applied to Kentucky State before he submitted an application to the university. According to Johnson, Atwood told him that he was making a "big mistake" since he had not applied to Kentucky State to learn whether the school had what he needed. Atwood assumed Johnson would have a stronger case if Atwood was allowed to contribute to the argument that Kentucky State did not offer equal programs. Johnson believed that proving educational equality did not exist in Kentucky was his lawyer's job, not Atwood's. During one exchange on the matter, Johnson recalled telling Atwood: "Mr. President you are assuming too much. You are taking away from me my right to go to any damn school in this state that we support with public taxes. Any of these schools," continued Johnson, "is my school and I have just as much right to go to anyone of those as a white student has."⁵⁶

Atwood's remarks to Johnson were reflective of his paternalistic behavior and his continuous plan to highlight the weaknesses of Kentucky State. Atwood believed he was the most informed black leader on inequality in education in Kentucky, and he was convinced that all activities surrounding the subject had to be cleared by him. Since opportunities at Kentucky State were limited, Atwood searched for every opportunity to press the state for larger appropriations. Regardless, Johnson's suit forced the state to choose between establishing an arrangement that offered equal education or an inevitable court order to desegregate higher learning institutions. White officials chose to adopt a solution that forbade the integration of the races.

On July 13, 1948, the State Board of Education and the University of Kentucky's board of trustees signed a contract in part planned to raise the standards of Kentucky State College to that of the University of Kentucky. Governor Clements allocated forty-five thousand dollars to the project. The staffs of State Attorney General A.E. Funk and University of Kentucky president Herman Donovan spent several weeks preparing the agreement. Their plan was intended to offer graduate and professional training similar to that being offered at the University of Kentucky on the campus of Kentucky State. Courses would be taught by professors of the university, and the laboratory facilities at the University of Kentucky would be made available to Kentucky State students during designated hours.[57]

Attorney General Funk admitted that the plan was developed in response to Johnson's lawsuit. "We want to get this set up," said Funk, "before we have to answer that suit." According to Funk, Atwood, Clements, and President Donovan were cognizant of the program and had approved it; however, A.E. Meyzeek, the only black member of the State Board of Education, called the plan a "subterfuge." "It sets up a Jim Crow system of education," he noted.[58]

The new academic arrangement and Johnson's lawsuit once again placed Atwood in the middle of the controversial struggle to desegregate the state's schools. Similar to the approach he had used during the Eubanks case, Atwood used the board's plan as sufficient reason to request greater funding. He observed that in order for the plan to meet the expectations of those who created it, the size of the plant at Kentucky State College would have to be expanded. He requested $2 million from the building commission, noting that the school needed more classrooms for graduate and professional students.[59] Despite this emphasis, Atwood gave the impression he was in favor of the state's plan. "While the plan is cumbersome," stated Atwood, "it can be made to work if given adequate financial support."[60]

Charles Thompson, editor of the *Journal of Negro Education*, was highly critical of Atwood's statement indicating the feasibility of the plan. In a 1948 editorial, Thompson wrote that he believed Atwood's comment "was both unwise and unnecessary, if not actually injurious to the cause."[61] To be sure, Atwood's statement was "unwise." It gave the impression to blacks and whites that he hoped the plan would work. In actuality, however, Atwood did not want Kentucky State tied to any makeshift programs that could jeopardize its accreditation. He believed Kentucky State should concentrate on building its undergraduate program rather than focus on all phases of graduate and professional training. But, instead of verbally attacking the board's plan and possibly distancing himself from white leadership, Atwood pretended to go along with the program, perhaps too much but realizing all the while it would fail.

Meanwhile, the first student required to attend classes under the board's awkward arrangement was John Hatch, who had been denied admission to the University of Kentucky's Law School. In the fall of 1948, Hatch began his law studies as seven professors from the University of Kentucky in Lexington drove back and forth to Frankfort to instruct him. However, after a few weeks, university officials decided to modify the arrangement. President Donovan announced that four Frankfort attorneys had been hired to teach Hatch. According to the university's administration, this procedure would improve Hatch's daily schedule of classes.

Donovan also revealed that Hatch's classwork would be shifted from the campus of Kentucky State to the state capitol, where there was a completed law library. The change would supposedly improve Hatch's chances of receiving an equal education; however, Atwood was very critical of the university's decision to alter the plans. He charged that the original contract had been violated since it stipulated that courses offered at Kentucky State would have to be instructed by regular teachers from the University of Kentucky. "Obviously the new plan does not meet these requirements," argued Atwood.[62]

While Atwood protested Hatch's law school program, the NAACP legal defense team geared up to win Johnson's suit against the University of Kentucky. Thurgood Marshall and Robert Carter, representing the national office of the NAACP; Ben Shobe of Lexington; and James A. Crumlin from Louisville comprised the principal legal team responsible for preparing Johnson's case. On March 17, 1949, depositions for the Johnson case were taken in Atwood's office. Atwood was one of the witnesses examined by Johnson's attorneys and he gave testimony that further supported their case against the University of Kentucky. Instead of tacitly endorsing segregation, Atwood was forthright in explaining how' the state had failed to expand his school. During his testimony, Atwood revealed that Kentucky State did not have an adequate library or physical facilities to meet the needs of graduate students. Attorney Carter asked Atwood, "How do you feel [the state] plan is going to work out in terms of affording adequate training at the graduate school?" Atwood replied, "I don't think it will work out. We are doing the best we can to give our registrants the very best education possible."[63]

The NAACP did not have to present this evidence at the trial, however. Judge H. Church Ford began the March 30 trial by stating the issue was whether the University of Kentucky was providing Johnson an equal education. The university had no evidence to submit in its defense; consequently, Ford ruled in Johnson's favor and the University of Kentucky was required to admit blacks to its graduate school as well as the colleges of law, pharmacy, and engineering, becauses these courses were not offered at Kentucky State.[64]

According to Atwood, President Donovan was concerned about the implications of Ford's historic decision. Atwood claimed years later that Donovan feared riots and activities from hate groups like the Ku Klux Klan. Furthermore, Atwood recalled that "just prior to the opening of the 1949 summer school session, he asked me to use my influence to see that only Lyman Johnson attended the school at that time, or if that failed, to carefully select the Negroes that were going to be the first to attend the University. To relieve his fears, I told him that I would do what I could. I did nothing, absolutely nothing."[65]

Although Atwood did not support the request of his colleague, he was pleased Donovan did not encounter problems during the summer school session. Donovan later expressed his appreciation to Atwood for sending a group of good students to the university. Rather than reveal the truth of the matter, Atwood simply accepted Donovan's compliment.[66]

Following the Johnson suit, segregation in higher education began to whither away in other parts of the South. On June 5, 1950, the Supreme Court ruled that the University of Texas had to admit Heman Sweatt. On the same day the Court decided in favor of George McLaurin and declared that segregation on the University of Oklahoma's campus was unconstitutional. On August 9, 1950, the Court of Chancery of Delaware determined that nine black plaintiffs were entitled to enroll in the undergraduate college of the University of Delaware in Newark and also ruled that Delaware State College did not offer blacks an education equal to whites and thus violated the Fourteenth Amendment.[67]

Between 1948 and 1950, as the movement to desegregate schools in southern and border states pushed forward, Governor Clements addressed the need to abolish Kentucky's Day Law. He got little support from University of Kentucky board of trustees members Richard C. Stoll and Judge Edward C. O'Rear, who opposed desegregration and considered appealing the Johnson case to the United States Supreme Court. During an April 5, 1949, board meeting a majority of those present voted to appeal the case. Judge O'Rear insisted that Clements call a special session of the state legislature so it could appropriate the necessary funds for a black university. Clements refused, and the two men almost became entangled in a fist fight during the discussion. Concerned that the controversy would not be good for the progress of the university, Vice-Chairman Stoll reluctantly asked board members to reconsider their position and vote not to appeal the Johnson case, which they agreed to do.[68]

The controversy at the University of Kentucky did not discourage Clements from considering the need to amend the Day Law. Meyzeek, Stanley, Timberlake, and black state representative Jessie Lawrence were among the black leaders who encouraged Clements to get the law amended. In 1950, Clements maneuvered an amendment through the legislature that allowed the governing board of institutions to decide whether to admit black students. During this process, Atwood was basically a cautious observer. Although Atwood favored amending the Day Law, he was concerned that such action might lead to the closing of Kentucky State.[69] He worried that the school's poor development would prevent it from successfully competing with the state's white institutions.

Atwood's concern for the future of Kentucky State was evident soon after the Johnson case was decided. In April 1949, he wrote President Donovan and Governor Clements explaining the financial needs of Kentucky State. He indicated to them how important appropriations from the Governor's Fund were toward the development of the school. Atwood wanted Kentucky State to continue receiving the forty-five thousand dollars originally set aside under the State Board's plan to raise the standards of the school. He explained the need to expand the departments of home economics, agriculture, and business administration. Atwood also expressed a desire to establish new departments in economics, psychology, dramatics, fine arts, and industrial arts and trades. According to Atwood, "if students who leave Kentucky State College to do graduate work at the University are to be in a position to do creditable work and not bend to lower academic standards, they must be given opportunities at the college level to obtain an education which is at least substantially equal to that given to undergraduate students at the University."[70] Atwood's genuine appeal to the governor and the president of the University of Kentucky was indicative of his concern for the future of Kentucky State. He was willing to utilize whatever resources he could to advance the college.

Following the amendment of the Day Law, several colleges opened their doors to blacks. Berea, Nazareth, and Bellarmine colleges revised their admission policies within the first year after the amendment was passed. As these schools became integrated, attention focused on the University of Louisville. The local chapter of the Louisville NAACP was preparing to file a suit against the institution in the event that the process of desegregation at the school was delayed. Instead of engaging in a legal battle, the university desegregated in the summer of 1950. The decision led to the closing of the Louisville Municipal College the next year.[71]

With the closing of the Louisville Municipal College, Kentucky State became the only four-year black college in the state. Atwood realized that the school was now vulnerable to the same fate as that of the Louisville Municipal College, and he fought even harder to see that it survived and expanded. He did this by proving the school could make significant contributions within an integrated system of education. Because Atwood had established a working relationship with the University of Kentucky and other white schools over the years, he was able to continue cooperating with them during desegregation.

In 1952, at a relatively early date in the period of desegregation, the University of Kentucky and Kentucky State debate teams participated in their first competition against each other. During the same year, Kentucky State scheduled a football game against all-white Taylor University, located in Upland, Indiana. These events were bold steps designed to improve race relations between students. The May 1954 Supreme Court decision outlawing segregation in education increased opportunities to obtain this objective. Five months after the decision, Geraldine Ogden was admitted as

Atwood and Dr. Ralph Bunche, 1950 commencement speaker at
Kentucky State University. Courtesy of Kentucky State University
Photographic Archives.

Kentucky State's first white student. While she did not remain at
the college, her admission was indicative of a new era in higher
education at Kentucky State.[72]

Although Atwood was not a pioneer in the desegregation of the
University of Kentucky, he did work vigorously to attract white
students to Kentucky State. In the fall 1954 issue of the *Kentucky
Teachers Association Journal*, Atwood published an article titled
"Kentucky State College and Integration." He cited several reasons
why Kentucky State should not be closed as a result of integration.

Frank Stanley, Sr., and Rufus Atwood with the 1957 Kentucky State
commencement speaker, Dr. Martin Luther King, Jr. Courtesy of Kentucky State University Photographic Archives.

He argued that the state needed the institution since Kentucky
ranked low among states in the area of education. Atwood believed
Kentucky State could be used to offer educational programs to state
government employees. A general education for students would
include courses in construction, farming, and secretarial work as
well as remedial instruction for students who had received a poor
primary and secondary education. Atwood emphasized that these
courses would attract black *and* white students.

Atwood also focused on the contribution Kentucky State could
make toward training teachers for the public school system. Because the state needed well-trained teachers this was a valuable
service the school could easily provide.[73] Not since the first decade
of his administration had Atwood offered an education program
that exemplified his creativity as an administrator. The struggle for
school desegregation had stifled Atwood's potential to guide Kentucky State to another level. When it ended, Atwood was able to
redirect his energy in seeking other ways of improving the institution.

Being the consummate politician that he was, Atwood mailed copies of his article to various Kentucky leaders, including Earle Clements, then a United States Senator; James Crumlin, president of the Kentucky NAACP; and Frank Dickey, University of Kentucky president. Dickey responded positively to Atwood's suggestions. In 1957, he and Atwood announced joint sponsorship of a new program of evening courses to be offered at Kentucky State. The program was formed to meet the educational needs of state government employees as well as business, industrial, and professional groups. More important, the program provided Kentucky State a greater opportunity to recruit students from white communities.[74]

By 1959, sixty-nine white students were enrolled in evening classes at Kentucky State. Total student enrollment for that year was 620, indicating an increase of 111 students since 1955.[75] While Atwood was pleased with this progress, his problems as a black educator in the South were far from over. The movement to desegregate education was only the first major phase of the civil rights movement. As the struggle pushed forward, Atwood and other black college presidents found themselves facing even greater challenges.

8
Spring 1960

In the spring of 1960, virtually every black president of a state-supported college faced a changing academic world. Black and white students alike questioned their leadership and led demonstrations against racial inequality. This time the dilemma facing black college presidents was influenced by the sit-in movement of February 1, 1960. On that date four students from North Carolina Agricultural and Technical College in Greensboro walked into a local Woolworth store and purchased a few items. They then sat at the segregated lunch counter and asked for coffee and doughnuts. Although the waitress refused to serve them, they remained in their seats until the store closed. The media publicized the students' "passive demand for service" and soon college students throughout the South were staging sit-ins at lunch counters that did not serve blacks.[1] By April 1960, at least fifty-four cities in nine states had experienced demonstrations similar to the one in Greensboro.[2] White city and state officials made a concerted effort to end the movement; more than a thousand students were arrested for demonstrating.[3] Yet, the sit-in movement continued, lifting the struggle for black equality to a new dimension.

The sit-ins were intended ultimately to bring positive changes in race relations. Instead, they ignited racial violence in America. A number of young black college and high-school students were beaten, spat on, and cursed by white racists who opposed equal access to public accommodations by blacks and whites. Of those who witnessed the sit-in movement, few experienced the dilemma shared by the black college presidents of publicly supported colleges. These men had to choose between supporting their students' protest for equal rights, possibly losing white support and funds, and maintaining the status quo preferred by the segregationists who controlled appropriations of the colleges.[4] Inevitably, "Some Negro college presidents," wrote New York magazine and television writer Louis Lomax, "are set to execute strange maneuvers. I would not be surprised, for example, if some of the student demonstrators who are studying under grants from foundations suddenly find their scholarships have been canceled on recommendation from their college presidents . . . for 'poor scholarship.'"[5]

Because of the mandates of white state officials, some black administrators did not have the freedom to support the student sit-in movement. In Georgia, the governor and the board of regents of the University of Georgia system warned the presidents of three state-supported black colleges to discipline any students who participated in demonstrations.[6] The State Board of Education in Louisiana similarly ordered officials at Southern University to expel eighteen student leaders who had been involved in protest movements. President Felton Clark proceeded to expel seventeen demonstrators and allegedly fire one faculty member.[7]

At Tuskegee, President Luther Foster chose not to renew the contract of Charles Hamilton after he led a march from the school into the center of downtown Tuskegee. Foster and the chairman of the social science division, Charles Gomillion, encountered strong criticism from students who decorated their lawns with placards that read "Are There Uncle Toms among Us?"[8] In Montgomery, Alabama, Governor John Patterson telephoned the president of Alabama State College, H. Council Trenholm, and demanded that he expel the students who had led a sit-in at the courthouse snack bar. After investigating the incident, Trenholm recommended that the students be placed on probation rather than expelled. However, the governor, who was an ex-officio member of the State Board of Education, insisted that nine of the students be expelled from the campus. According to the governor, the students were guilty of "conduct detrimental to the welfare of the school." Patterson's actions generated demonstrations that ultimately resulted in a stand-off between police and students near the college campus.[9]

Not all black college presidents felt compelled to expel students and dismiss faculty who participated in civil rights demonstrations. President Stephen Wright at Fisk University publicly endorsed the sit-in demonstrations. Black educators in North Carolina tried to avoid having to dismiss faculty and students by claiming the demonstrators were acting as citizens and not students. In Alabama, Talladega College president Arthur Gray fully supported his students and faculty, but a permanent injunction forbidding protest in Talladega forced him to take a conservative position. He was concerned that the school would lose its charter if students and faculty participated in further demonstrations, so he urged them to fight illiteracy and to register black voters.[10]

By the end of March 1960, a growing number of black college presidents throughout the South had witnessed the participation of their students in the sit-in movement. Yet, Atwood was an exception to this number. None of his students had yet demonstrated against local businesses. That situation changed during the months of April and May, when Kentucky State students became simultaneously involved in efforts to liberalize campus regulations and to put an end to segregation at local lunch counters. In the process, conflict and confusion permeated the campus, and Atwood finally expelled twelve students and fired two faculty members. The episode provided one of the most controversial chapters in Atwood's thirty-three-year career as president of Kentucky State College.

As the civil rights movement mounted, Kentucky State students expressed little interest in recalling Atwood's past contributions toward the growth of the institution. In the spring of 1960 they were more concerned with his response to the contemporary problems they were experiencing on the campus and in the community. Because of Atwood's decision to dismiss students and faculty members during the peak of the sit-in demonstration, he was criticized by civil rights workers. Not surprisingly, Atwood vehemently defended his decision, arguing that he took such action to eliminate student protest against campus regulations.

President Atwood's controversial response to the Kentucky State student demonstrations caused some to question whether conservative whites influenced his decision to dismiss students and faculty protesting segregation in Frankfort. To assess properly Atwood's response to the student demonstrations requires a full explanation of the situation he confronted in the spring of 1960.

Unlike most other black college presidents who had experienced the participation of their students in the sit-ins during February and March 1960, Atwood and his executive council were already in the midst of negotiating with the Kentucky State Student Council over school regulations. Between October 1959 and March 1960, Student Council representatives had expressed common student grievances concerning several campus matters. Among their concerns were the administration's decision to bar students from the Lavilla, a local club located off campus, and the need to enforce lunchroom regulations that required cafeteria workers to wear aprons and paper caps or hair nets. In addition to these matters, the Student Council wanted "more power and a freer and more efficient hand in settling student problems."[11]

As the sit-in movement spread, the Atwood administration was forced to deal with even more student activism. In late February 1960, a rumor circulated that students were planning to stage a sit-in at a Frankfort restaurant. On February 25, President Atwood called an emergency meeting of the executive council to discuss the situation. Selected and chaired by Atwood and composed of ten department heads, the council assisted the president in overseeing the school's business affairs and in resolving disciplinary problems. At the beginning of the meeting the council agreed that "a demonstration would definitely be against the best interest of the college and of the advancement of integration and race relations in Kentucky" and "that integration should proceed, but that it should be done in a legal and orderly manner." Atwood favored establishing a commission on human rights, an idea that at the time was being considered in the legislative session. Convinced a demonstration would work to the detriment of the college, the executive council agreed to investigate the credibility of the rumored sit-in.[12]

Arthur Norman, an assistant professor in the Department of Education and Psychology, was called to the meeting to answer questions pertaining to his connection with the rumored sit-in. He was known to have held discussions with students on segregation in and out of class, and the council believed he could provide information about the rumor. Norman informed the council that he and Lester Tripp, a Kentucky State student, had recently visited a Frish's restaurant near the campus and had been denied service. Although they left the restaurant without incident, Norman stated that the matter had been discussed in his psychology class and during a weekly coffee-hour discussion he held with students majoring in psychology. Norman, however, denied any knowledge of the rumored demonstration.[13] The Student Council president, Owen Carter, also met with the executive council and he, too, was not aware of the exact plans for the rumored sit-in. Instead, Carter, a twenty-two-year-old senior from Cincinnati, Ohio, emphasized that the Student Council was more concerned with settling on-campus matters. He and other student leaders had met and decided to resolve these problems before they attempted to address the larger problem of segregation in the city of Frankfort.[14]

The executive council, after listening to the statements of Norman and Carter, ended the meeting by choosing not to hold a student assembly to discuss the sit-in rumor. Their reasons for making this decision were not disclosed in the council's minutes; however, the body agreed that each faculty member would talk with students on the proposed day of the sit-in to encourage them to support a council on human relations instead of arranging a sit-in movement in the city of Frankfort.[15]

For a few weeks the executive council's suggestion that students not engage in a sit-in demonstration was not challenged. In the meantime, a group of Kentucky State students who had participated in Arthur Norman's informal coffee-hour discussions on segregation remained interested in the idea of organizing a sit-in movement. On March 18, 1960, Norman and Tripp wrote a letter to the Congress of Racial Equality (CORE) inquiring about the possibility of establishing a chapter in Frankfort. The letter, which included four other signatures of support, claimed to represent a biracial group in Frankfort seeking to establish better race relations. Within two weeks the Students For Civil Rights, a Frankfort CORE affiliate, was officially recognized by the national chapter. Since the Greensboro sit-ins, CORE had taken the leading role in advocating sit-in demonstrations. Founded in Chicago in the spring of 1942 by black and white Christian pacifists, CORE fought racism with "interracial, nonviolent direct action." The Students For Civil Rights, while meeting at the St. John AME Church in Frankfort, sought to interest others in participating in the newly formed local organization. Within three days of receiving recognition from the national office, the group published their first newsletter defining CORE, its policies, and the expectations of those willing to participate. The newsletter was distributed throughout the campus to generate student interest.[16]

The activity of the Students For Civil Rights instigated the emergence of two student movements on the Kentucky State campus. One sought to revise campus regulations and improve student rights; the other focused on community problems and civil rights for blacks. The situation at Kentucky State was different from the black student protest movements on other black college campuses. The first demonstrations held by black students in the early 1960s were value-oriented and centered around the community. By the late 1960s, after experiencing a degree of success in the civil rights struggle, students began to devote their attention to problems on their respective campuses.[17] Kentucky State College was an exception. In 1960, its students were involved in two demonstrations at the same time, which forced Atwood to take questionable action in response to the movements for student rights *and* civil rights.

Prior to Atwood's actions, the Students For Civil Rights claimed to have received a mixed response from the college's administration concerning their organizing activities. When the group first organized, Atwood did not publicly support them. The Frankfort CORE newsletter reported that the administration had warned students who had participated in demonstrations that they could be subject to revocation of their scholarships or to expulsion. But in the same newsletter, dean of students Ann Hunter was reported to have supported the Students For Civil Rights; however, Hunter claimed in a later interview that she did not publicly support the students. Instead, she "played it easy" in order to allow the students to have control of their own organization.[18]

Although confusion existed over the exact position of the administration, the Students For Civil Rights continued to advocate racial equality. On April 2, 1960, fifty members of the organization divided into groups of three and visited public eating places in Frankfort. Their objective was not to demonstrate but to determine if racial discrimination was the policy of the establishment. In each store, restaurant, and hotel visited, the students requested service in a "friendly and courteous manner." In most instances their request was denied; however, the students were persistent in their efforts to negotiate with owners who practiced segregation, and they were also prepared to demonstrate if negotiations proved unsuccessful.[19]

The sincerity of their efforts was outlined in an April 6, 1960, letter to Frankfort Mayor Paul Judd. The Students For Civil Rights called upon Judd to assist in removing racial discrimination in the city. He was urged to send letters to all business owners in Frankfort requesting them to "serve all regardless of race, creed, or color" and to introduce "an ordinance making it unlawful to practice segregation in public businesses."[20]

On the same day this letter was sent to the mayor, Atwood for the first time publicly acknowledged his support of the Students For Civil Rights. In a statement submitted to the group, Atwood overemphasized his contribution to the civil rights movement by claiming that throughout his life he had worked to end segregation. He added that during his tenure at Kentucky State, many methods of attacking segregation had been necessary; undoubtedly, in the future other methods and techniques would be used. But, he continued, "they will not be more sincere merely because they are different."[21]

In response to Atwood's support, the newsletter staff of the

Students For Civil Rights met with the president to discuss a joint effort between CORE and the administration to improve race relations in Frankfort. Although no immediate plans were made, Atwood explained why he had waited to support the Students For Civil Rights. He said he had preferred to wait until after the state legislature approved House Bill 163, which had been approved a month before with Governor Bert Combs's support, creating a Kentucky Council on Human Relations. Atwood believed the commission would be a major step toward improving race relations. Its purpose would be to study racial problems and to "encourage fair treatment for, to foster mutual understanding and respect among, and to discourage discrimination against any racial ethnic group or its members."[22] As chairman of the executive committee of the Kentucky Council on Human Relations, Atwood had supported the bill in its early stages; thus he did not want to do anything that might have hindered its passage. The meeting between Atwood and the student group ended in a positive manner. Representatives from the Students For Civil Rights recognized his situation and expressed appreciation of his endorsement of their activities. That evening, April 6, CORE held its first mass meeting on the campus. Those in attendance were informed about Atwood's recognition of CORE as well as about the aims and achievements of the organization.[23]

The following day, the local newspaper reported that students were planning sit-ins at restaurants in the community. The demonstrations, however, were called off when the mayor responded to the students' concerns by meeting with several black and white leaders representing the Frankfort community. This group included Atwood, the chief of police, the city commissioner, and the Franklin County school superintendent. At this meeting Mayor Judd agreed to meet later with separate groups of Frankfort merchants to discuss segregation, but he emphasized he would "do nothing under duress or pressure." The students decided not to demonstrate for three weeks in order to allow the mayor ample time to meet with various owners of public establishments. Meanwhile, CORE continued to hold workshops on nonviolence while they negotiated with store owners.[24]

At the same time CORE was working to eliminate segregation in Frankfort, the Kentucky State Student Council continued to search for ways to increase student privileges. On April 26, 1960, the new president of the Student Council, Rufus Slaton, a junior from

Madisonville, called a mass meeting of students to discuss the grievances they wanted their representatives to present to the executive council. Included among the twenty-six demands were relaxed rules for students who owned cars, permission for female students to go home on the weekends, better food in the cafeteria, and expanded operating hours for the student union recreation room and library. But when the Student Council presented the list to Atwood, he told them not to "demand anything." He was willing to talk things over with them but he would not submit to their demand that changes be made.[25]

When it appeared the executive council was not going to take action on the complaints, the students began to boycott the cafeteria. On April 29, three hundred students went to the cafeteria, ordered their breakfast, and immediately threw it away. During lunch the male students collected money to buy bread and luncheon meat for those students desiring to eat. A table was set up in the picnic area of the campus where students sometimes gathered for lunch. The dean of students, Ann Hunter, did not approve of these activities and interrupted the picnic by overturning the tables of food. This episode heightened the tension between students and faculty. On the same day this incident took place, the college's board of regents was meeting on the campus in Blazer Library. The students used the opportunity to call more attention to their concerns. About four hundred students organized and surrounded the library, singing songs and holding signs that read: "We Want Freedom" and "Kentucky State Concentration Camp." Because most students had to return to their classes, the demonstration was short,[26] but it captured Atwood's attention. He decided to convene a meeting of the student body that night to discuss the campus situation.

Atwood informed the students that if the demonstrations did not cease immediately it could become necessary to close the college for the remainder of the semester. He added that when the demonstrations stopped he would be willing to negotiate with students about their concerns. Atwood's most unexpected comment related to the Students For Civil Rights. He announced that because the organization had acted contrary to the spirit of its recognition by the college, the executive council was withdrawing its recognition of the group. The leaders of the Students For Civil Rights Frankfort CORE affiliate were warned that they would be expelled if they met on the college grounds "to arouse unrest among the students."[27]

Despite the efforts of students to persuade Atwood that CORE had nothing to do with leading protests against the school's regulations, the president remained firmly behind the decision. The students then planned a march from the campus to the state capitol to protest school regulations. But on Sunday, May 1, the scheduled day of the march, the executive council met in a special session and decided to expel twelve students from the campus. In addition, two faculty members, Arthur Norman and Robert Boyd, instructors in the biology and chemistry departments, were fired by the administration. The council's swift decision proved to be a significant obstacle in CORE's attempt to end segregation in Frankfort. Eleven of the students were members of CORE's steering committee, scheduled to meet with a group of restaurant owners on May 3. This meeting was canceled since all the expelled students were directed to leave the campus immediately. Although no exact details were included in the letters to the students explaining the reasons for dismissal, the administration had documented specific charges against each of them. During a special meeting of the executive council, Atwood and council members reported that they had witnessed the students either verbally criticizing the administration or instructing fellow classmates on when and how to demonstrate.[28]

Instead of improving the situation, the expulsions led to further disturbances on campus, culminating with the burning of the school gymnasium during the early morning hours of May 2. It deeply saddened Atwood to watch this particular building explode into flames. Bell gymnasium had been the first building constructed under his administration and thus held sentimental value for him. But now it was gone, ruined by events surrounding an unfortunate campus demonstration. Damage to the gym was more than a hundred thousand dollars. An investigation attributed the disaster to arson. In the wake of the confusion on campus, a majority of the 611 students enrolled packed their bags and went home. A few days later Atwood announced that some of the campus regulations would be relaxed, but students would have to return to the campus within a week in order not to lose their credits for the semester.[29]

Following the burning of the gymnasium, the expulsion of twelve students and dismissal of two faculty members, demonstrations on campus and negotiations with city officials came to a halt. Instead, a bitter debate began between the dismissed students and faculty members on one side and Atwood and the executive council

Atwood poses with other Kentucky educators in the late 1950s. Left to right: Robert R. Martin, superintendent of public instruction; Presidents W. F. O'Donnell, Eastern Kentucky State College; Ralph H. Woods, Murray State College; Frank G. Dickey, University of Kentucky; Adron Doran, Morehead State College; Kelly Thompson, Western Kentucky State College; and Atwood. Courtesy of Kentucky State University Photographic Archives.

on the other. Those dismissed by the college insisted that their removal was part of Atwood's effort to destroy CORE's activities in Frankfort. They argued that Atwood was being pressured by white businessmen to end student protest and that he merely used the campus demonstrations as an excuse for interfering with CORE's efforts to abolish segregation in Frankfort. One of CORE's representatives, Ulysses Prince, noted that it was not part of the organization's program in Frankfort to lead student demonstrations against the college. Atwood, however, insisted that CORE was behind the demonstrations on campus. He further stated that "one of the goals of CORE is to discredit present Negro leadership and the NAACP."[30]

To the white citizens of Kentucky, Atwood had responded effectively to the student demonstrations. An editorial in the Frankfort *State Journal* claimed Atwood "acted wisely" in handling the school's problems. "If school administrators are to operate institutions in the proper manner," wrote the Lexington *Leader*, "then they sometimes must act in a manner that may appear arbitrary and harsh to outsiders."[31]

In contrast, CORE's national office denounced Atwood's treatment of the students and faculty members affiliated with the local chapter. During its July 1960 national convention in St. Louis, CORE drew up a resolution blasting Atwood along with presidents Felton Clark, H. Council Trenholm, George Gore of Florida A & M, and Chancellor Harvey Branscombe of Vanderbilt University for "abdicating their responsibility." Each of the four presidents had dismissed students and/or faculty during the height of the sit-in demonstrations. Yet Atwood denied the charges made by the civil rights organization. "No question of racial equality was involved," he insisted. "The college did not consider non-violent protests for racial equality as the causes for disciplinary action." The Lousiville *Courier Journal* defended Atwood, noting that "he could give lessons in practical restraint and in practical achievement to the newcomers."[32]

But according to those forced to leave the campus, Atwood's argument was pathetically weak. Both of the dismissed faculty members, Norman and Boyd, had served as consultants on the Students For Civil Rights newsletter and offered sharp criticisms of Atwood's administration. Boyd said: "I had nothing to do with the students' campus demonstrations and my dismissal is ill-founded." Norman claimed that Atwood's reaction and "his character exemplified Uncle Tom behavior." The president of the local CORE affiliate, Lester Tripp, who was a freshman and one of the expelled students, said the dismissals were "an expression that President Atwood does not care whether or not equal rights are obtained for Negro citizens in the Frankfort community."[33]

Atwood received numerous letters from across the country criticizing his actions. George Mahin, whose son was one of the students expelled, even wrote a letter to Atwood that was published in the Louisville *Defender*. Mahin wrote that he was "shocked" to learn what had transpired at the school because Atwood had earlier informed him that he supported CORE. "We certainly feel," wrote Mahin, "that your administration has betrayed the trust and confidence which the affected parents had placed in you."[34]

The editor of the Lousiville *Defender*, Frank Stanley, began his editorial indicating that he "sorely" regretted the problems that had

Rufus and Mabel returning from a trip to Europe in 195? Courtesy of Kentucky State University Photographic Archives.

erupted at Kentucky State. "As always," Stanley said, "there is some merit to be found in the contentions of both sides. However, regardless of who or what is right or wrong, the well-being of the insititution remains paramount." Stanley did observe, however, that it was time for the college to be evaluated by professionals to determine how it compared with other state colleges in terms of programs and regulations. While Stanley credited the administration at Kentucky State for compromising with students on some terms, his comments, overall, implicitly sided with the students. "Opposition to any and all campus regulations that limit individual freedom of movement is to be expected. The conflict," noted Stanley, "comes in an aggressive and impatient insistence on relief and stubborn and crude persistence to maintain the old order."[35]

Edward King, Jr., co-chairman of the dormitory council and one of the twelve suspended students, summed up what he thought was the problem in an editorial published in the *New York Times*. "The elder Negro of the South learned all of his life," King wrote, "that he had a particular place in his society and that the white man had absolute control over him. Today's young Negro student has never had a chance to learn this fear." According to King, his generation had been exposed to more cultural and educational opportunities and could not "adjust to a southern way of life that [was] wrong."[36]

Although Atwood received criticism from the black community, some blacks supported his position and were sensitive to the situation he found himself in. For instance, Ersa Poston, an alumna of Kentucky State, was the regional director of the New York State

Youth Commission. She read Edward King's editorial and responded to it by writing him a letter and forwarding a copy to Atwood. Poston reminded King that the organization and early work of the NAACP and Urban League "depended largely on the foresight leadership and contributions of 'elder' Negro Leaders" whom he had critically referred to in his article. While Poston praised King and other students for their willingness to take up the fight for equality, she informed him that various strategies would have to be tested. "Many of these steps were taken by your elders," wrote Poston, "in order to make each generation's move toward ultimate defeat of those conditions that eat as cancers upon our dignity a bit more meaningful and dynamic."[37]

On July 14, 1960, the Kentucky State College board of regents held a hearing for the expelled students. Atwood revealed facts he had gathered from faculty members who had observed the students disseminating information concerning when to demonstrate on campus. Although each student denied being a leader of campus demonstrations, the board of regents supported the executive council's action. The board contended that Atwood and the council had to react quickly in order to prevent violence and that the expulsions were necessary to avert a possible riot.[38] The board, however, did suggest that Atwood and the executive council review information gathered at the hearing for the expelled students and consider the evidence against each. Furthermore, the board recommended that Atwood and the council "take appropriate steps with reference to adjustments and changes in disciplinary action."[39]

The council accepted the board's recommendation and met to reconsider the action taken against each student. The council concluded that because each of the twelve dismissed students had provided different levels of leadership for campus demonstrations, the penalties for some should be less severe. Thus the council permitted six students to reapply to Kentucky State one year after their suspension.[40]

The executive council's reconsideration did not lessen the friction between Atwood and those dismissed from the college. In May 1961, the two faculty members who were fired along with eleven of the expelled students filed suit against Atwood, the executive council of Kentucky State, and the board of regents. The suit demanded fifty thousand dollars for each of the dismissed students and faculty members. Harry McAlpin, the Louisville attorney who represented the group, argued that "there was a conspiracy to prevent those people from petitioning for redress of grievances, that they were denied due process in the expulsions, and that all this violated their constitutional rights." Moreover, McAlpin claimed that the executive council did not want students to demonstrate because it feared such activities would diminish the school's opportunity to secure a favorable budget from the state legislature.[41]

The suit against Atwood and the board of regents languished in the judicial system for more than two years. In September 1963, a United States District Court jury, after a thirty-five minute deliberation, exonerated the administrators of Kentucky State College. The jury ruled that the administration did not conspire against the dismissed students and faculty members. With the announcement of the verdict, United States District Court judge H. Church Ford dismissed the suit against the school officials, and the incidents of spring 1960 were finally put to rest. According to Atwood, it was not until after the court's decision that he felt "completely free of the whole business."[42] But President Atwood's response to the student demonstrations left an important question unanswered. Did he yield to the pressure of white officials in deciding to punish those affiliated with CORE?

Because of the circumstances Atwood confronted in the spring of 1960, his situation must be measured differently from that of other black college presidents. Whereas several were either pressured by state officials to expel students for demonstrating or were, like some presidents of privately owned colleges, in a position to support the movements, Atwood was caught between two different student movements. Atwood's actions, according to Joseph Fletcher, who served on the executive council under him, were not controlled by whites. Fletcher said that Atwood was no "weakling" and that he "did not allow whites to dictate to him what he should do."[43] While Fletcher overstressed Atwood's independence, he clearly did not believe whites had pressured him to respond to the campus or community demonstrations.

Atwood was not opposed to civil rights activities. He had long been involved in the black struggle for equality in Frankfort and in the rest of Kentucky. He was a member of the NAACP and chairman of the Kentucky Council on Human Rights, an affiliate of the Southern Regional Council. He chaired the Frankfort's Citizens Committee, which was a local interracial group of twenty faculty and community members working to desegregate facilities in Frankfort. Atwood preferred working with whites on civil rights goals instead of protesting against them, but he did not oppose the other activities of civil rights workers. Helen Holmes, a professor at Kentucky State, recalled that Atwood did not question her civil rights activities. Holmes, who was president of the Frankfort chapter of the NAACP, led a protest march through the city's business community in December 1961. Atwood, who was out of the city at the time, sent a telegram informing the marchers that he supported their demonstration.[44]

On another occasion Atwood adroitly allowed one of the college's employees to participate in a protest movement. During a Christmas break in the early 1960s, the local chapter of the NAACP boycotted the local cab company. In support of the NAACP, Atwood permitted the director of maintenance to drive by the bus and train stations three to four times a day to pick up the luggage of Kentucky State students. The college's assistance contributed to the success of the boycott while minimizing Atwood's connection to the demonstration.[45]

In February 1962, Genevie Hughes, a CORE representative, visited Frankfort and found Atwood actively involved in the local civil rights movement. He was part of a steering committee comprised of NAACP members and other community activists interested in leading demonstrations in the Frankfort community. Hughes met with the group and observed him as one of the more outspoken participants. In her field report, she wrote: "According to reports and to my own assessment he is anxious to repair his bad reputation in some quarters by doing something to achieve integration before going out of office. He in fact had offered the motion to go ahead with sit-ins." Hughes noted Atwood had also indicated that students would not be penalized for their participation in civil rights demonstrations. Although he did not lower academic standards, teachers were free to deal with that concern as they deemed necessary.[46]

It was the tragedy of Atwood's career that his strategy for attaining civil rights became an anachronism. At the time of the sit-ins, Atwood was sixty-three years old. His generation's style of confronting segregation obviously conflicted with that of his students. President Atwood and the older faculty members were accustomed to advocating black equality through the NAACP, which geared its efforts toward negotiation, litigation, and remedial legislation.[47] Consequently, Atwood became angry, bewildered, and even embarrassed by the events that evolved in the spring of 1960. It was difficult for him to accept the impatience of his students, who insisted upon immediate improvements in civil rights as well as student rights.

As the civil rights movement gained momentum, students looked for leaders who were willing to challenge the racist system of Kentucky and to sacrifice personal opportunities if necessary in order to claim black equality. Atwood was never able or willing to make that kind of commitment. Still, it would be unfair to characterize Atwood as an "Uncle Tom." He did speak out against racial discrimination. This fact is perhaps best represented in a speech he delivered at Berea College in 1949. In rejecting the notion that civil rights would give special privileges, Atwood stated: "We feel that our friends know that we are not asking for any special privilege, if anything we want to do away with some of those special privileges so ungraciously accorded us. We don't want the special privilege of being the last hired and the first fired . . . Our purpose is only to remove the discrimination of race and stand with our fellow Americans as equals in responsibilities, equals in treatment. We ask no more, we accept no less."[48]

Although Atwood had spoken and worked in support of racial equality, he was guilty of failing to comprehend the feelings of his students and the changed racial climate of the early 1960s. Atwood failed to realize that his students had a much brighter vision of the future than he did when he was their age. He failed to understand that Kentucky State students were frustrated with conditions on and off the campus and that they, too, wanted to play a significant role in the struggle for civil rights. But, most important, Atwood did not recognize that whites were using negotiations, as they had always done, to stave off integration, while black Americans in general were tired of waiting for equality. Unfortunately the struggle for student rights became inseparable from the struggle for civil rights, forcing Atwood to discipline students in search of both.

To be sure, the civil rights years placed the presidents of state-supported black colleges in a delicate situation. They had to be concerned with the educational and financial progress of their institutions and yet serve as proponents of civil rights in the face of opposition from white state officials.

Atwood probably did as much as he could to promote racial equality, considering the circumstances he confronted in Kentucky, a rural state that had a poor record for supporting education and a historical reputation for keeping the conditions of blacks below that of whites. Throughout Atwood's presidency, he wrote articles and gave speeches in favor of equal rights for blacks. And, though he was not as outspoken as others might have preferred, he was at least operating in the best way he knew. Atwood's method for achieving racial equality was succinctly presented in his autobiography: "I have this philosophy never give up the goal of full equality. But sometimes, in my judgement, it becomes necessary to accept an advanced step, use it well, and enlist the help of white friends to take the next step."[49] By the early 1960s, this approach was unacceptable to many young black students, and it led to significant criticism of Atwood's commitment to the freedom movement.

As his years at Kentucky State wound down, Atwood found it more difficult to administer the school he had developed. Student demonstrations and subsequent local opposition calling for the school to be closed overshadowed the years of dedication he had rendered to Kentucky State. While his last three years at the college were difficult, Atwood continued to promote and protect the college with the same resiliency he had shown when he first arrived there more than three decades earlier.

9
Measuring the Years

On March 30, 1962, in a simple, two-paragraph letter, Atwood informed the board of regents of his decision to retire. For several years Atwood had considered leaving the college for other work. In November 1952, he had written his good friend John Davis, expressing an interest in alternative employment. Davis had retired from West Virginia State College to accept an appointment by President Harry Truman as the director of American Technical Assistance to Liberia. In wishing the best for his "very good friend," Atwood wrote: "if you see a job in the foreign service which your fellow president in Kentucky might fill, by all means, do not fail to drop my name in the right place."[1]

Whether Davis recommended Atwood for any "foreign service" positions is unknown, but, as each year passed, Atwood's work at Kentucky State became more challenging. The integration of Kentucky's schools and the concern that Kentucky State could be closed, the Mahatma White incident, and the constant need to further expand Kentucky State made the 1950s a stressful period in his administration. The 1960 campus demonstrations probably did little to convince Atwood to reconsider his pending decision. He knew the lawsuit filed by the dismissed students and faculty, the burning of the gymnasium, and the charge of Uncle Tomism would leave an indelible mark on his career. Despite being distressed, though, Atwood did not want to end his administration in the midst of controversy, so he pressed on. Yet the longer he remained as president of Kentucky State, the greater the challenges to develop the school became.

In December 1961, S.C. Van Curon, editor of the Frankfort *State Journal*, began a campaign to close down Kentucky State. Van Curon suggested in a series of editorials that the 1962 Kentucky General Assembly close Kentucky State in order to turn the facilities over to the Kentucky Training Home in Frankfort, which cared for the retarded children of the state. The Kentucky Training Home needed extensive repairs. Van Curon admitted he was sensitive to the well-being of retarded children since his son was mentally ill. But, to substantiate his arguments for closing Kentucky State, Van Curon highlighted an observation by Governor Bert Combs, who had earlier noted that it would be less expensive to move the home to a new location. Van Curon recommended that the new location be Kentucky State, since black students were permitted to enroll in white institutions.[2]

Atwood and blacks throughout the state were appalled over Van Curon's proposal. Atwood believed Van Curon was attacking Kentucky State in response to the demonstrations that students had planned for Frankfort and that he was disturbed about the number of out-of-state students who attended Kentucky State College. According to Atwood, Van Curon believed they were the ones encouraging the racial protests in Frankfort. In several editorials Van Curon made the point of mentioning that 35.8 percent of the school's 708 students were from states outside Kentucky. He also pointed out that the state was paying $534 per student at Kentucky State compared to $365 for each student attending Morehead College.[3] By presenting his argument in this manner, Van Curon gave the impression he was concerned with the state saving money and assisting retarded children rather than the impact student demonstrations were having on race relations.

Because of Van Curon's suggestion, Atwood was locked into another major struggle on behalf of Kentucky State. Although Van Curon did not want the college to close until after Atwood's retirement, the gesture did not lessen Atwood's determination to see that the school remained open. Within a week of Van Curon's editorial, Atwood called a faculty meeting to discuss the article. During the meeting Atwood announced to the group that he did not think Van Curon's suggestion was feasible. He read an open letter to be released to the public in reply to Van Curon's editorial. In order to make sure that he had discussed all the arguments in the school's favor, Atwood organized a committee to make any necessary revisions. In addition, the faculty was asked to make suggestions on ways to improve the image of Kentucky State College. Each member wanted the college to attract the support of not only the black community but of the white community as well. Some of their suggestions included improving the campus atmosphere, publicizing the names of Kentucky State students who obtained graduate and professional degrees from outstanding universities in the country, and publishing facts, figures, and future programs of the institution in order to give the public a broader view of the school's role in the Frankfort community.[4] Through these measures and others, the administration of Kentucky State prepared to defend the school against Van Curon's attacks.

On December 21, 1961, Atwood's letter defending Kentucky State appeared in the *State Journal*. In the first part of his discussion, Atwood agreed with Governor Combs that conditions at Kentucky Training Home were unsatisfactory and that something had to be done to improve its facilities. "However," wrote Atwood, "those who are conversant with developments in the field of care for the mentally retarded recognize that a specialized plant should be developed on the cottage plan (that is C-O-T-T-A-G-E plan, not C-O-L-L-E-G-E plan)." Atwood did not believe that the facilities of Kentucky State College would solve the needs of the state's retarded children. An institution for the mentally retarded needed clinics for therapy, testing, and diagnosis. A reception center and training workshops would also be essential to the institution's objectives. "The buildings at Kentucky State College," noted Atwood, "would be newer but fundamentally just as unsuitable."[5]

The second part of Atwood's letter addressed the positive conditions of Kentucky State College. The school's estimated value was $5,500,000 including significant acreage for expansion. The faculty consisted of forty-eight teachers who had earned degrees from various universities including Atlanta University, Columbia University, Cornell University, Fisk University, and Stanford University. All except two of the teaching faculty possessed either a masters or doctorate degree. Atwood was confident that the institution could make a significant contribution to education in Kentucky. He wrote: "Kentucky State College is a valuable resource which apparently many of the leaders of Frankfort somehow have never come to fully appreciate. . . . I doubt seriously that the people of Frankfort in general know that they have in their community such a reservoir of knowledge, skills and resource personnel as is represented by the faculty of Kentucky State College." It bothered Atwood that white citizens of Frankfort were not taking advantage of the institution's resources. Atwood realized that he could not encourage whites to enroll in the college by himself. Therefore, his letter argued that Frankfort leaders would have to assist the school in its effort to attract white student enrollment. Atwood informed Frankfort leaders that they played an important role in determining whether Kentucky State would remain an all-black college or become a state college for all residents.[6]

Atwood's arguments did not alter the opinion of editor Van Curon. In his reply to Atwood's letter, Van Curon reminded readers of the problems the school experienced in the spring of 1960. He further pointed out that no arrests had been made in regard to the burning of the college's gymnasium. Van Curon believed that all those affiliated with the college owed the "state and community a moral obligation to assist in tracking down those responsible for destroying the school property at a great loss to the taxpayers." He was not satisfied that the matter was being reviewed by the State Police and state officials from the Department of Public Safety. Yet, in his reply to the Atwood letter, Van Curon pretended to be sensitive to Atwood's request that the school remain open. He argued that in order for Kentucky State College to achieve the status Atwood hoped for, the school would have to speed up the process of integration. He suggested the school select a white president to succeed Atwood upon his retirement. Moreover, Van Curon proposed the hiring of more white faculty at the college to replace those blacks who retired. Because Atwood had placed much of the credit for Kentucky State's growth with the community, Van Curon wanted the citizens of Frankfort to have some influence on the college's presidential selection.[7]

According to Atwood, Van Curon wanted black Kentuckians to pay a price for equality, and abolishing Kentucky State College would be the cost.[8] Based on Van Curon's comments to Atwood's open letter, it is evident that he wanted blacks to give something in their struggle for equality. Van Curon preferred blacks to decide between closing Kentucky State or accepting a white president at the college; although he mentioned both options, Van Curon continued to focus his efforts on closing the school.

On March 1, 1962, George J. Ellis, Jr., state representative from Glasgow, introduced House Bill No. 517 to the General Assembly. The bill was designed to close Kentucky State College and transform the institution into a junior college in the University of Kentucky's community college system. The proposal did not surprise Atwood, who claimed that he had received a telephone call a few days before the bill was introduced forewarning him that a legislator and Van Curon were meeting at Frankfort's Holiday Inn. The bill did not gain enough support and died in the House; still, the debate concerning the existence of Kentucky State did not end.[9]

The attack on Kentucky State prompted the board of regents to authorize an "objective study" outlining the future of the school. The board passed a resolution requesting "that the Council on

Public Higher Education be requested to make a study in depth of the college to determine the most effective use to which the plant and facilities of the college can be put."[10] The council employed the services of three distinguished educators to examine the status of Kentucky State College and to make recommendations for its future. The committee consisted of Merritt M. Chambers, Executive Director of the Michigan Council of State College Presidents; Thomas G. Pullen, state superintendent of schools and chairman of the Maryland State Department of Education; and Broadus E. Sawyer, on leave from his position as Associate Professor of Economics at Morgan State College and serving as assistant director of the Michigan Council of State College Presidents.[11]

Between May 25 and June 1, 1962, the team of consultants examined the history, problems, and status of Kentucky State. They held a public hearing in the college's library to give those interested in the future of the institution a chance to express their views. Van Curon was among the twenty-one persons who spoke before the panel. He proposed the school serve as a two-year community college under the auspices of the University of Kentucky. According to Van Curon, it cost the state too much money to educate students at the college and all facilities were not being fully used by the institution.

The Frankfort Chamber of Commerce also believed Kentucky State should occupy a different role in higher education. Jack Bolton, vice-president-elect of the group, read a statement at the hearing. Bolton indicated that "the majority of community leaders of Frankfort" believed higher education in the state could "best be served by changing the status of Kentucky State College to a truly integrated institution of higher learning with a broadened curriculum," rather than transforming the school into a two-year community college, as Van Curon proposed. According to Bolton's statement "larger numbers of *Kentucky* young people should be encouraged to avail themselves of these facilities [Kentucky State], rather than the present system, which includes an abnormally large number of out-of-state students."[12]

Not surprisingly, students, faculty, and alumni of Kentucky State favored the retention of Kentucky State College as a four-year college. Clayton Jones, assistant director of the Kentucky Commission on Human Rights, revealed that Kentucky State was actually leading "the field in its efforts to provide a truly desegregated college environment." The school had ten white instructors while

Atwood upon retirement in 1962. Courtesy of the *Courier Journal* and *Louisville Times*.

none of the state's other higher learning institutions employed a black faculty member. Kentucky State had twenty-two white students while none of the other institutions, with the exception of the University of Kentucky, had more than twenty-five black students. Jones also noted that white students attending Kentucky State College were accorded equal privileges to participate in campus activities, unlike the situation black students confronted on the predominately white campuses.[13]

Several persons speaking before the committee argued that those blacks attending Kentucky State would not attend the available white institutions since they did not offer a similar social life or nurturing academic environment. "Only the Negro understands the Negro as of now," said Reverend Homer Nutter, a member of the Kentucky State College board of regents. "Our good white friends mean well, but as to completely understanding the Negro, they can't do it at this stage of the game."[14]

On June 25, 1962, the committee filed its report, titled "The Future of Kentucky State College." The committee recommended to the council that the state increase appropriations for Kentucky State, that the school continue to be governed by its own board of regents, and that the college not be reduced to a two-year community college. The committee reported: "With a physical plant well-adapted for college use, worth $5½ million and having a replacement value much greater than that, on an excellent site in the capital city of the Commonwealth, and in view of the oncoming increased need for higher education facilities throughout the state, it would be a great error to consider closing the college or transferring its facilities to some other agency such as a home for mentally retarded children. Remodeling the plant for a purpose of this kind would be enormously costly and the result would never be fully satisfactory."[15]

Indeed, the committee's recommendation in this matter was a significant victory for the supporters of Kentucky State College. Yet, while the committee rejected Van Curon's suggestion to close the school, it did acknowledge that Kentucky State would have to make some changes for future growth. They suggested the college provide two-year community junior college courses and strengthen instruction in public administration, business administration, and political science.

The consultants recommended that the college also serve the Frankfort region by providing opportunities for high school graduates and adults wishing to advance their education beyond the high school level. The committee urged the school to serve the state by educating state government employees in Frankfort, as well as blacks from Kentucky through the completion of desegregation. Yet the committee believed the "college should not attempt unilaterally and at a single stroke to correct the practice of partial de facto segregation in public education throughout Kentucky." The committee also refused to establish a percentage of out-of-state students for the school but indicated that Kentucky State should continue to encourage the enrollment of out-of-state students since their presence on the campus reduced the chances of "provincialism from growing in the Frankfort area."[16]

The Kentucky Council on Public Higher Education reviewed the report and approved the recommendations of the committee.[17] Although Kentucky State would not be closed, the school's administrators had to prepare the institution for the future. The task would be more difficult considering it would have to be accomplished through the leadership of another president; Atwood was scheduled to retire. At sixty-five Atwood could have remained at the college until he reached the mandatory retirement of age of seventy, but he wisely recognized that school needed "younger more vigorous leadership to see it through the next period." "I was beginning to feel," wrote Atwood years later, "that maybe my mind was not accustomed to so much change. Maybe because I had seen the college make such great strides, I would begin to feel content with what we had, and not go on to further and greater goals."[18]

Although Atwood had submitted his letter of resignation to the board in March, he remained administrator of Kentucky State College until December 1962. Meanwhile, University of Kentucky president Frank Dickey informed Atwood of the school's decision to bestow on him one of its highest honors, the Algernon Sydney Sullivan Citizens Award.[19] The award was established by the New York Southern Society. The University of Kentucky was among the fifteen institutions chosen by the society annually to present three of the forty-five awards. The Sullivan medallions were to be given to a graduating man and woman as well as a distinguished citizen. That Atwood had contributed to the process of school desegregation and actively participated with volunteer programs and state and national educational committees during his thirty-three years as president of Kentucky State fully qualified him for the award.

Yet it was an ironic twist that the university chose Atwood, since it had for years participated in the efforts to keep African-Americans from attending the institution. Yet, Atwood overlooked those days and graciously accepted the recognition the university extended. He considered the award the "highlight" of his personal career because it stood for an ideal he believed in—service to others. Atwood had "tried" to demonstrate his concern for his fellow man all his life. His work in black education and his role as an interracial diplomat signified his concern for other people.

During Atwood's last semester at the college, the new Bell Health and Physical Education Building was officially dedicated. The building was the thirteenth built during his administration. It replaced the Bell Gymnasium that had been destroyed by arson during the student demonstrations of 1960.[20] Besides participating in the search for a new president and handling other routine administrative duties, Atwood encouraged the faculty to "contribute [their] utmost for the highest welfare and best interest of the college." Because the future of Kentucky State had been questioned, Atwood wanted the faculty to engage in a personal campaign to promote the image of the school to alumni, students, parents, and citizens. He also suggested they be committed to the needs of the students, that they support all of the college's activities, and that they offer constructive criticism to the administration in order to better the institution.[21]

Atwood's suggestions to the faculty reiterated the kind of expectations he had always held for those whom he hired. He believed faculty should be involved in the affairs of the college. He was receptive to new ideas and delegated responsiblity to those who earned his confidence. Thus, unlike some college presidents, Atwood was not a ruthless campus dictator; instead, he was a stern supervisor who did not allow his authority to disrupt the chances of establishing positive relationships with his faculty. Several faculty members even chose to spend most of their career in education employed at Kentucky State. Faculty members Henry Cheaney, Minnie Johnson Hitch (Mebane), William W. Jones, Eugene Raines, A.J. Richards, Pattye Simpson, Harold Smith, and dean and registrar David Bradford had worked under Atwood's administration since the 1930s.[22] They were a steady and loyal force that Atwood could depend on for general advice as well as suggestions for making Kentucky State a better institution.

Atwood considered his faculty to be a major resource enabling him to serve the needs of black Kentuckians. For example, on

November 5, 1959, Frank Stanley wrote Atwood requesting him to list the state jobs for which he believed blacks should be employed and to give justification for hiring them. Stanley planned to include the suggestions in a proposal he was submitting to the state administration. Atwood referred the matter to two of his able professors, Harold Smith and Henry Cheaney. A month later they submitted to Atwood a five-page report titled "The Employment of Negroes by the State Government." Atwood mailed the report to Stanley and gave proper recognition to Smith and Cheaney for conducting the survey.[23]

Atwood appreciated and respected his faculty, and they admired him as well. On November 9, 1962, about two hundred friends of Rufus and Mabel gathered for a banquet to honor the Atwood era. The faculty and staff presented the Atwoods with a $550 gift certificate and a sterling silver punch bowl. Three faculty members, Helen Holmes, Henry Cheaney, and Harold Smith, presented a skit that highlighted humorous personal incidents of Atwood's presidency. George Wilson, professor and head of the Department of English and Psychology, read a poem he had written titled "How Shall We Measure His Years?" In his tribute, the author observed that the success of Atwood's leadership could be measured by his long tenure at Kentucky State, the expansion of the campus, and the well-trained faculty he recruited to teach there. Wilson also praised Atwood for guiding the institution through some of the most difficult periods of the twentieth century.[24]

Indeed, Wilson's analysis of Atwood's role in the development of Kentucky State College was accurate. Atwood was a highly capable administrator and educator. That he guided the institution through the 1930s depression and from segregation to desegregation is indicative of his loyalty to the college. Yet Atwood's contributions to Kentucky State were not solely the result of his own capabilities. David Bradford anchored the college's faculty and extended exemplary leadership in directing academic changes at the college. It was "difficult to separate Bradford from Atwood," said William Exxum. According to him, Atwood allowed "Bradford great leeway to do what he thought was best. And I think Bradford was the kind of person who was going to demand that he be given leeway—as far as what it is [sic] he thought was best for the university [college]."[25] That Bradford was a well-educated, creative, articulate leader convinced Atwood to give him latitude in handling campus-related administrative duties. Since he was busy

Atwood, Governor Bert
Combs, and new Kentuc
State College president, (
M. Hill, in 1962. Courtes
Kentucky State Universit
Photographic Archives.

in black educational organizations and lobbying financial support for the college, Atwood found it to his advantage to have someone of Bradford's caliber in charge of the institution during his absence, but Atwood never completely relinquished his control of the affairs of the college. He took his job as president personally. Kentucky State College was *his* school and whatever happened there was *his* responsibility.

On December 4, 1962, Carl M. Hill succeeded Atwood as president of Kentucky State College.[26] Hill won the job over forty applicants, mostly black, who had applied for the position. A native of Norfolk, Virginia, Hill had a bachelor of science degree from Hampton Institute and a masters and doctorate in chemistry from Cornell University. Hill was a chemistry professor, dean of the faculty, and dean of the School of Arts and Sciences at Tennessee Agricultural and Industrial State University when he accepted the offer to become president of Kentucky State. His wife, Mary, was also an associate professor in the chemistry department.

Unlike Atwood and his wife Mabel, the Hills were scholars in their field. They had coauthored fifty-two research papers published in several different scientific journals. Carl Hill had coauthored a textbook titled *General College Chemistry* and had also received national recognition for being an outstanding chemistry teacher. He had also developed and supervised research projects sponsored by the National Science Foundation, the United States Air Force Research Command, and the Tennessee Valley Authority.[27]

Ten months after officially succeeding Atwood, Hill was inaugurated as the seventh president of Kentucky State. Kentucky governor Bert Combs gave the principal address in observance of the occasion. While proclaiming the state was "fortunate" to have Hill "succeed another distinguished man of learning, Dr. Rufus B. Atwood," Combs expressed confidence in Hill's ability to be an effective president at Kentucky State. Combs also indicated he was optimistic about the future of Kentucky State, encouraging the college to "be a cathedral, not of bricks and mortar, but of ideas and principles."[28]

As Hill began his duties, Atwood became president emeritus of Kentucky State College. Although he was a consultant for the new administration, he did not want to interfere with Hill's tenure so he and Mabel decided to move away from Frankfort so they did not impose on the new president.[29] Unable to find a satisfactory home in Louisville or Lexington, the Atwoods decided to relocate to Cincinnati. Cincinnati would allow them to remain close to their many friends in Lexington and throughout the state of Kentucky. Furthermore, their nephew Rufus Mitchell, Atwood's namesake, lived in Columbus and his son Roy resided in Cincinnati, thus making their choice convenient for visiting with the family. Because they had never had any children of their own, Rufus and Mabel were especially fond of their nephews and nieces, who lived in various parts of the country. They looked forward to spending more time visiting their family.

The last twenty years of Atwood's life were not nearly so eventful as his earlier life. His withdrawal from the state he had given so much to ended his participation and influence on the events that had shaped black education and the civil rights movement in Kentucky. By the early 1960s, a new generation of young black leaders, aggressive and impatient with the progress of civil rights, were actively pursuing solutions to racial inequality throughout the country. As a new resident of Cincinnati with moderate racial views, Atwood became merely one of the lesser known participants of the civil rights movement.

The Cincinnati CORE chapter was busy attacking racial segregation in the community. As of 1961 the organization was demonstrating against segregation at swimming pools and roller rinks. CORE had also successfully protested the Coney Island Amusement Park's policy of excluding blacks from swimming in its pools by the time the Atwoods moved to the city in 1962. In 1964 and 1965, CORE sponsored demonstrations for employment in the building trades. It also organized a rent strike and sit-in at City Hall that resulted in better housing and health codes.[30]

Atwood spent most of his retirement engaged in activities that were less demanding than those he faced at Kentucky State. He appreciated not having the burdens he had shouldered for thirty-three years at the college. While Atwood did not abandon his involvement in community activities, he wanted his retirement to be one of reflection and relaxation. He was particularly concerned about the management of his personal business. He wanted to make sure he and Mabel could live comfortably for the rest of their lives, even after death claimed one of them. Atwood hired as their family attorney the prominent Cincinnati lawyer Reuven Katz, who at the time represented several professional sports figures. Because they were financially secure, Atwood and his wife were able to enjoy their senior years in Cincinnati to the fullest. They first moved to in a nice middle-class home on Eaton Lane. After living there for several years, they moved onto the twenty-first floor of The Regency, a high-rise apartment building in Hyde Park, an upper-class suburb of Cincinnati. In March 1969, the Atwoods took a cruise to Jamaica. While this was not their first foreign travel experience, it was a pleasant vacation for them, especially since they both were in their seventies at the time.

Rufus and Mabel became involved in a variety of activities while living in Cincinnati. Mabel renewed her interest in teaching music and gave lessons to a few students. She also became involved in several clubs as well as those at the church she and Rufus attended, St. Andrew's Episcopal. Rufus was also active in the predominately black parish. He served on several committees, coordinated the usher board, and served as a member of the vestry. Because of their "faithful" church participation, both Rufus and Mabel were regarded highly by the other members.[31]

Atwood became active in the Cincinnati branch of the NAACP. He contributed significantly to the organization's activities during the

1960s and early 1970s. From 1962 to 1966, he served as chair of the Education Committee, and he was appointed to the branch's Executive Committee in 1969. While he was chairman of the Education Committee, Atwood represented the NAACP in assisting with the preparation of the book, *The Negro In American Life*, which was to be used in the public schools. Because of his contributions to education in the city, Atwood was recognized with an award from the Cincinnati branch of the NAACP in 1966.[32] His brief involvement with the chapter was indicative of his continued interest in the betterment of black education, even within the era of desegregation.

By the mid-1970s, as school systems across the nation began to desegregate in large numbers, Atwood was no longer actively involved in local civil rights activities. His physical condition began to decline with age, and he no longer possessed the energy to engage in the various activities he had formerly enjoyed so much. In April 1982, he and Mabel moved into the Marjorie P. Lee retirement home. He had begun to exhibit symptoms of Alzheimer's disease, making it necessary for them to have access to immediate care.

Atwood did not live one full year in the new residence. He died on Friday, March 18, 1983, in the Our Lady of Mercy Hospital as a result of arteriosclerotic heart disease.[33] He was eighty-six years old. Funeral services were held at the St. Andrew's Episcopal Church, and a memorial service was held at Bradford auditorium on the Kentucky State Campus in Frankfort.[34] Following the campus service, Atwood was laid to rest in the north end of the Frankfort cemetery.

In 1986, Kentucky State celebrated its centennial anniversary. This was an emotional and inspirational year for all those who were alumni of this historic black institution. Special programs were held in observance of the school's milestones. In August 1986, the school renamed one of its older buildings after the former president. The Rufus B. Atwood Research Facility was named as a tribute to his many contributions to the school.

To be sure, Kentucky State did make significant progress between 1929 and 1962. Atwood provided sound and capable leadership during his presidency. Unlike his predecessors, Atwood was very careful in making political connections, and he kept the college from being used as a political plum. Because of his political maneuvering, the size of the campus doubled, student enrollment tripled, the institution was accredited as a four-year college, and educational and administrative programs were revised and expanded during his administration. All of these accomplishments had occurred in the context of an unpredictable white political arena.

Without doubt, the Atwood administration deserves much credit for Kentucky State's growth during the second half of the twentieth century. And, though Atwood was unable to acquire facilities equal to Kentucky's other institutions of higher learning, his leadership at least laid an educational foundation for future generations to build on.

In November 1962, Whitney M. Young, Jr., executive director of the National Urban League, and Charles Parrish, Jr., the first black faculty member hired by the University of Louisville, were among the many friends who contributed to a testimonial volume of letters congratulating Atwood on his service to Kentucky State. A 1941 graduate of the college, Young wrote:

As one of your graduates and a consistent admirer over the years, I naturally react with mixed feelings on the occasion of your retirement. I am not only personally grateful for the rich education which you made possible for me under your able administration, but I am sure that I voice the appreciation of thousands of young Negro citizens—and even the more mature ones like myself—who, because of your interest and dedication, became better prepared to make what I hope are great contributions to society-at-large.

I will always admire your great capacity for dignity as well as humanness—for strong conviction as well as flexibility. You have been a scholar as well as an administrator, and yet you have never lost the common touch or the ability to make each individual feel that he is something special.[35]

In his letter of congratulations to Atwood, Parrish eloquently expressed the significance of the Atwood administration. He wrote: "it seems to me that the unique contribution you have made is measured rather by the way in which the College, under your leadership, has responded creatively to the changing needs of its constituents. It would have been easy to have guaranteed the continued existence of Kentucky State merely by insistence upon the maintenance of previously established standards. Instead, your plans for the development of the College have always revealed a proper regard for tradition but never abject subservience to it."[36] Parrish continued his letter by noting that "Kentucky State College and Rufus B. Atwood have been linked together for so many years that it will be difficult to think of one without thinking of the other."

In concluding his remarks, Parrish told Atwood: "The heritage you are leaving is a rich one. Its beneficiaries will not soon forget you. Unborn generations will bless you."[37]

In spite of the difficulties he encountered, Atwood never gave up hoping for a better Kentucky State. When he retired there were 868 students enrolled in the college, 53 full-time faculty members, and 13 undergraduate departments.[38] Because of his untiring efforts to obtain funding for the school, several new buildings were constructed, including a science building, three dormitories, two gymnasiums, a library, an alumni house, and a heating plant. Kentucky State also gained accreditation from the Southern Association of Colleges and Secondary Schools and the National Council for Accreditation of Teacher Education during the Atwood years.[39] Atwood's most enduring legacy, however, was the appreciation of the students who graduated from the college and whose lives he influenced. Many of them became teachers, principals, doctors, ministers, lawyers, politicians, and owners of businesses in Kentucky. Several alumni besides Whitney M. Young, Jr., achieved distinguished success. For example, 1939 graduate Luska Twyman served a number of terms as mayor of Glasgow, Kentucky; Harvey C. Russell, Jr., a 1939 graduate became the first black vice-president at Pepsi-Cola; Ersa H. Poston, who graduated in 1942, was appointed by President Jimmy Carter to serve as vice-chair of the U.S. Merit Systems Protection Board.[40]

Producing outstanding graduates and earning regional and national academic recognition were impressive achievements for a small black college located in a southern state that was conservative in its support of education. Yet Kentucky State's noteworthy progress was similar to that of other state schools struggling during the same period. As President Atwood was working to build a better Kentucky State, other African-American college presidents were also making historic marks on their institutions. For instance, presidents Lawrence Davis of Arkansas A & M, J.R. Lee at Florida A & M, and H. Council Trenholm representing Alabama A & M guided their schools to unprecedented growth during the pre-civil rights years. Like Atwood, these men and others faced racial and political obstacles in gaining equal treatment for the colleges they represented.[41] Moreover, their leadership was critically appraised by black contemporaries who failed to grasp the complications of their job.

Ralph Ellison's fictional character, Dr. Bledsoe, a villain in *Invisi-*

ble Man, served to validate the tarnished characteristics found in some black college presidents. However, as Christopher Jencks and David Riesman have written, "while there were plenty of President Bledsoes in the Negro Colleges, there were also courageous and progressive men who did as much as their institutions would allow—and more." [42]

Unlike Dr. Bledsoe, Atwood did not completely avoid civil rights issues. He spoke in favor of racial equality on more than one occasion. Although it was difficult for his generation to endorse the protests of the 1950s and 1960s, Atwood offered more support to young civil rights activists than some of his contemporaries.

Atwood's ability to remain at Kentucky State for thirty-three years and to direct the college through turbulent periods is only a partial indication of his determination and keen abilities as an interracial diplomat. To be sure, Atwood was a crafty politician like Dr. Bledsoe, yet he did not employ the fictional character's ruthless administrative style. Instead, Atwood was approachable, ambitious, and astute—a black educator who earned significant respect from his colleagues. And, while whites may have preferred Atwood serve simply as the caretaker of Kentucky State, he chose to advance conditions at the college by whatever means necessary. In so doing, Atwood created for blacks Kentuckians a better Kentucky State and encouraged its graduates to develop the skills necessary to meet the needs of the community at large.

Notes

INTRODUCTION

1. Ralph Ellison, *Invisible Man* (New York: Random House, 1952), passim.

2. Louis Harlan, *Booker T. Washington: The Making of a Black Leader, 1865-1901* (New York: Oxford University Press, 1972), 272.

3. Interview with Minnie Hitch Mebane, tape #2.

4. William C. Hine claims "many regarded" Turner "as an insufferable tyrant" ("South Carolina's Challenge to Civil Rights: The Case of South Carolina State College, Unpublished Paper Presented to the Southern Historical Association, Lexington, Kentucky, Nov. 10, 1989), 14-15.

5. Harlan, *Leader*, 157-58.

6. Ibid., 169; Raymond Wolters, *The New Negro on Campus* (Princeton: Princeton Univ. Press, 1975), 144-45.

7. David R. Goldfield, *Black, White, and Southern: Race Relations and Southern Culture 1940 to the Present* (Baton Rouge: Lousiana State Univ. Press, 1990), 2.

8. Most discussions of black college presidents are included in books on black education in general or in histories of particular black colleges and universities. Among the noteworthy are Harlan, *Leader* and *Booker T. Washington: The Wizard of Tuskegee, 1901-1915* (New York: Oxford University Press, 1983); Gordon D. Morgan, *Lawrence A. Davis: Arkansas Educator* (New York: Associated Faculty Press Incorporated, 1985); Martia Graham Goodson, ed., *Chronicles of Faith: The Autobiography of Frederick D. Patterson* (Tuscaloosa: The University of Alabama Press, 1991); Benjamin E. Mays, *Born To Rebel: An Autobiography by Benjamin E. Mays* (New York: Charles Scribners Sons, 1971); Arnold Cooper, *Between Struggle and Hope: Four Black Educators in the South, 1894-1915* (Ames: Iowa State University Press, 1989); Angel Patricia Johnson, "A Study of the Life and Work of A Pioneer Black Educator: John W. Davis" (Ed.D. diss., Rutgers University, 1987); Cynthia Griggs Fleming, "The Plight of Black Educators In Postwar Tennessee, 1865-1920" (*Journal of Negro History* [Fall 1979]:355-76); Raymond Gavins, *The Perils and Prospects of Southern Black Leadership: Gordon Blaine Hancock, 1884-1970* (Durham: Duke University Press, 1977); Lathardus Goggins, "The Evolution of Central State College Under Dr. Charles H. Wesley From 1942-1965: An Analysis" (Ed.D. dissertation University of Akron, 1983).

9. Goodson, *Chronicles*, 49.

10. "The End of Uncle Tom Teachers," *Ebony* 12 (8) (June 1957):68.

11. JoAnn Gibson Robinson, *Montgomery Bus Boycott and the Women Who Started It* (Knoxville: The University of Tennessee Press, 1987), 45-50.

12. William Chafe, *Civilities and Civil Rights* (New York: Oxford Univ. Press, 1981), 21-22, 61.

13. Maurice F. Seay, "A Report On Education" found in *Reports of Committee For*

Kentucky (Oct. 4, 1945), 8. See also, Harry W. Schacter, *Kentucky On The March* (New York: Harper, 1949), passim; "The Report of the Kentucky Commission On Negro Affairs" (Frankfort, Nov. 1, 1945), 30; Amy Porter, "Weep No More, Kentucky" (*Colliers Magazine* 117 (Mar. 30, 1946), passim.

14. Louisville *Courier-Journal*, June 17, 1962.

15. Atwood was a specialist in agricultural education. He never earned a doctorate degree; however, he was awarded two honorary doctorates during his tenure at Kentucky State. From Lane College he received an honorary doctorate of laws and from Monrovia College and Industrial Institute a doctorate of education. The highest degree he earned was a masters from the University of Chicago. Atwood's publication record was not nearly as scholarly or extensive as other black college presidents such as Horace Mann Bond, Benjamin Mays, and Charles Wesley.

16. I adopted the term "interracial diplomat" from Wolters's reference to Robert Russa Moton. According to Wolters, the Tuskegee president "was more in character as an interracial diplomat than as a combative man-at-arms." Moton "knew that no black man in the South could defy the white powers consistently." See Wolters, *New Negro*, 165. A good description of black leadership can be found in Bunche, "A Brief and Tentative Analysis of Negro Leadership" (Sept. 1940), a Research memorandum prepared for the Carnegie-Myrdal Study of the Negro In America.

17. Christopher Jencks and David Riesman, "The American Negro College" *Harvard Educational Review* 37 (Winter 1967): 18.

1. THE HOMEPLACE

Note: The epigraph for this chapter comes from "The House On Moscow Street," a poem by Marilyn Nelson Waniek, from her book *The Homeplace* (Baton Rouge: Louisiana State Univ. Press, 1990).

1. Although some of Atwood's recollections of his presidency are in the form of handwritten notes, he did write an autobiography, which provides significant information on his family history and the activities and events that shaped his experiences as a black college president; but, as with any autobiography, it does contain serveral errors. See his notes, Atwood papers, boxes 2 and 18. Paul G. Blazer Library Archives, Kentucky State University, Frankfort. See also Atwood, "From Segregation to Integration, 1929-1962: The Autobiography of Dr. Rufus B. Atwood," (unpublished manuscript, n.d., [1968]), 30; See also, Frank Dickey letter to Atwood, Apr. 27, 1962, Dickey papers, box 25, Department of Special Collections and Archives, University of Kentucky Libraries.

2. Atwood, "From Segregation To Integration," 4-9.

3. The census does not list the number of blacks living in Hickman town. However, blacks living in Fulton County, which included Hickman town and three other magisterial districts, combined for 18.1 percent of the population in 1900. See, U.S. Census Bureau, *Twelfth Census*, 178; U.S. Census Bureau, *Negro Populaton*, 781; *Fulton County History, 1845* (Paducah, Ky.: Fulton County Historical Society, 1983), 21-23; Atwood, "From Segregation to Integration," 11-13, 30.

4. In a taped oral interview several years after writing his autobiography, Atwood stated that he was unsure about the origin of his surname. It is worth noting that there was a white family in Hickman with the same name. Thomas Letcher Atwood, born in Virginia in 1843, moved with his family to Hickman County around the mid-nineteenth century. He later became a "well-known"

surveyor. It is not known whether Diverne was associated with Thomas Letcher Atwood's family, but it is a possibility since Hickman was a small rural area. I chose to accept Atwood's explanation for Diverne's arrival in Hickman since I found no definite linkage between Diverne and Thomas Letcher. See *Hickman County History*, vol. 1 (Clinton, Ky.: Hickman County Historical Society, 1983), 78-79; Atwood, "From Segregation to Integration,", 14-17; and Oral History Project, Mar. 19, 1974, part 2. Marilyn Nelson Waniek, one of Atwood's great-nieces and a professor of English at the University of Connecticut at Storrs, has written a collection of poems based on her research of the Atwood family history. See *Homeplace*, 3, 10, 15.

5. Atwood, Oral History Project, Mar. 19, 1974, part 2; and "From Segregation to Integration," 14-15.

6. Herbert G. Gutman, *The Black Family in Slavery and Freedom, 1750-1925* (New York: Vintage, 1976), 251-52.

7. Atwood suspected that Diverne's master was Pomp's father. For information concerning Rufus's paternal grandfather, see his "From Segregation to Integration," 14, 22; Waniek, *Homeplace*, 3, 10, 15 and telephone interview, Feb. 21, 1991; Atwood, Oral History Project, Mar. 18, 1974, part 1.

8. Waniek, *Homeplace*, 6.

9. For a more detailed account of the movement to equalize the funding of black schools, see Victor Howard, *Black Liberation in Kentucky: Emancipation and Freedom, 1862-1884* (Lexington: Univ. Press of Kentucky, 1983), 160-76; J. Morgan Kousser, "Making Separate Equal: Integration of Black and White School Funds in Kentucky," *Journal of Interdisciplinary History* 10 (Winter 1980), 399-428.

10. Atwood, "From Segregation to Integration," 13, 16;

11. Several years ago, Blanche Atwood Anderson, Rufus's second-oldest sister, was interviewed by her niece, Johnnie Nelson, the daughter of Rufus's oldest sister, Ray. During this undated interview Blanche briefly discusses Annie's background. The interview between Nelson and Anderson is in the possession of the author. See also, Atwood, "From Segregation to Integration," 16-17; Hickman *Courier*, May 23, 1929.

12. Atwood, "From Segregation to Integration," 18; Waniek, telephone interview, Mar. 6, 1991.

13. George C. Wright's study of racial violence in Kentucky reveals that blacks living in the Bluegrass state were often the victims of racial hostility. He found that at least two hundred fifty-eight blacks were lynched in the state between the years 1865 and 1940. See *Racial Violence in Kentucky, 1865-1940* (Baton Rouge: Louisiana State Univ. Press, 1990), 131-32; Atwood, "From Segregation to Integration," 18;

14. *Fulton County History, 1845*, 24; Atwood, "From Segregation to Integration," 18.

15. Hickman *Courier*, June 1898.

16. Hickman *Courier*, Sept. 19, 1902.

17. Ibid.

18. Hickman *Courier*, Jan. 9, 1891.

19. Hickman *Courier*, June 1898 and Jan. 9, 1891.

20. *Fulton County History, 1845*, 24; Atwood, "From Segregation to Integration, 19.

21. Kappa Alpha Psi, Alpha Upsilon Chapter, "Biographical Sketches of Kentucky State College Presidents, 1887-1937," Paul G. Blazer Library, Kentucky State University, Frankfort, 11; Atwood, "From Segregation to Integration," 13, 20.

22. Ibid., 21-22.

23. Atwood, "From Segregation to Integration," 26-27.

24. *Fulton County History*, 24; Atwood, "From Segregation to Integration," 25;

25. Atwood, "From Segregation to Integration," 27.

26. Ibid., 25, 28.

27. Wright, *Racial Violence*, 131-32.

28. Ibid., 134.

29. Ibid., 123, 134-35.

30. Ibid., 123-24.

31. Atwood, "From Segregation to Integration," 28-30.

32. Fisk University *News*, vol. 3, no. 2, Nov. 1917, 35; Atwood, "From Segregation to Integration," 33-34;

33. *Fulton County History 1845*, 451; Atwood, "From Segregation to Integration," 31.

34. Atwood, "From Segregation to Integration," 32-33.

35. Ibid., 33-34.

36. Ibid., 33-34.

37. Fisk University catalog, 1913-14, 50-51, 69; Atwood, "From Segregation to Integration," 34.

2. GOODBYE, "SKULLBUSTER"

1. Fisk University *News*, Oct. 1915, 25-26.

2. Fisk University *News*, vol. 3; catalog 9, 1915-16, 77.

3. U.S. Bureau of Education, Jones, Thomas Jesse, ed., *Negro Education: A Study of the Private and Higher Schools For Colored People in the United States*. vol. 1, Bulletin 38, Washington, D.C., 1917., 60.

4. Joe M. Richardson, *A History of Fisk University, 1865-1946* (Tuscaloosa: Univ. of Alabama Press, 1980), 3-4.

5. Ibid., 22-24, 46-47, 160.

6. Richardson, *History of Fisk*, 47; Harlan, *Wizard*, 181.

7. Fisk University *News*, vol. 3, catalog 9, 1915-16, 31; Atwood, "From Segregation to Integration," 36-37.

8. Fisk University *News*, vol. 3, catalog 9, 1915-16, 25; Atwood, Oral History Project, Mar. 18, 1974, part 1; Fisk University Yearbook, 1916, 67.

9. Fisk University Yearbook, 1916, 81, 92; Atwood, "From Segregation to Integration," 37; Mabel Atwood interview, Nov. 9, 1985.

10. Richardson, *History of Fisk*, 71-72; Lester C. Lamon, *Black Tennesseans 1900-1930* (Knoxville: Univ. of Tennessee Press, 1977), 276-78; James D. Anderson, *The Education of Blacks in the South, 1860-1935* (Chapel Hill: The University of North Carolina Press, 1988), 264.

11. Anderson, *Education of Blacks*, 264-65.

12. Richardson, *History of Fisk*, 84-86; Fisk University *News*, vol. 3, catalog 9, 1915-16, 17.

13. Richardson, *History of Fisk*, 84-86.

14. Atwood, "From Segregation to Integration," 37; Mabel Atwood interview, Nov. 9, 1985; Kentucky *Thorobred*, Sept. 1962, 1; See videotape of Atwood titled, "Distinguished Kentuckian," Kentucky Education Television, Feb. 19, 1976, Paul G. Blazer Library, Kentucky State Univ., Frankfort.

15. Emmett J. Scott, *The American Negro In The World War* (Washington, D.C., n.p., 1919), 40; John Hope Franklin, *From Slavery to Freedom: A History of Negro Americans* 6th ed. (New York: Knopf, 1988), 294-95; Richardson, *History of Fisk*, 76.

16. World War I service records of black veterans were destroyed in a fire at the National Personnel Records Center in St. Louis, Missouri, in 1973. However, Atwood's enlistment record and honorable discharge from the United States Army, no. 1974547, Feb. 3, 1918-Sept. 2, 1919, is in a collection of personal family papers in the possession of Atwood's great-nephew, Roy Mitchell, in Cincinnati, Ohio (hereafter Atwood Family Papers). See also, Atwood, "From Segregation to Integration," 38-39; Scott, *American Negro*, 130-31.

17. *Fisk University News*, Feb. 1918, 39; Franklin, *Slavery to Freedom*, 295-96; Scott, *American Negro*, 130-31; Atwood, Oral History Project, Mar. 18, 1974, part 1.

18. Atwood, "From Segregation to Integration," 38-39; Scott, *American Negro*, 130-31.

19. The author was unable to ascertain General Martin's first name, which was not recorded with the citation. See Scott, *American Negro*, 186; Atwood, "From Segregation to Integration," 40-41.

20. *Hickman Courier*, Jan. 23, 1919; Scott, *American Negro*, 186; *Fisk University News*, Feb. 1919, 24.

21. Atwood's enlistment record; Atwood, Oral History Project, Mar. 18, 1974, part 1; Atwood, transcript of oral interview with George Caulton, edited in 1975-76, Atwood Family Papers.

22. Wright, *Racial Violence*, 119-20; Bernard C. Nalty, *Strength For The Fight: A History of Black Americans in the Military* (New York: Free Press, 1986), 126.

23. Atwood, "From Segregation to Integration," 42.

24. Atwood's honorable discharge; Atwood, "From Segregation to Integration," 42-43.

25. Articles written by Atwood can be found in the *Fisk University News*, Nov. 1919 and Dec. 1919; Knoxville College was a black institution operated by Presbyterians. For more information regarding the debate between Fisk and Knoxville see *Fisk University News*, Apr. 1920.

26. Frank Joseph Loesch, counsel for the Pennsylvania Road Lines, gave the commencement address. For excerpts of his speech and additional information concerning commencement exercises, see *Fisk University News*, May 1920; general anniversary program of Fisk University, Apr. 4-May 27, 1920. Special Collections, Fisk Memorial Library, Nashville, Tennessee.

27. Earle D. Ross, *A History of The Iowa State College of Agriculture and Mechanic Arts* (Ames: Iowa State College Press, 1942), 17-21, 325; Goodson, *Chronicles*, 11-12, 25-26, 187; Atwood, Oral History Project, Mar. 18, 1974, part 1; Mar. 19, 1974, part 2.

28. Goodson, *Chronicles*, 11, 187.

29. Ibid., 15.

30. Atwood, "From Segregation to Integration," 44-45

31. Mabel Atwood, interview, Nov. 9, 1985; Atwood, "From Segregation to Integration,", 45-46.

32. Atwood, interview, Mar. 19, 1974, part 2; Atwood, "From Segregation to Integration," 45-46; Mabel Atwood, interview, Nov. 9, 1985; *Kentucky Thorobred*, Sept. 1962, 1.

33. Goodson, *Chronicles*, 9; Ruble Woolfolk, *Prairie View: A Study in Public Conscience, 1878-1946* (New York: Pageant, 1962), 32-33; Annie Mae Vaught White,

"The Development of the Program of Studies of the Prairie View State Normal & Industrial College" (M.A. thesis University of Texas, Austin, August 1938), 2; Atwood, "From Segregation to Integration," 46. For additional information about the salaries paid to faculty at Prairie View, see Biennial Budget, Prairie View State Normal and Industrial College Fiscal Years ending Aug. 31, 1926, and Aug. 31, 1927, 29-31.

34. White, "Studies of Prairie View," 56; Woolfolk, *Prairie View*, 178-79; Atwood, Oral History Project, Mar. 18, 1974, part 1.

35. *American Baptist*, June 2, 1937; *The Prairie*, 1926, 32.

36. Bulletin of the Prairie View State Normal and Industrial College Annual Report For The Fiscal Year 1923-24, vol. 3, No. 1, Jan. 1, 1925, 20-21; White, "Studies of Prairie View," 59; Annual catalogue of the Prairie View State Normal and Industrial College for the School Year 1924-25, 15.

37. Houston *Informer*, June 16, 1928.

38. *American Baptist*, June 2, 1937; Houston *Informer*, Feb. 23, 1924.

39. Prairie View *Standard*, Oct. 15, 1927.

40. Atwood, Oral History Project, Mar. 18, 1974, part 1; Atwood, "From Segregation to Integration," 47.

41. Woolfolk, *Prairie View*, 213-19, 231, 245-48; Atwood, Oral History Project, Mar. 18, 1974, part 1; *American Baptist*, June 2, 1937.

42. Vera Edwards, interview, Aug. 1, 1987.

43. Atwood, "From Segregation to Integration," 47-48.

44. Ibid.

45. Houston *Informer*, June 8, 1929; Kentucky State Industrial College board of trustee minutes, 28-29; Atwood, "From Segregation to Integration," 48.

46. Kentucky State Industrial College, board of trustees minutes (May 29, 1929), 28-29.

47. Atwood, "From Segregation to Integration," 48-49.

3. THE NEW ADMINISTRATION

1. Atwood, "From Segregation to Integration," 55.

2. Kentucky *Thorobred*, Nov. 23, 1929.

3. Anderson, *Education of Blacks*, 248.

4. Ibid., 244-49; U.S. Bureau of Education, *Negro Education*, 16-17.

5. Additional information on black higher learning institutions in Kentucky can be found in Thomas Calvin Venable, "A History of Negro Education in Kentucky" (Ph.D. diss., George Peabody College, Sept. 1952), 165-66; George Wright, "The Founding of Lincoln Institute," *Filson Club Quarterly* 49 (Jan. 1975), 60-63; See also Wright, "The Faith Plan: A Black Institution Grows During the Depression," *Filson Club Quarterly* 51 (Oct. 1977), 336; Alice Dunnigan, *The Fascinating Story of Black Kentuckians: Their Heritage and Tradition* (Washington, D.C.: Associated, 1982), 182, 184, 188; Oscar F. Galloway, *Higher Education for Negroes in Kentucky* 5, Bulletin of the Bureau of School Service, College of Education, University of Kentucky (Lexington, Ky.: University of Kentucky, 1932), 17, 20-21; James Blaine Hudson, III, "The History of Louisville Municipal College: Events Leading to the Desegregation of the University of Louisville" (PhD. diss., University of Kentucky, 1981); and John Arthur Hardin, "Hope Versus Reality: Black Higher Education in

Kentucky 1904-1954" (Ph.D. diss., Univ. of Michigan, 1989) Superintendent of Public Instruction, Biennial Report for Two Years Ending Dec. 31, 1919, 364.

6. Paul W.L. Jones, *A History of Kentucky Normal and Industrial Institute* (Frankfort, Ky.: Frankfort Printing, 1912), 11-19; Lena Mae Coleman, "A History of Kentucky State College for Negroes" (M.A. thesis, Indiana University, Aug. 5, 1938), 13.

7. The name of the Kentucky Normal and Industrial Institute for Colored Persons was changed in 1926 to Kentucky State Industrial College for Colored Persons as a result of an act passed by the General Assembly. See Acts of the General Assembly of the Commonwealth of Kentucky, 1926, Chapter 90, 304-5. For biographical information on Russell, see Kappa Alpha Psi, "Biographical Sketches," 6-9.

8. Ann J. Heartwell-Hunter, *Against the Tide* (Georgetown, Ky.: Kreative, 1987), 13. The best general history of Kentucky State University has been written by John Hardin. See John Hardin, *Onward and Upward: A Centennial History of Kentucky State University, 1886-1986* (Frankfort, Ky.: Kentucky State University, 1987), 20.

9. U.S. Bureau of Education, *Negro Education*, vol. 2, bulletin 39 (Washington, D.C., 1917), 267.

10. Heartwell-Hunter mailed out a questionnaire to several alumni of Kentucky State requesting them to write about their years at the school. Mary E. Tracy Ellis's comments were published along with various others. See *Against the Tide*, 135. President Russell's poor relationship with the students was reported in several editions of *The Starr*, a weekly newspaper published in Frankfort. See editions for Oct. 24 and Oct. 31, 1914; and Nov. 7, 1914.

11. Hardin writes extensively about the Russell controversy, including significant information on the political problems the school experienced during both of his administrations. The quote from the Hopkinsville newspaper was printed in his study on Kentucky State. See *Onward and Upward*, 17-33. For information on the Morrill Land Grant Act and Smith-Lever Fund, see John E. Sullivan, "A Historical Investigation of the Negro Land-Grant College from 1890 to 1964" (Ed.D. diss., Loyola University, Feb. 1969), 43.

12. Hardin, *Onward and Upward*, 21

13. Ibid., 23; Lexington *Herald*, May 6, 1923.

14. Fred Allen Engle, Jr., *The Superintendents and the Issues: A Study of the Superintendents of Public Instruction in Kentucky* 3 (Kentucky Department of Education, Mar. 1968), 47-48; Lexington *Herald*, May 9, 1923 and May 20, 1923; ibid., 23-25.

15. Lexington *Herald*, May 20, 1923; Hardin, *Onward and Upward*, 25.

16. Hardin, *Onward and Upward*, 25-28.

17. Ibid., 30-31.

18. Ibid., 28-31.

19. H.S. Smith, "Kentucky State College and Its President," *Wilberforce Quarterly* 2 (July 1941): 77; *American Baptist* June 2, 1937; Galloway, *Higher Education*, 106. Superintendent of Public Instruction, Biennial Report for the Years Ending June 30, 1929, part 1, 166.

20. Louisville *Courier-Journal*, Sept. 21, 1929; Louisville *Leader*, Apr. 11, 1931.

21. Kentucky State Industrial College, board of trustees minutes (July 26, 1929), 1-2.

22. Pittsburgh *Courier*, Aug. 17, 1929.

23. Atwood, "From Segregation to Integration," 60-64.

24. Kentucky State Industrial College, board of trustees minutes (Jan. 20, 1931), 127-28.

25. Atwood, "Kentucky Faces the Problem of Training Colored Teachers," *Kentucky Negro Education Association Journal* 1 (Feb. 1931): 23

26. L.N. Taylor's report titled "Our Colored Schools" is in Superintendent of Public Instruction, Biennial Report for the Biennium Ended June 30, 1931, part 1, 147-60.

27. George T. Blakey, *Hard Times and New Deal in Kentucky, 1929-1939* (Lexington: The University Press of Kentucky, 1986), 6-12.

28. Atwood, "From Segregation to Integration," 64-65.

29. Ibid.

30. Superintendent of Public Instruction, Biennial Report for the Biennium Ended June 30, 1931, part 1, 50, 53; Kentucky *Thorobred*, Mar. 15, 1930; Atwood, "From Segregation to Integration," 65-66.

31. Acts of the General Assembly of the Commonwealth of Kentucky, 1930, Chapter 187, 677; Atwood, "From Segregation to Integration," 66-67.

32. Atwood to McVey, Dec. 20, 1930; McVey to Atwood, Dec. 31, 1930; McVey papers, box 37.

33. Atwood to McVey, Feb. 7, 1931, McVey papers, box 37.

34. Boyd to Atwood, Apr. 7, 1931, included in President's Recommendations to the State Board of Education, series 119, archives, Paul G. Blazer Library, Kentucky State University; Galloway, *Higher Education*, 17.

35. Louisville *Leader*, Apr. 11, 1931.

36. Atwood, "From Segregation to Integration," 78-79.

37. Kentucky State Industrial College, board of trustees minutes, May 6, 1932, 184; Louisville *Leader*, May 14, 1932.

38. Franklin, *Slavery to Freedom*, 393-95.

39. U.S. Department of Labor, Employment Service, L.A. Oxley files, State Reports, "Kentucky State Employment Service Survey," part 2, n.d., found in *New Deal Agencies and Black America*, microfilm edition, reel 10, frame 00535.

40. Blakey, *Hard Times*, 72-73.

41. Atwood, "From Segregation to Integration," 97-98.

42. Harvard Sitkoff, *A New Deal for Blacks* (New York: Oxford University Press, 1978), 35, 66-68.

43. See H.B. 810 in the *Journal of the House of Representatives of the Commonwealth of Kentucky Regular Session*, vol. 3, 1934; Atwood, "From Segregation to Integration," 98-101.

44. The financial allotment for the construction of the men's dormitory was later increased to $133,000. The new dormitory, dedicated Oct. 20, 1935, provided housing for 128 students and seven faculty members. For additional business information on the dormitory, see Kentucky State Board of Education, minutes, Dec. 18, 1935; State *Journal*, Aug. 18, 1934 and Mar. 20, 1934; Atwood, "From Segregation to Integration," 98-101.

45. Louisville *Defender*, Aug. 3, 1935.

46. State *Journal*, Mar. 18, 1936.

47. Atwood to Governor A.B. Chandler, Apr. 4, 1936, Chandler papers, box 72, Department of Special Collections and Archives, University of Kentucky Libraries.

48. Atwood to Governor A.B. Chandler, Apr. 22, 1937, Chandler papers, box 72.

49. Atwood's report is included in State Board of Education, minutes, Dec. 16, 1936.

50. "Factual Brochure of Kentucky State College, Home of the 'Thorobreds,' 1886-1952," complied in the Office of Public Relations, Director Charles King, Blazer Library Archives, Kentucky State University, Frankfort.

51. Kentucky State College, "Ten Year Report," May 1939. The information in the preceding paragraphs is also from this source.

52. Hardin, *Onward and Upward*, 36, 41; Kentucky State Industrial College, Bulletin, 1930, 8-10.

53. Kentucky State Industrial College, faculty minutes, Sept. 8, 1930 and Feb. 3, 1931.

54. Kentucky State Industrial College, faculty minutes, Sept. 8, 1930.

55. Kentucky *Thorobred*, Oct. 1935.

56. Charles Quillings, interview, Aug. 5, 1990; Heartwell-Hunter, *Against the Tide*, 152.

57. Russell is quoted in Nancy J. Weiss, *Whitney M. Young, Jr., and the Struggle For Civil Rights* (Princeton: Princeton Univ. Press, 1989), 22-23.

58. John T. Williams was chosen in 1947 as the first and only president of Maryland State College. He held this position for twenty-three years. For more information on Williams's administration there, see Ruth Ellen Wennersten, "The Historical Evolution Of A Black Land Grant College: The University of Maryland, Eastern Shore, 1886-1970" (M.A. thesis, University of Maryland, 1976). See also Kentucky State Industrial College, Bulletin, June 1937, 10-11.

59. Atwood, "From Segregation to Integration."

60. Minnie Hitch Mebane, interview, Aug. 4, 1990, tape 1; Joseph Fletcher, interview, May 25, 1989; William Exxum, interview, July 30, 1987, Frankfort.

61. Kentucky *Thorobred*, Sept. 1962.

62. Pittsburgh *Courier*, Oct. 22, 1938.

63. Langston Hughes to Mabel Atwood, Oct. 15, 1957, Atwood family papers.

64. Anderson, *Education of Blacks*, 250; Hardin, *Onward and Upward*, 41.

65. Acts of the General Assembly of the Commonwealth of Kentucky, 1938, chapter 29, 1038-91.

66. Atwood to McVey, Oct. 26, 1938, McVey papers, box 37. See also McVey to Atwood, Nov. 5, 1938, McVey papers, box 37. It is not known exactly when Atwood wrote Donovan, but, from a subsequent letter informing him of the school's accreditation, it is evident Atwood had written him before. See Atwood to Donovan, Apr. 18, 1939, Herman Donovan papers, box 2, Eastern Kentucky University Library, Richmond.

67. Atwood to McVey, Dec. 16, 1938, McVey papers, box 37; Hardin, *Onward and Upward*, 41.

68. Donovan to Atwood, Apr. 22, 1939, Donovan papers, box 2.

69. Anderson, *Education of Blacks*, 274-75.

70. Ibid., 274-76.

71. Ibid., 276-78.

4. WALKING A TIGHTROPE

1. Woolfolk, *Prairie View*, passim.

2. The quotation from the Washington *Afro-American* was found in Goggins's study on Wilberforce. For more information on the controversy at Wilberforce, see Goggins, "Evolution of Central State College," 62-66. See also Washington *Afro-American*, Aug. 5, 1944; Mays, *Born To Rebel*, 190.

3. Joseph Winthrop Holley, *You Can't Build a Chimney from the Top: The South through the Life of A Negro Educator* (New York: William-Frederick, 1948), 112; Berkley Carlyle Ramsey, "The Public Black College in Georgia: A History of Albany State College 1903-1965" (Ph.D. diss., Florida State University, 1975), 163-64; Atwood, Oral History Project, Mar. 19, 1974, part 2; Roger M. Williams, *The Bonds: An American Family* (New York: Atheneum, 1917), 89-90.

4. Leedell W. Neyland and John W. Riley, *The History of Florida Agricultural Mechanical University* (Gainesville: Univ. of Florida Press, 1963), 79-84, 110.

5. John Clifford Harlan, *History of West Virginia State College 1890-1965* (Dubuque: Brown, 1968), 48-57.

6. Johnson, "Study," 14-21.

7. Ibid., passim; J.C. Harlan, *History*, 48-57, 85.

8. Johnson, "Study," 38-39.

9. Atwood, Oral History Project, Mar. 19, 1974, part 2.

10. Ibid., Mar. 18, 1974, part 1.

11. Joseph J. Boris, ed., *Who's Who in Colored America*, 2d ed., 1928-1929 (New York: Who's Who In Colored America), 17; Thomas Yenser, ed., *Who's Who In Colored America*, 5th ed., 1938, 1939, 1940 (New York: Yenser), 34.

12. Mabel had strong family ties to the Episcopalian Church. She was the niece of Rev. George Freeman Bragg, a noted black Episcopalian minister and pastor of St. James in Baltimore, Md., one of the oldest black Episcopalian churches in the nation. Father Wilson H. Willard, Jr., telephone interview, Aug. 1 1991; Atwood, Oral History Project, Mar. 18, 1974, part 1; Mabel Atwood, interview, Aug. 1, 1987; Louisville *Courier-Journal*, June 17, 1962.

13. Neal R. Peirce, *The Border South States* (New York: Norton, 1975), 218.

14. James B. Skaggs, "The Rise and Fall of Flem D. Sampson, 1927-1931" (M.A. thesis, Eastern Kentucky University, Aug. 1976), 16.

15. James C. Klotter and John W. Muir, "Boss Ben Johnson, the Highway Commission and Kentucky Politics, 1927-1937," *Register of The Kentucky Historical Society* 84 (Winter 1986), passim.

16. Atwood, "From Segregation to Integration," 67.

17. Heartwell-Hunter, *Against the Tide*, 17; Atwood, "From Segregation to Integration," 52.

18. An editorial in the Louisville *Courier-Journal* briefly acknowledges the political connection between Russell and Klair; see Feb. 25, 1929. Atwood mentions Klair's insurance contracts at Kentucky State in a video interview on his life and work at Kentucky State College. See "Distinguished Kentuckian." See also Atwood "From Segregation to Integration," 71; Klotter and Muir, "Boss Ben Johnson," 33; Robert Fenimore Sexton, "Kentucky Politics and Society: 1919-1932" (Ph.D. diss., Washington University, 1970), 69. Generally black Lexingtonians did not support Klair or Democratic candidates during the early 1900s; Russell was an exception. For more information on Klair's background and political career as well as Chandler's recollections of the Lexington political boss, see James Duane Bolin, "Bossism and Reform: Politics in Lexington, Kentucky, 1880-1940" (Ph.D. diss., University of Kentucky, 1988), 50, 53-54, 59, 70-72.

19. Klotter and Muir, "Boss Ben Johnson," 20, 32-33.

20. Ibid., 38; Atwood, "From Segregation to Integration," 71-72; Atwood, Oral History Project, Mar. 18, 1974, part 1.

21. Louisville *Leader*, Oct. 10 and Oct. 31, 1931; Klotter and Muir, "Boss Ben Johnson," 38-39.

22. *American Baptist*, Nov. 27, 1931.

23. Louisville *Leader*, Dec. 12, 1931; for a more thorough discussion of Governor Ruby Laffoon's 1931 inaugural parade, see Atwood, Oral History Project, Mar. 18, 1974, part 1. See also Atwood, "Distinguished Kentuckian."

24. Atwood to McVey, Dec. 1, 1931, McVey papers, box 37; see also Atwood to Donovan, Dec. 1, 1931, Donovan papers, box 2.

25. McVey to Atwood, Dec. 11, 1931, McVey papers, box 37.

26. Donovan to Atwood, Dec. 5, 1931, Donovan papers, box 2.

27. Louisville *Leader*, Jan. 30, 1932.

28. Atwood, "From Segregation to Integration," 73-74.

29. Elvis Stahr, Sr., was a prominent lawyer and later judge from Fulton County. For a number of years Stahr served as the Fulton County Democratic chair. According to Dr. Esther Nelson, Stahr had some influence in the original decision to hire Atwood as president of Kentucky State in 1929. Dr. Nelson, a native of Hickman, interviewed members of the Atwood family in the late 1960s and has conducted research on the black community. It is not known how true this claim is; however, it is possible considering Stahr's political connections. For more information on Stahr, see *Fulton County History*, 483; Esther Nelson, telephone interview, July 25, 1991, Memphis, Tenn.; Atwood, "From Segregation to Integration," 74; Hickman *Courier*, Dec. 10, 1931. Sheriff Goalder Johnson's political career was discussed in the Hickman *Courier*, Nov. 7, 1929.

30. Atwood, "From Segregation to Integration," 73-75; Atwood, Oral History Project, Mar. 18, 1974, part 1.

31. Kentucky Statutes, Carroll's Edition, 1915, section 4527, chapter 113, article 16, 5th ed., vol. 2 (Louisville: Baldwin Law Book, 1915), 2307. Osceola A. Dawson, *The Timberlake Story* (Carbondale, Ill.: Dunaway-Sinclair, 1959), 15. See also Harlan, *Onward and Upward*, 1

32. Dawson, *Timberlake Story*, 15; Clarence Timberlake, "Politics and the Schools," 9. Timberlake papers, box 5, Murray State University, Pogue Library.

33. Acts of the General Assembly of the Commonwealth of Kentucky, 1918, Chapter 30, 93.

34. Atwood, "From Segregation to Integration," 61-62.

35. In his autobiography, Atwood records that he submitted Ezra Gillis's name along with that of Callahan. This is incorrect. Gillis was already on the board when Callahan was appointed. See Atwood, "From Segregation to Integration," 75-77; Sexton, "Kentucky Politics," passim.

36. Atwood, "From Segregation to Integration," 75-77; William E. Ellis, *Patrick Henry Callahan (1886-1940): Progressive Catholic Layman In The American South* (Lewiston, N.Y.: Mellon, 1989), 8, 112-13.

37. Atwood, "From Segregation to Integration," 75-77; Louisville *Courier-Journal*, May 4, 1932; Kentucky State Industrial College, board of trustees minutes, May 6, 1932. Reference is made to the hiring of Chancellor Morris in Kentucky State Industrial College, board of trustees minutes, Jan. 20, 1933.

38. Weiss, *Farewell*, xiv, 180.

39. Blakey, *Hard Times*, 81; *Kentucky's Black Heritage*, 85.

40. Louisville *Leader*, Feb. 16, 1935.

41. John, Ed Pearce, *Divide and Dissent: Kentucky Politics, 1930-1963* (Lexington: Univ. Press of Kentucky, 1987), 41; Atwood, Oral History Project, Mar. 18, 1974, part 2.

42. Oden to Chandler, June 3, 1936, Chandler papers, box 72.

43. State Board of Education, minutes, Dec. 18, 1935.
44. Klotter and Muir, "Boss Ben Johnson," 45-46.
45. Atwood to Davis, Dec. 14, 1943, Davis papers.
46. Louisville *Leader*, Oct. 25, 1947; Louisville *Defender*, Nov. 8, 1947.
47. Representative Ralph Gilbert of Shelby County endorsed the bill permitting the governor to control state agencies in 1934. See the *State Journal*, Mar. 14, 1934. Governor Earle Clements led the proposal to get the 1934 Ouster Act overturned. He was prompted to do so by the Southern Association of Secondary Schools and Colleges (SACSS) and the Association of Teachers Colleges of America (ACTA), which opposed the political interference presidents of southern colleges were subjected to. SACSS and ACTA were particularly concerned about the 1946 dismissal of W.H. Vaughn, president of Morehead State University, who was fired allegedly because of his political connections. See Louisville *Courier-Journal*, Feb. 29, and Mar. 2, 1948. For details on Clement's role in getting the Ouster Act repealed, see Thomas H. Syvertsen, "Earle Chester Clements and the Democratic Party, 1920-1950" (Ph.D. diss., University of Kentucky, 1982), 333-40; Kentucky Revised Statutes, 1948, chapter 63, section 080, 4th biennial ed. (Kentucky Statute Revision Commission), 390.
48. Lawrence Wetherby, interview, July 27, 1991, Frankfort.
49. Adron Doran, interview, Apr. 12, 1991, Lexington, Kentucky.
50. Louisville *Defender*, Nov. 29, 1947; Wetherby interview.
51. Chicago *Defender*, Mar. 5, 1938.
52. Chandler to Mabel Atwood, May 9, 1984, Atwood family papers. Hardin, *Onward and Upward*, 43.
53. See "Factual Brochure of Kentucky State College, Home of the Thorobreds, 1886-1952"; Atwood, "From Segregation to Integration," 102.
54. Atwood shares these recollections more in oral interviews than he does in his unpublished autobiography. See Atwood, Oral History Project, Mar. 18, 1974, part 1; Atwood, "From Segregation to Integration," 122-23; Louisville *Defender*, June 4, 1959.

5. Beyond the Campus

1. Atwood, address before the 1945 freshmen class, n.d., Atwood papers, box 29.
2. Atwood, address delivered at the inauguration of Dr. J.D. Boyd, president, Alcorn A & M College, Lorman, Mississippi, n.d., Rufus Atwood Collection, Box 30.
3. Atwood, "The Role of Negro Higher Education in Post-War Reconstruction: The Negro Land Grant College," *Journal of Negro Education* 11 (July 1942): 393-98.
4. Sitkoff, *New Deal for Blacks*, 53; U.S. Census Bureau, *Fifteenth Census*, 56, 598, 600; U.S. Census Bureau, *Sixteenth Census*, 144, 147, 174.
5. Atwood, "Role Of Negro," 398.
6. During Atwood's presidency of the Association of Colleges and Secondary Schools for Negroes, "The Cooperative Negro College Study" was established. The study was designed to promote professional services for black colleges that wanted to improve their instructional program. For more information on this study, see Atwood's discussion of "The Cooperative Negro College Study," proceedings of the Conference of Presidents of Negro Land Grant Colleges, 1941, 57-59; *Midwestern*

Athletic Association Bulletin, passim, n.d., n.p. See also Louisville *Leader,* Mar. 12, 1932.

7. Clyde L. Orr, "An Analytical Study of the Conference of Presidents of Negro Land-Grant Colleges" (Ed.D. diss., University of Kentucky, 1959) 22; Atwood, "From Segregation to Integration," 32

8. Orr, "Analytical Study," 14; Atwood, "From Segregation to Integration," 89.

9. Issac Fisher, "Ten Years of the Conference of Presidents of Negro Land-Grant Colleges 1923-1933," in proceedings of the Conference of Presidents, 1923-1933; 1935-1938, 93-94; Orr, "Analytical Study," 13, 19.

10. Fisher, "Ten Years," passim; Atwood, "From Segregation to Integration," 84-85; Orr, "Analytical Study," 94.

11. Proceedings of the Conference of Presidents, 1935, 45-46.

12. On several occasions during the 1930s, Atwood appealed to President Frank McVey of the University of Kentucky for support in establishing Cooperative Extension work among blacks at Kentucky State, but he was unable to get McVey's support. In a June 21, 1938, letter to Atwood, McVey said the arrangement would be expensive. See Cooper to McVey, Oct. 5, 1933; Atwood to McVey, Feb. 8, 1937; Atwood to McVey, June 3, 1938; McVey to Atwood, June 21, 1938, McVey papers, box 37; proceedings, Conference of Presidents, 1937, 67-72.

13. Proceedings of the Conference of Presidents, 1937, 80-81.

14. Atwood, "A Confidential Report" to members of the Conference of Presidents, Committee on Federal Funds, Feb. 21, 1946, Atwood papers.

15. See Atwood, "A Confidential Report"; Orr, "Analytical Study," 96; Kentucky *Thorobred,* Apr. 1946.

16. Monroe Billington, "Civil Rights, President Truman and the South" *Journal of Negro History* 58 (Apr. 1973): 131; Harvard Sitkoff, "Harry Truman and the Election of 1948: The Coming of Age of Civil Rights in American Politics," *The Journal of Southern History* 37 (Nov. 1971): 597-600.

17. For a copy of the Executive Committee's statement, see proceedings of the Conference of Presidents, 1946, 15-16; Washington *Afro-American,* Oct. 26, 1946.

18. Orr, "Analytical Study," 96-97; see also proceedings of the Conference of Presidents, 1935, 54; 1937, 97; 1938, 69.

19. Orr, "Analytical Study," 97; see also proceedings of the Conference of Presidents, 1942, 20; 1948, 24-33. The latter includes a report by Coordinator E. Franklin Frazier that explains in greater detail the problems of the Social Studies Project.

20. Minutes of the various November 1953 meetings to merge the Conference of Presidents of Negro Land Grant Colleges with the Association of Land Grant Colleges as well as Atwood's remarks to the Senate were published in the October edition of the proceedings of the Conference of Presidents, 97-103.

21. Proceedings of the Conference of Presidents, 1953, 104-05; the final proceedings of the conference include the recommendation of the Executive Committee to the senate of the association. See proceedings of the Conference of Presidents, 1954 and 1955, 2, 106.

22. Evans to Atwood, Dec. 8, 1954, Atwood, Office of President, Correspondence Files, series 101, box 1.

23. The members of the conference discuss their organization and the relationships they shared with each other in Orr, "Analytical Study," 112.

24. Atwood, "From Segregation to Integration," 85-90.

25. Harvey C. Russell, "the Kentucky Negro Education Association, 1877-1946" (Norfolk, Va.: Guide Quality, 1946), 5-11, in A.S. Wilson and H.C. Russell, *History of KNEA, 1877 to 1957*, n.d., n.p.

26. Russell, "Kentucky Negro Education Association," 19-55. Periodically the minutes of the KNEA were included in its journal. The membership of the organization is broken into districts in *KNEA Journal* 1 (Oct. 1930): 19-23.

27. Ibid., 6-7.

28. Atwood, "From Segregation to Integration," 94, 110-11; Louisville *Leader*, Apr. 30, 1927.

29. Louisville *Independent News*, Apr. 29, 1933; Kentucky *Thorobred*, Apr. 1933; Atwood, "From Segregation to Integration" 110-11.

30. *KNEA Journal* 5 (Oct.-Nov. 1934), 3; Atwood, "The Kentucky Educational Commission and the Negro," *KNEA Journal* 4 (Oct.-Nov. 1933): 23-25; Russell, "Kentucky Negro Education Association," 30-31.

31. Lyman T. Johnson, interview, May 10, 1991, Louisville.

32. "Report of the Efficiency Commission," vols. 1 and 2, in *The Government of Kentucky* (Frankfort: State Journal Company, Jan. 1, 1924), 7, 408.

33. Louisville *Leader*, Oct. 22, 1932; Nov. 29, 1936.

34. Hardin, "Hope Versus Reality," 73.

35. In his autobiography, Atwood claims he opposed the closing of WKIC; however, the evidence supports a different conclusion. See Atwood to Chandler, Oct. 27, 1937, Chandler papers, box 72.

36. See Atwood's report to Chandler, Nov. 5, 1937, Chandler papers, box 72.

37. While Atwood does not specifically mention SACSS, he was probably referring to this accrediting association. He does state that Kentucky State had been rated "B" since 1931, and, according to the evidence, the school was reviewed by SACSS. Atwood to Chandler, June 30, 1937, Chandler papers, box 72.

38. Atwood to Chandler, June 30, 1937; Atwood to Chandler, Apr. 22, 1937, Chandler papers, box 72.

39. Louisville *Courier-Journal*, Dec. 12, 1937; "KNEA Board of Directors Meeting," *KNEA Journal* 9 (Jan.-Feb. 1938): 18

40. Victor K. Perry, member of the KNEA board of directors, A.E. Meyzeek, chairman of the KNEA Committee on Legislation, and J. Bryant Cooper, representing the Principal's Committee of Louisville Public Schools, cosigned the letter to Chandler urging him to reconsider his actions. See their letter to Chandler, Dec. 16, 1937, Chandler papers, box 186.

41. "KNEA Board of Directors Meeting," Dec. 18, 1937, *KNEA Journal* 9 (Jan.-Feb. 1938): 17-20; Wilson to Chandler, Chandler papers, box 86.

42. J.A. Thomas, "Introducing Kentucky's Legislator," *Opportunity* 18 (Mar. 1940): 76; Louisville *Leader*, Jan. 8, 1938; Atlanta *Daily World*, Dec. 30, 1937.

43. See Atwood to Chandler, Jan. 3, 1937, Chandler papers, box 86. This letter is apparently dated incorrectly, because the controversy had not begun at that time. Atwood said he was enclosing a signed statement from Charles Anderson attesting that he would support and sponsor the merger. The author did not locate this information or other letters from blacks who supported the merger in the Chandler papers.

44. Fouse, "Proposed Merger," 22-23; Meyzeek, "Arguments against the Merger," 24-25; Atwood, "Advantages of the Merger," 21-22 in *KNEA Journal* 9 (Jan.-Feb. 1938): 21-22.

45. *Acts of the Kentucky General Assembly*, 1938, Chapter 29, 1083-1091; Hardin, "Hope Versus Reality," 77-78.

6. Difficult Days

1. Mays, *Born to Rebel*, 196.

2. With the exception of Eastern Kentucky and Morehead State colleges, Governor Keen Johnson recommended lower appropriations for all state higher learning institutions. While Kentucky State's budget was the lowest of state schools, it did not, at least, receive a reduction in appropriations. For the governor's budget recommendations, see *Executive Budget*, for Biennium 1940-42, Commonwealth of Kentucky, 124-37. The actual appropriations for the state colleges are reported in *Acts of the Kentucky General Assembly*, 1940, Chapter 16, 131-34; Louisville *Courier-Journal* Aug. 9, 1940; Hardin, *Onward and Upward*, 39.

3. Louisville *Courier-Journal*, Sept. 10, 1941.

4. "The Report of the Kentucky Commission on Negro Affairs," 29; Louisville *Courier-Journal*, Aug. 9, 1940; Louisville *Defender*, Mar. 14, 1942; Kentucky *Thorobred* n.d., Oct. 1943.

5. Louisville *Courier-Journal*, Dec. 2, 1941.

6. See Atwood's report, State Board of Education minutes, June 20, 1941.

7. State Board of Education minutes, June 20, 1941; Louisville *Courier-Journal*, Oct. 2, 1941. For information on Kentucky State's appropriations, see "Factual Brochure of Kentucky State College, Home of the 'Thorobreds,' 1886-1952," 7.

8. Morgan D. Gordon, *Lawrence A. Davis: Arkansas Educator*, 19-20, 72.

9. "The End of Uncle Tom Teachers," *Ebony* 12 (June 1957): 68.

10. Lamon, *Black Tennesseans*, 100-3.

11. Neyland and Riley, *History of Florida Agricultural and Mechanical University*, 110; Williams, 89-90.

12. Atwood, "From Segregation to Integration" 124-25, 135-36; Adron Doran interview, Apr. 11, 1991.

13. Russell's quotes were taken from Nancy Weiss's *Whitney M. Young*, 24.

14. Donovan left Eastern Kentucky State Teachers College to head the University of Kentucky in 1941. He remained in that position until 1956. See "Report on Kentucky State College," University of Kentucky Committee, Oct. 23, 1945.

15. Ibid.

16. "Report of the Kentucky Commission on Negro Affairs," Nov. 1, 1945, 6.

17. Ibid.

18. *Kentucky's Black Heritage*, 98; "Report on Kentucky State College," 11-12.

19. James C. Klotter, Edmund D. Lyon and C. David Dalton, *The Public Papers of Governor Simeon Willis 1943-1947* (Lexington: University of Kentucky Press, 1988), 303; Louisville *Defender*, Mar. 30, 1946; Kentucky State College, "Factual Brochure," 6-7.

20. Kentucky State College, "Factual Brochure," 7

21. Martin named the meeting room of the presidents "the room of the big knives." Martin was appointed commissioner of finance by Governor Bert Combs in December 1959. He was appointed president of Eastern Kentucky State College in July 1960. See the biographical sketch of Robert Richard Martin included with the Robert Martin Papers, Eastern Kentucky University; Adron Doran, interview, Apr. 12, 1991; Kentucky, *Acts of the General Assembly*, 1960, chapter 45, 160-61.

22. Clements to Gerow, Aug. 6, 1948; Gerow to Clements, Aug. 3, 1948; Clements papers, box 81.

23. Houser to Chapman, Mar. 1, 1950, Clements papers, box 81; Rufus Atwood to Farras, Jan. 2, 1950, Clements papers, box 81.

24. Louisville *Courier-Journal*, Feb. 20, 1953; Hardin, *Onward and Upward*, 46, 48, 61.

25. Louisville *Courier-Journal*, Nov. 30, Dec. 7, Dec. 14, 1948; Jan. 6, 149; Lexington *Herald*, Feb. 17, 1949.

26. Louisville *Courier-Journal*, June 1 and June 15, 1950.

27. Louisville *Courier-Journal*, Feb. 2, 1952; Hardin, *Onward and Upward*, 46.

28. Louisville *Courier-Journal*, Feb. 2, 1952; Louisville *Defender*, Feb. 9, 1952; Kentucky State College board of regents minutes, Sept. 26, 1952.

29. Frankfort *State Journal*, May 12, 1953; Louisville *Courier-Journal*, May 26, 1953.

30. Kentucky *Thorobred*, Oct. 1935.

31. Archie Surratt interview, May 22, 1989.

32. Louisville *Defender*, Mar. 28, 1957; Apr. 4, 1957; July 3, 1957; Minnie Hitch Mebane interview, Aug. 4, 1990, part 1; Frankfort *State Journal*, Mar. 19, 1957.

33. Lexington *Herald*, June 20, 1957.

34. Frankfort *State Journal*, Oct. 17, 1957; Louisville *Courier-Journal*, Apr. 20, 1958; Frankfort *State Journal*, Oct. 30, 1958; *Courier-Journal*, Dec. 20, 1958; Frankfort *State Journal*, June 6, 1958.

35. Joseph Fletcher interview, May 25, 1989.

36. Kentucky *Thorobred*, Sept. 1957.

37. Kentucky State College faculty minutes, Dec. 9, 1957; Louisville *Courier-Journal*, June 21, 1959.

38. W.S. Hall, "Kentucky State College of the Future: An Initial Study," Jan. 15, 1958, 9-13, 18-19.

39. Hardin, *Onward and Upward*, 48, 50.

40. Louisville *Courier-Journal*, Aug. 7, 1949.

7. School Desegregation

1. White to Atwood, May 17, 1939, NAACP papers, reel 4, part 3, series A, frame 00249.

2. Louisville *Leader*, May 11, 1935.

3. "Adopted Program of the Negro State Co-Ordinating Committee in Session at Louisville, Kentucky," Dec. 19, 1936, Chandler collection, box 72; KNEA *Journal 7*, 13.

4. Kluger, *Simple Justice*, 132-36.

5. Ibid., 187-92.

6. *Acts of the General Assembly of the Commonwealth of Kentucky*, 1904, chapter 85, 181-82; *Kentucky's Black Heritage*, 62.

7. *Acts of the General Assembly of the Commonwealth of Kentucky* 1936, chapter 43, 110-12; Louisville *Courier-Journal*, Dec. 8, 1938; Rufus E. Clement, "Legal Provisions for Graduate and Professional Instruction for Negroes in States Operating School Systems," *Journal of Negro Education* (April 1939): 142-47; Venable, "History," 229-31; Louisville *Courier-Journal*, Jan. 29, 1939.

8. Louisville *Courier-Journal*, Jan. 28, 1939; Louisville *Leader* Feb. 4, 1939; Anderson to Houston, Feb. 8, 1939, NAACP papers, reel 4, part 3, series A, frame 00234.

9. Atwood to Chandler, Feb. 8, 1939, Chandler papers, box 72.

10. Anderson to Charles Houston, Feb. 8, 1939, NAACP papers, reel 4, part 3, series A, frame 00234; Marshall to Anderson, Apr. 5, 1939, NAACP papers, reel 4, part 3, series A, frame 00247.

11. Louisville *Courier-Journal*, Mar. 12, 1939.

12. Hudson, "History of Louisville Municipal College," 42, 47-48.

13. Louisville *Courier-Journal*, Mar. 12, 1939.

14. Atwood to White, Mar. 14, 1939, NAACP papers, reel 4, part 3, series A, frame 00245.

15. Ibid.

16. Shepard did express concern for racial violence. In December 1935 he sent a letter to southern governors requesting them to protect the rights of prisoners and oppose lynching, and, although Miller F. Whitaker agreed to assist the Regional Educational Council during the 1940s, he did support the work of the Southern Regional Council, which promoted better race relations after World War II. See Hine, "South Carolina's Challenge" 8-9; Cleveland *Call and Post*, Mar. 2, 1939; Kluger, *Simple Justice*, 157-58; Pittsburgh *Courier*, Dec. 14, 1935; Augustus M. Burns III, "Graduate Education for Blacks in North Carolina, 1930-51," *Journal of Southern History* 46 (May 1980): 195-96.

17. Burns, "Graduate Education," 196-206.

18. Governor's Advisory Committee minutes, Nov. 24, 1939, McVey papers, box 73.

19. Lizzie Fouse, the wife of W.H. Fouse, had mailed White a copy of the Governor's Advisory Committee's minutes for her husband, who was ill at the time. White to Lizzie B. Fouse, Dec. 14, 1939, NAACP papers, reel 4, part 3, series A, frame 00276.

20. E. Franklin Frazier, "Human, All Too Human," *Survey Graphics* 36 (January 1947): 74-75, 99; Jack M. Bloom, *Class, Race and the Civil Rights Movement* (Bloomington: Indiana Univ. Press, 1987), 164, 171.

21. The quote from Atwood was taken from Harrison, *Western Kentucky University*, 145.

22. Kentucky, "Report of Sub-Committee," Jan. 15, 1940; Governor's Advisory Committee minutes, Jan. 30, 1940, McVey papers, box 73.

23. Louisville *Courier-Journal*, Mar. 8, 1940; Kentucky, "Report of Sub-Committee"; and "Report of the Governor's Advisory Committee," n.d., McVey papers, box 73.

24. White to McVey, Mar. 20, 1940; NAACP papers, reel 4, part 3, series A, frames 00289-00290.

25. White to McVey, Mar. 20, 1940; McVey to White, Apr. 3, 1940, NAACP papers, reel 4, part 3, series A, frame 00293.

26. Norrell, *Reaping*, 46-48.

27. In 1940 the NAACP successfully won cases to equalize the salaries of blacks with whites in several counties in Maryland and in Norfolk, Va. The NAACP papers are the best source for information on the teacher's salary case in Louisville; they discuss the organization of the Education Equalization Committee and give significant information on the suit filed by Valla Dudley Abbington, a black teacher at Jackson Junior High School. See NAACP papers, reel 8, part 3, series B; see also,

Louisville *Courier-Journal*, Apr. 2, 1941. The teacher's salary cases in Maryland and Norfolk, Va., are briefly discussed in *Crisis*, Mar. 1940, 85-86; Sept. 1940, 290.

28. In 1938 Charles Houston resigned from his position as the special counsel of the NAACP in order to re-enter private practice, yet he remained an active member of the NAACP legal advisory team. Thurgood Marshall succeeded Houston as head of the NAACP legal defense committee. See Kluger, *Simple Justice*, 204-5, 229. Houston to Thomas, Jan. 22, 1940, NAACP papers, reel 11, part 3, series B, frame 00688; Thomas to Houston, Jan. 26, 1940, NAACP papers, reel 4, part 3, series A, frame 00285; Thomas to Houston, NAACP papers, June 23, 1941, reel 11, part 3, series B, frame 00692; Hardin, "Hope Versus Reality," 108-9.

29. Louisville *Courier-Journal*, Oct. 5, 1941; Louisville *Courier-Journal*, Feb. 2, 1941.

30. *Charles Lamont Eubanks by His Next Friend, Bodie Henderson vs. Herman Lee Donovan, president, Leo Chamberlain, registrar, the Board of Trustees of the University of Kentucky*, Petition for Writ of Mandamus, Fayette Circuit Court, n.d., included in the NAACP papers, reel 11, part 3, series B, frame 00722. This suit was later dropped and another one was filed requesting three thousand dollars in damages and an injuction against the university; see Chamberlain to Eubanks, Sept. 6, 1941, NAACP papers, reel 11, part 3, series B, frame 00706; Thomas to Marshall, Sept. 9, 1941, frame 00708; Thomas to Ransom, Sept. 10, 1941, frame 00713; Thomas to Marshall, Sept. 15, 1941, frame 00728; see NAACP Papers, reel 11, part 3, series B.

31. Thomas to Goodloe, Sept. 18, 1941, NAACP papers, reel 11, part 3, series B, frame 00737; see "Eubanks Files New Suit against University of Kentucky," Oct. 17, 1941, NAACP papers, reel 11, part 3, series B, frame 00798.

32. Louisville *Courier-Journal*, Nov. 6, 1941.

33. Thomas to Marshall, May 4, 1942, NAACP papers, reel 11, part 3, series B, frame 00913.

34. Kentucky State College, "Factual Brochure," 6-7; see also Houston's report of "Eubanks Case," Nov. 18, 1943, NAACP papers, reel 11, part 3, series B, frame 01098.

35. Thomas to Jones Feb. 24, 1942, frame 00890; Thomas to Marshall, Apr. 1, 1942, frame 00894; Henderson to Thomas, Mar. 14, 1943, frame 01006; Thomas to Burnley, Mar. 24, 1943, frame 01011; Thomas to Rowe, Feb. 6, 1943, frame 00988; see NAACP papers, reel 11, part 3, series B.

36. Louisville *Defender*, Jan. 13, 1945.

37. Kentucky *Thorobred*, Nov., 1944.

38. Louisville *Courier-Journal*, Feb. 5, 1944; Atwood, "From Segregation to Integration," 115-16, 126-27.

39. Anderson to Wilkins and Marshall, Mar. 16, 1944, NAACP papers, reel 12, part 3, series B, frame 00595; Louisville *Courier-Journal*, Feb. 9, 1944; Louisville *News* Mar. 11, 1944; Hardin, "Hope Versus Reality," 111-12.

40. Louisville *Courier-Journal*, Feb. 26, 1944.

41. Ibid., Mar. 7, 1944.

42. Anderson to Wilkins and Marshall, Mar. 16, 1944, NAACP papers, reel 11, part 3, series B, frame 00595.

43. Louisville *Defender*, Oct. 21, 1944; Louisville *Courier-Journal*, Mar. 2, 1944.

44. Louisville *Defender*, Oct. 21, 1944; Louisville *Leader*, Oct. 21, 1944.

45. "Report of the Legislative Committee of the Kentucky Negro Education Association," *KNEA Journal* 16 (Apr.-May 1945): 20-21.

46. Atwood, "From Segregation to Integration," 127.

47. Louisville *Courier-Journal*, Oct. 18, 1945.

48. *Kentucky Reporter*, Mar. 30, 1945; Pittsburgh *Courier*, Dec. 1, 1945.

49. Kluger, *Simple Justice*, 258-61.

50. Ibid.

51. Ibid., 266-68.

52. Pittsburgh *Courier*, Feb. 14, 1948; Thompson, "Why Negroes Are Opposed," 1-2.

53. Thompson, "Why Negroes Are Opposed," 4-8; Atwood to Ivey, Nov. 8, 1948, Correspondence files, series 101, box 2.

54. Louisville *Defender*, Nov. 29, 1947; Lattimore, Meyzeek, Steele, and Stanley to Clements, Mar. 6, 1950, Stanley papers, series 5.

55. The facts of the suit are discussed in *Lyman T. Johnson v. Board of Trustees of the University of Kentucky, et al.*, Lexington—No. 625 United States District Court for the Eastern District of Kentucky, filed: Apr. 27, 1949. For a copy of this information see the NAACP papers, reel 12, part 3, series B, frame 00511.

56. Lyman T. Johnson interview, May 10, 1991.

57. *Lyman T. Johnson v. Board of Trustees of the University of Kentucky*; Louisville *Courier-Journal*, July 14 and Sept. 12, 1948.

58. Louisville *Courier-Journal*, July 7 and July 14, 1948.

59. Louisville *Courier-Journal*, July 14, 1948.

60. Regarding the contract between the State Board of Education and the University of Kentucky board of trustees, see Atwood's "Statement For The Press," NAACP papers, reel 12, part 3, series B, frame 00520.

61. Thompson wrote Atwood a letter before he published his editorial and informed him that he got the impression that Atwood believed training could be provided to blacks under the board's plan. He also told Atwood that he was going to give the board's plan as well as Atwood's statement "wide and unfavorable publicity." See Thompson to Atwood, NAACP papers, reel 12, part 3, series B, frame 00188; see also Thompson, "Administrators Of Negro Colleges," 441.

62. Louisville *Courier-Journal*, undated clipping [Nov. 1948].

63. *Lyman T. Johnson v. Board of Trustees of the University of Kentucky, et al.*, Deposition For Plaintiff, Civil Action No. 625, Frankfort, Kentucky, Mar. 17, 1949, NAACP papers, reel 12, part 3, series B, frames 00454-00492; Lyman Johnson interview, May 10, 1991, 14, 19.

64. Press release, NAACP papers, reel 12, part 3, series B, frame 000276.

65. Atwood, "From Segregation to Integration," 144.

66. Ibid.

67. Kluger, *Simple Justice*, 281-83; Louis L. Redding, "Desegregation in Higher Education in Delaware," *Journal Of Negro Education* 27 (Summer 1958): 253-54.

68. For more details on the University of Kentucky's board of trustees' response to the Lyman Johnson case, see, Donovan, "Keeping the University Free and Growing," Donovan papers, UK, box 137. See also Syvertsen, "Earle Chester Clements," 351-52. Hardin offers significant information on school desegregation in Kentucky in "Hope Versus Reality."

69. According to then lieutenant governor Lawrence Wetherby, he and Governor Clements had informed Atwood that they "expected to amend the Day Law and later repeal it" during a private luncheon at the executive mansion. The meeting, which centered around a discussion of Kentucky State's budget, was held

in either December 1947 or January 1948. Wetherby recalled Atwood noting the luncheon as being his first at the governor's mansion. The three men agreed that he was probably the first invited black guest to eat there in the state's history. Wetherby interview, July 27, 1991; *Kentucky's Black Heritage*, 100-1.

70. Atwood to Clements, Apr. 12, 1949, Clements papers, box 81; Atwood to Donovan, Apr. 12, 1949, Donovan papers, UK box 6.

71. C.H. Parrish, "Desegregated Higher Education in Kentucky," *The Journal of Negro Education* 27 (Summer 1958): 264; *Kentucky's Black Heritage*, 100-1; Hudson, "History of Louisville Municipal College," 76-85.

72. Louisville *Courier-Journal*, Apr. 2 and Nov. 2, 1952; Hardin, *Onward and Upward*, 46.

73. *Kentucky Teachers Association Journal* 2 (Oct.-Nov. 1954): 6-8.

74. Atwood to Clements, Crumlin, and Dickey, Jan. 7, 1955, unprocessed box of Atwood's presidential papers; Frankfort *State Journal*, June 20 and June 23, 1957; University of Kentucky board of trustees minutes, June 11, 1957.

75. Louisville *Courier-Journal*, July 19, 1959.

8. Spring 1960

Note: An earlier version of this chapter was published by the *Register*, 1990.

1. Harvard Sitkoff, *The Struggle for Black Equality, 1954 to 1980* (New York: Oxford University Press, 1981), 60; William Chafe, *Civilities and Civil Rights* (New York: Oxford Univ. Press, 1981), 71.

2. Chafe, *Civilities*, 71.

3. Pittsburgh *Courier*, Apr. 16, 1960.

4. Hurley Doddy, "The Sit-In Demonstrations and the Dilemma of the Negro College Presidents," *Journal of Negro Education* 30 (1961): 1-2.

5. Louis E. Lomax, "The Negro Revolt against 'The Negro Leaders,'" *Harper's Magazine* 220 (June 1960): 48.

6. For a brief discussion on the response of college presidents to sit-in demonstrations, see Robert Weisbrot, *Freedom Bound: A History of America's Civil Rights Movement* (New York: Norton, 1990), 31-32; Pittsburgh *Courier*, May 21, 1960.

7. Pittsburgh *Courier*, Apr. 16, 1960; Louisville *Defender*, July 7, 1960; Pittsburgh *Courier*, July 30, 1960.

8. Norrell, *Reaping The Whirlwind*, 170-72; Pittsburgh *Courier*, Apr. 23, 1960.

9. L.D. Reddick, "The State vs. The Student," *Dissent* 2 (1960): 219-24; Pittsburgh *Courier*, Mar. 5, 1960; Pittsburgh *Courier*, Mar. 12, 1960.

10. Pittsburgh *Courier*, Mar. 5, 1960; Birmingham *World*, Mar. 20, 1960; Maxine D. Jones and Joe M. Richardson, *Talladega College: The First Century* (Tuscaloosa: The University of Alabama Press, 1990), 181-85.

11. Proceedings of the Board of Regents Hearing for Expelled Students, July 14, 1960, 13-14, Atwood papers, box 5 (hereafter Expelled Students). This source provides the best information on the events leading to the student demonstrations of April and May 1960 and includes significant primary information including excerpts from the Frankfort CORE meetings, a letter to Frankfort Mayor Paul Judd, and the Executive Council's charges against each student.

12. Kentucky State College, Executive Council minutes, Feb. 25, 1960; Heartwell-Hunter interview, July 20, 1989; Joseph Fletcher interview, May 25, 1989.

13. Kentucky State College, Executive Council minutes, Feb. 25, 1960.

14. Ibid.; Expelled Students, 13-14; "Dossier of Twelve Students Expelled from Kentucky State College," May 1, 1960, Atwood Collection, box 18.

15. Kentucky State College, Executive Council minutes, Feb. 25, 1960.

16. Expelled Students, 16-17; Arthur Norman et al., letter to Congress of Racial Equality, Mar. 18, 1960, Papers of the Congress of Racial Equality, reel 40, series 5, film no. 8522, vol. 345, frame 00912; August Meier and Elliott Rudwick, CORE, 4-10.

17. E.C. Harrison, "Student Unrest," 117; H. Edwards, Black Students, 61-62.

18. Students for Civil Rights, CORE Newsletter, Apr. 6, 1960; Heartwell-Hunter interview, July 20, 1989.

19. Frankfort State Journal, Apr. 3, 1960; Students for Civil Rights CORE Newsletter, Apr. 6, 1960.

20. Students for Civil Rights CORE Newsletter, Apr. 6, 1960.

21. Expelled Students, 21-22.

22. Louisville Defender, Mar. 24, 1960; Students For Civil Rights CORE Newsletter, Apr. 14, 1960.

23. Students For Civil Rights CORE Newsletter, Apr. 14, 1960; Atwood to Friends of the Kentucky Council on Human Relations, Feb. 12, 1960, George D. Wilson Papers, box 3, Ekstrom Library, University of Louisville.

24. Frankfort State Journal, Apr. 8, 1960; Expelled Students, 24-25, 27.

25. Frankfort State Journal, Apr. 28 and 29, 1960; Expelled Students, 27-30; Louisville Defender, May 5, 1960.

26. Louisville Defender, May 5, 1960; Expelled Students, 28-30.

27. Louisville Courier-Journal, Apr. 30, 1960; Frankfort State Journal, May 1, 1960.

28. Demonstrations in Frankfort resumed in December 1961. By February 1962 there were three groups in the city working toward racial equality: the Capital City Human Relations Committee, the Frankfort Citizens Committee, and the Steering Committee. By this time desegregation had begun in restaurants and at lunch counters of drug stores and dime stores. As of late 1961, the city had hired two blacks, James C. Griffen on the city police force and Camellia Millon as a clerk typist in the police department. See Louisville Defender, Dec. 14, 1960, and Feb. 15, 1962. Kentucky State College, Executive Council minutes, May 1, 1960; Louisville Courier-Journal, May 1, 1960; Expelled Students, 6; Louisville Defender, May 5 and Dec. 8, 1960; Frankfort State Journal, May 2, 1960.

29. Louisville Courier-Journal, May 4, 1960; Frankfort State Journal, May 9, 1960; Louisville Defender, May 5, 1950.

30. Louisville Defender, May 5, 1960.

31. Frankfort State Journal, May 3 and July 5 and 6, 1960; the Lexington Leader's response to Atwood's handling of the demonstrations was published in the Louisville Defender, May 12, 1960.

32. State Journal, May 3 and July 5 and 6, 1960: Louisville Defender, July 7, 1960; Louisville Courier-Journal, July 6, 1960.

33. Louisville Defender, May 5, 1960; Louisville Courier-Journal, May 4, 1960.

34. Atwood, "From Segregation to Integration," 189-91; Louisville Defender, May 19, 1960.

35. Louisville Defender, May 12, 1960.

36. New York Times, Apr. 11, 1960.

37. Poston to King, Apr. 13, 1960, Atwood Collection, box 12.

38. Frankfort State Journal, July 15, 1960; Expelled Students, 5-137, passim.

39. Kentucky State College, Executive Council minutes, July 20, 1960.

40. Ibid.

41. Louisville *Defender*, July 8, 1961; Lexington *Leader*, June 29, 1962; Louisville *Courier-Journal*, Sept. 3, 1963; *State Journal*, Sept. 4, 1963.

42. Louisville *Courier-Journal*, Sept. 11, 1963; Atwood, "From Segregation to Integration," 197.

43. Joseph Fletcher interview, May 25, 1989.

44. Helen Holmes interview, June 27, 1988; Louisville *Defender*, Dec. 14, 1961.

45. Archie Surrat interview, May 22, 1989.

46. Genevie Hughes, "Field Report," Feb. 5-8, 1962, CORE papers, reel 40, series 5, no. 8522, vol. 345, frame 00932.

47. Kesselman, "Interim Report." Kentucky

48. Rufus Atwood, Address before Berea College, Dec. 15, 1949, Atwood collection, box 29.

49. Throughout his presidency Atwood wrote several articles on African-Americans. Most of them were published in newspapers, but several were printed in other publications. Articles published in the Louisville *Courier-Journal* include "Vocational Training Needed So Negroes Can Find Jobs," Apr. 30, 1940; and "Give Kentucky Negro Doctors a Chance to Help Their Race," May 21, 1940. Atwood discussed the issue of civil rights in "Enactment of Civil Rights Program Now," *Kentucky Negro Education Association Journal* 22 (April 1951): 17-18.

9. MEASURING THE YEARS

1. Atwood's letter of resignation was filed in the Minutes of the Board of Regents of Kentucky State College, Mar. 30, 1962; Atwood to Davis, Nov. 7, 1952, Correspondence Files, series 101, box 1; Johnson, "A Study of The Life And Work of A Pioneer Black Educator: John W. Davis," 99.

2. Frankfort *State Journal*, Dec. 10, 12, and 22, 1961.

3. Atwood, "From Segregation to Integration," 199-200; Frankfort *State Journal* Dec. 10, 13, and 22, 1961, and Jan. 2, 1962.

4. Kentucky State College Faculty Meeting minutes, Dec. 14, 1961; Frankfort *State Journal*, Dec. 17, 1961.

5. Frankfort *State Journal*, Dec. 21, 1961.

6. Ibid.

7. Ibid., Dec. 22, 1961.

8. Atwood, "From Segregation to Integration," 199-200.

9. Kentucky House of Representatives journal, 1962, 1145; Atwood, "From Segregation to Integration," 200; Wilson, *Foot Prints in the Sand*, 308; Louisville *Courier-Journal*, Mar. 31, 1962.

10. Kentucky State College Board of Regents minutes, Mar. 30, 1962.

11. Kentucky State College, "Future of Kentucky State College," iv.

12. Statement From Board of Directors Frankfort Chamber of Commerce to Council on Higher Education, in "Future of Kentucky State College," 34; Louisville *Courier-Journal*, May 30, 1962.

13. Louisville *Courier-Journal*, May 30, 1962; see also "Statement By Clayton Jones, Commission on Human Rights Frankfort, Kentucky-Speaking As An Individual" in "Future of Kentucky State College," 35-36.

14. Louisville *Courier-Journal*, May 30, 1962.

15. "Future of Kentucky State," 1.

16. Ibid., passim.

17. Louisville *Times*, July 10, 1962.

18. Louisville *Courier-Journal*, June 17, 1962; Atwood, "From Segregation to Integration," 210-11; Louisville *Courier-Journal*, Mar. 31, 1962.

19. Dickey to Atwood, Apr. 27, 1962, Dickey papers, box 25.

20. In March 1960, the Paul G. Blazer Library was dedicated, making it the twelfth building erected during Atwood's tenure; see announcement in Louisville *Courier-Journal*, Feb. 29, 1960, and Oct. 21, 1962.

21. Atwood memorandum to faculty and employees of Kentucky State College, Sept. 17, 1962.

22. Kentucky State College *Bulletin*, 1961-1963.

23. Stanley to Atwood, Nov. 5, 1959; Atwood to Stanley, Dec. 5, 1959, Rufus B. Atwood/Carl M. Hill Correspondence Files, series 102, box 3.

24. Kentucky *Thorobred*, Dec. 1962; Wilson, *Foot Prints in the Sand*, 357-58.

25. Exxum interview, July 30, 1937.

26. Louisville *Courier-Journal*, Oct. 12, 1963.

27. Ibid., Aug. 21, 1962.

28. Robinson, *Public Papers*, 463-66.

29. Atwood, "From Segregation to Integration," 211-212; Atwood Oral History Project, Mar. 19, 1974, part 2; Louisville *Courier-Journal*, Aug. 21, 1962.

30. Meier and Rudwick, CORE, 159, 377-78.

31. Father Wilson H. Willard, Jr., telephone interview, Aug. 1, 1991.

32. Cincinnati *Herald*, Dec. 13, 1969.

33. Ohio Department of Health, Division of Vital Statistics, certificate of death, Mar. 18, 1983.

34. Frankfort *State Journal*, Mar. 20, 1983.

35. Young to Atwood, Nov. 27, 1962, Atwood Collection, box 2.

36. Parrish to Atwood, Nov. 30, 1962, Parrish papers, box 24.

37. Ibid.

38. See Carl M. Hill, "Kentucky State University Academic and Service Programs: 1962 to 1975, and Beyond," summary report, (Apr. 1975, found in Whitney M. Young, Sr., papers, "miscellaneous envelope," unlisted box number. Kentucky State University Archives).

39. Hardin, *Onward and Upward*, 48; Heartwell-Hunter, *Against the Tide*, 30.

40. Heartwell-Hunter, *Against the Tide*, 137, 146-47, 149.

41. Neyland and Riley, *History of Florida Agricultural and Mechanical University*, passim; Morgan, *Lawrence A. Davis*, passim; Robinson, *Montgomery Bus Boycot*, 47-48.

42. Jencks and Riesman, "American Negro College," 18.

Selected Bibliography

PRIMARY SOURCES

Manuscript Collections

Atwood, Rufus B. Association Correspondence. Paul G. Blazer Library, Archives, Kentucky State University, Frankfort.

———. Collection. Paul G. Blazer Library Archives, Kentucky State University, Frankfort.

———. Correspondence Files. Paul G. Blazer Library Archives, Kentucky State University, Frankfort.

Chandler, Albert B. Papers. University of Kentucky, Department of Special Collections and Archives, Lexington.

Clements, Earl. Papers. University of Kentucky, Department of Special Collections and Archives, Lexington.

Congress of Racial Equality Papers. Microfilm. John Willard Brister Library, Memphis State University.

Davis, John W. Papers. Drain-Jordan Library Archives, West Virginia State College, Institute, W.V.

Donovan, Herman. Papers. University of Kentucky, Department of Special Collections and Archives, Lexington.

———. Papers. John Grant Crabbe Library, Eastern Kentucky University, Richmond, Kentucky.

McVey, Frank. Papers. University of Kentucky, Department of Special Collections and Archives, Lexington.

National Association for the Advancement of Colored People. Papers. Microfilm. John Willard Brister Library, Memphis State University.

Parrish, Charles H., Jr. Papers. Ekstrom Library Archives Department, University of Louisville.

Stanley, Frank, Sr. Papers. Ekstrom Library Archives Department, University of Louisville.

Timberlake, Clarence L. Papers. Forrest C. Pogue Library, Special Collections and Archives, Murray State University, Murray, Ky.

Young, Whitney M., Sr. Papers. Paul G. Blazer Library Archives, Kentucky State University.

Public Documents

Kentucky, Commonwealth of. Acts of the General Assembly, 1904, 1930, 1934, 1936, 1938, 1950.

————. House of Representatives of the General Assembly of the Commonwealth. Journal. Regular sess., vol. 3, 1934.

————. House of Representatives of the General Assembly of the Commonwealth. Journal. Regular Sess., vol. 1, 1962.

————. *Revised Statutes.* 4th ed. Frankfort: Kentucky Statute Revision Commission, 1948.

————. *Kentucky Statutes.* Carroll's ed. Vol. 2. Louisville: Baldwin Law Book, 1915.

Ohio Department of Health Division of Vital Statistics. Certificate of Death, Rufus Ballard Atwood, March 18, 1983.

Prairie View State Normal and Industrial College. Biennial Budget for fiscal years ending Aug. 31, 1926 and 1927.

U.S. Bureau of Education, Jones,Thomas Jessie, ed., *Negro Education: A Study of the Private and Higher Schools for Colored People in the United States.* Vol. 1. Bulletin 38. Washington, D.C.: GPO, 1917.

U.S. Census Bureau. *Negro Population in the United States, 1790-1915.* Washington, D.C.: GPO, 1918.

————. *Twelfth Census of the United States, 1900.* Vol. 1, part 1. Washington, D.C.: GPO, 1901.

————. *Fifteenth Census of the United States, 1930.* Vols. 2 and 4. Washington, D.C.: GPO, 1933.

————. *Sixteenth Census of the United States, 1940.* Vol. 2, part 3, and vol. 3. Washington, D.C.: GPO, 1943.

Proceedings

Kentucky, Commonwealth of. Board of Education. Minutes, 1935, 1941.

Kentucky Negro Education Association. Board of Directors. Minutes. Jan.-Feb. 1938.

————. Legislative Committee. Minutes. Jan.-Feb. 1938.

Kentucky State College. Board of Regents. Minutes. Sept. 26, 1952; Mar. 30, 1962.

————. Board of Trustees. Minutes. 1929-1932.

————. Faculty and Executive Council. Minutes. 1929-1962.

Presidents of Negro Land Grant Colleges, Conference Proceedings, 1935-1955, Paul G. Blazer Library, Archives, Kentucky State University, Frankfort.

University of Kentucky. Board of Trustees. Minutes. April 5, 1949.

Reports

Atwood, Rufus B. "A Confidential Report." Committee on Federal Funds. Conference of Presidents of Negro Land Grant Colleges. Feb. 21, 1946.

Chambers, M.M., Thomas G. Pullen, and Broadus E. Sawyer. "The Future of Kentucky State College: A Report with Recommendations to the Kentucky Council on Public Higher Education." Frankfort: Kentucky Council on Public Higher Education, June 25, 1962.

Hall, W. Scott. "Kentucky State College of the Future: An Intial Study." Paul G. Blazer Library, Archives, Kentucky State University: Jan. 15, 1958.

Kentucky, Commonwealth of. Department of Education. "Negro Education in Kentucky." *Educational Bulletin* 11 (May 1943).

———. Superintendent of Public Instruction. Biennial Reports. For the biennium ending June 30, 1929, 1931 1933, 1935, 1937, 1953.

———. "Report of the Efficiency Commission." 2 vols. Frankfort: State Journal Company, Jan. 1, 1924.

———. "Report of the Governor's Advisory Committee on the Equalization of Higher Educational Opportunities For Negroes," n.d.

———. "Report of the Kentucky Commission on Negro Affairs." Frankfort, Nov. 1, 1945.

———. "Report of Sub-Committee on the Equalization of Higher Educational Opportunities for Negroes." Special Collections and Archives, University of Kentucky, Jan. 15, 1940.

Kesselman, Louis C. "Interim Report Kentucky State College Situation." Academic Freedom Committee, Kentucky Civil Liberties Union, May 12, 1960. Atwood Collection, box 18.

Prairie View State Normal and Industrial College. Bulletin of the Annual Report for the Fiscal Year 1923-1924.

Seay, Maurice F. "A Report on Education (October 4, 1945)." In *Reports of Committee For Kentucky*, 1943-1945.

"Ten-Year Report of Kentucky State College, 1929-1939." Frankfort: Kentucky State College, May 1939.

U.S. Department of Labor. Employment Service. L.A. Oxley Files, State Reports, "Kentucky State Employment Service Survey in New Deal Agencies and Black America." Microfilm. Brister Library, Memphis State University.

Memoirs, Autobiographies, and Public Papers

Atwood, Rufus B. "From Segregation to Integration, 1929-62: The Autobiography of Dr. Rufus B. Atwood." Unpublished manuscript, n.d.

———. "Distinguished Kentuckian." Kentucky Educational Television video recording. Feb. 19, 1976.

———. Oral History Project. March 18 and 19, 1974. Department of Special Collections, University of Kentucky, Lexington.

———. Transcript. Oral interview with George Caulton, edited 1975-76.

Atwood, Rufus B., and Mabel Atwood. Family Papers. In the possession of Roy Mitchell, Cincinnati, Ohio.

Goodson, Martia Graham, ed. *Chronicles of Faith: The Autobiography of Frederick D. Patterson*. Tuscaloosa: Univ. of Alabama Press, 1991.

Hall, Wade. *The Rest of the Dream: The Black Odyssey of Lyman Johnson*. Lexington: Univ. Press of Kentucky, 1988.

Holley, Josephy Winthrop. *You Can't Build a Chimney from the Top: The South through the Life of a Negro Educator*. New York: William-Frederick, 1948.

Klotter, James C., Edmund D. Lyon, and C. David Dalton. *The Public Papers Of Governor Simeon Willis, 1943-1947*. Lexington: Univ. Press of Kentucky, 1988.

Mays, Benjamin E. *Born To Rebel: An Autobiography by Benjamin E. Mays*. New York: Scribners, 1971

McVey, Frank. *The Gates Open Sowly*. Lexington: Univ. of Kentucky Press, 1949.

Robinson, George W., ed. *The Public Papers of Governor Bert T. Combs, 1959-1963*. Lexington: Univ. Press of Kentucky, 1979.

Wilson, George. *Foot Prints in the Sand—Kentucky Sand*. Decorah, Iowa: Anindson, 1982.

Interviews with Author

Atwood, Mabel C. Nov. 9, 1985; August 1, 1987, Cincinnati.

Butler, Wendell. May 25, 1989, Frankfort.

Doran, Adron. Apr. 12, 1991, Lexington.

Edwards, A.J. Aug. 1, 1987, Cincinnati

Edwards, Vera. Aug. 1, 1987, Cincinnati.

Exxum, William. July 30, 1987, Frankfort.

Fletcher, Joseph. May 25, 1989, Frankfort.

Heartwell-Hunter, Ann J. July 20, 1989, Lexington.

Holmes, Helen. June 27, 1988, Frankfort.

Johnson, Lyman T. May 10, 1991, Louisville.

Mebane, Minnie Hitch. Aug. 4, 1990, Paris.

Mitchell, Rufus. Telephone interview, July 24, 1991, Cincinnati.

Nelson, Esther. Telephone interview, July 25, 1991, Sacramento.

Quillings, Charles. Aug. 5, 1990, Lexington.

Ross, Charles. Aug. 1, 1987, Cincinnati.

Surratt, Archie. May 22, 1989, Frankfort.

Waniek, Marilyn Nelson. Telephone interview, Feb. 21, 1991. Mansfield, Connecticut.

Wetherby, Lawrence. July 27, 1991, Frankfort.

Newspapers, Catalogues, and Bulletins

American Baptist

Atlanta *Daily World*

Birmingham *World*

Cleveland *Call and Post*

Crisis

Fisk University News

Fisk University yearbook

Frankfort *State Journal*

Hickman *Courier*

Hopkinsville *New Age*

Houston *Informer*

Kentucky State College Bulletin
Kentucky Thorobred
Lexington *Herald*
Louisville *Courier-Journal*
Louisville *Defender*
Louisville *Independent News*
Louisville *Leader*
Louisville *Times*
Midwestern Athletic Association Bulletin
New York *Times*
Paducah *Sun-Democrat*
Pittsburgh *Courier*
Prairie View State Normal and Industrial College Catalogue 1924-1926
Prairie View Standard
Students For Civil Rights Newsletter
The Starr
Washington *Afro-American*

SECONDARY SOURCES

Books

Anderson, James D. *The Education of Blacks In The South 1860-1935*. Chapel Hill: Univ. of North Carolina Press, 1988.

Bacote, Clarence A. *The Story of Atlanta University: A Century of Service 1865-1965*. Atlanta: Atlanta University, 1969.

Bardolf, Richard. *The Negro Vanguard*. New York: Vintage, 1961.

Blakey, George T. *Hard Times and New Deal in Kentucky, 1929-1939*. Lexington: Univ. Press of Kentucky, 1986.

Bloom, Jack M. *Class, Race, and the Civil Rights Movement*. Bloomington: Indiana Univ. Press, 1987.

Boris, Joseph J., ed. *Who's Who in Colored America, 1928-1929*. Second edition. New York: Who's Who in Colored America, 1930.

Chafe, William. *Civilities and Civil Rights*. New York: Oxford Univ. Press, 1981.

Chambers, Frederick. *Black Higher Education in the United States: A Selected Bibliography on Negro Higher Education and Historically Black Colleges and Universities*. Connecticut: Greenwood, 1978.

Cooper, Arnold, *Between Struggle and Hope: Four Black Educators in the South, 1894-1915*. Ames: Iowa State Univ. Press, 1989.

Cozart, Leland Stanford. *A History of the Association of Colleges and Secondary Schools, 1934-1965*. Charlotte, N.C.: Heritage, 1967.

Dawson, Osceola A. *The Timberlake Story*. Carbondale, Illinois: Dunaway-Sinclair, 1959.

Dunnigan, Alice A. *The Fascinating Story of Black Kentuckians: Their Heritage and Tradition*. Washington, D.C.: Associated, 1982.

Dykeman, Wilma, and James Stokley. *Seeds of Southern Change: The Life of Will Alexander.* Chicago: University of Chicago Press, 1962.

Edwards, Harry. *Black Students.* New York: Free Press, 1970.

Ellis, William E. *Patrick Henry Callahan (1866-1940) Progressive Catholic Layman in the American South.* Lewiston, N.Y.: Mellon, 1989.

Ellison, Ralph. *Invisible Man.* New York: Random, 1952.

Engle, Fred Allen, Jr. *The Superintendents and the Issues: A Study of the Superintendents of Public Instruction in Kentucky.* Frankfort: Department of Education. 1968.

Franklin, John Hope. *From Slavery to Freedom: A History of Negro Americans.* 5th ed. New York: Knopf, 1980.

Fulton County History, 1945. Paducah: Fulton County Historical Society, 1983.

Galloway, Oscar F. *Higher Education for Negroes in Kentucky.* Vol. 5, no. 1. Bulletin of the Bureau of School Service, College of Education, University of Kentucky, September 1932.

Gavins, Raymond. *The Perils and Prospects of Southern Black Leadership: Gordon Blaine Hancock, 1884-1974.* Durham: Duke Univ. Press, 1977.

Gutman, Herbert. *The Black Family in Slavery and Freedom, 1750-1925.* New York: Vintage, 1976.

Hardin, John. *Onward and Upward: A Centennial History of Kentucky State University.* Frankfort: Kentucky State University, 1987.

Harlan, John Clifford. *History of West Virginia State College, 1890-1965.* Dubuque: Brown, 1968.

Harlan, Louis. *Booker T. Washington, The Making of a Black Leader, 1865-1901.* New York: Oxford Univ. Press, 1972.

———. *Booker T. Washington: The Wizard of Tuskegee, 1901-1915.* New York: Oxford Univ. Press, 1983.

Harrison, Lowell H. *Western Kentucky University.* Lexington: Univ. Press of Kentucky, 1987.

Heartwell-Hunter, Ann J. *Against the Tide.* Georgetown, Ky.: Kreative Grafiks, 1987.

Hickman County History, Clinton, Kentucky. Vol. 1. Clinton, Ky.: Hickman County Historical Society, 1983.

Howard, Victor. *Black Liberation in Kentucky: Emancipation and Freedom, 1862-1884.* Lexington: Univ. Press of Kentucky, 1983.

Jones, Ann. *Uncle Tom's Campus.* New York: Praeger, 1973.

Jones, Maxine D., and Joe M. Richardson, *Talladega College: The First Century.* Tuscaloosa: Univ. of Alabama Press, 1990.

Jones, Paul W. L. *A History of the Kentucky Normal and Industrial Institute.* Frankfort: Frankfort Printing, 1912.

Kentucky's Black Heritage. Frankfort: Kentucky Commission on Human Rights, 1971.

Kluger, Richard. *Simple Justice.* New York: Vintage, 1975.

Kramer, Carl E. *Capital on the Kentucky: A Two Hundred Year History of Frankfort and Franklin County.* Frankfort: Historic Frankfort, 1986.

Lamon, Lester C. *Black Tennesseans, 1900-1930.* Lexington: Univ. of Kentucky Press, 1977.

Meier, August, and Elliot Rudwick. *CORE: A Study in the Civil Rights Movement, 1942-1968.* Chicago: Univ. of Illinois Press, 1975.

Morgan, Gordon D. *Lawrence A. Davis: Arkansas Educator.* New York: Associated Faculty Press, 1985.

Nalty, Bernard. *Strength for the Fight: A History of Black Americans in the Military.* New York: Free Press, 1986.

Neyland, Leedell W., and John W. Riley, *The History of Florida Agricultural and Mechanical University.* Gainsville: Univ. of Florida Press, 1963.

Norrell, Robert J. *Reaping The Whirlwind: The Civil Rights Movement in Tuskegee.* New York: Vintage, 1986.

Orum, Anthony. *Black Students in Protest: A Study of the Orgins of the Black Student Movement.* Urbana, Ill.: Arnold M. and Caroline Rose Monograph Series, American Sociological Association, 1972.

Pearce, John Ed. *Divide and Dissent: Kentucky Politics, 1930-1963.* Lexington: Univ. Press of Kentucky, 1982.

Peirce, Neal R. *The Border South States.* New York: Norton, 1975.

Robinson, JoAnn Gibson. *The Montgomery Bus Boycott and the Women Who Started It.* Knoxville: Univ. of Tennessee Press, 1987.

Ross, Earle D. *A History of the Iowa State College of Agriculture and Mechanic Arts.* Ames: Iowa State College Press, 1942.

Russell, Harvey C. "The Kentucky Negro Education Association 1877-1946." Norfolk, Va.: Guide Quality Press, 1946. In *History of KNEA, 1877 to 1922 to 1957,* ed. A.S. Wilson and H.C. Russell, n.d., n.p.

Schacter, Harry. *Kentucky on the March.* New York: Harper, 1949.

Scott, Emmett J. *The American Negro in the World War.* Washington, D.C.: n.p., 1919.

Sitkoff, Harvard. *A New Deal for Blacks.* New York: Oxford Univ. Press, 1978.

———. *The Struggle for Black Equality, 1954-1980.* New York: Hill and Wang, 1981.

Thompson, Daniel C. *The Negro Leadership Class.* Englewood Cliffs, N.J.: Prentice-Hall, 1963.

Waniek, Marilyn Nelson. *The Homeplace.* Baton Rouge: Louisiana State Univ. Press, 1990.

Weisbrot, Robert. *Freedom Bound: A History of America's Civil Rights Movement.* New York: Norton, 1990.

Weiss, Nancy J. *Farewell to the Party of Lincoln.* Princeton: Princeton Univ. Press, 1983.

———. *Whitney M. Young, Jr., and the Struggle for Civil Rights.* Princeton: Princeton Univ. Press, 1989.

Williams, Lawrence H. *Black Higher Education in Kentucky: The History of Simmons University.* New York: Mellon, 1987.

Williams, Roger M. *The Bonds: An American Family.* New York: Atheneum, 1971.

Wolters, Raymond. *The New Negro on Campus.* Princeton: Princeton Univ. Press, 1975.

Woolfolk, Ruble. *Prairie View: A Study in Public Conscience, 1878-1946.* New York: Pageant, 1962.

Wright, George C. *Life behind a Veil: Blacks in Louisville, Kentucky, 1865-1930.* Baton Rouge: Louisiana State Press, 1985.

———. *Racial Violence in Kentucky, 1865-1940.* Baton Rouge: Louisiana State Univ. Press, 1990.

Yenser, Thomas, ed. *Who's Who in Colored America, 1938, 1939, 1940.* New York: Thomas Yenser, n.d.

Journal Articles

Atwood, Rufus B. "Advantages of the Merger." KNEA *Journal* 9 (Jan.-Feb. 1938): 21-22.

———. "Enactment of Civil Rights Program Now." KNEA *Journal* 2 (Apr. 1951): 17-18.

———. "Financing Schools for Negro Children from State School Funds in Kentucky." *Journal of Negro Education* 3 (Oct. 1939): 659-66.

———. "The Kentucky Educational Commission and the Negro." KNEA *Journal* 4 (Oct.-Nov. 1933):23-25.

———. "Kentucky Faces the Problem of Training Colored Teachers." KNEA *Journal* 1 (Feb. 1931): 21-26.

———. "Kentucky State College and Integration." *Kentucky Teachers Association Journal* 2 (Oct.-Nov. 1954): 6-8.

———. "The Negro in Kentucky." KNEA *Journal* 12 (Jan.-Feb. 1942): 9-10.

Billington, Monroe, "Civil Rights, President Truman and the South." *Journal of Negro History* 58 (Apr. 1973): 127-39.

Burns, Augustus M., III. "Graduate Education for Blacks in North Carolina, 1930-1951." *Journal of Southern History* 46 (May 1980): 195-218.

Davis, Lenwood G. "A History of Blacks in Higher Education, 1875-1975: A Working Bibliography." *Council of Planning,* Librarians Exchange Bibliography #720 (1975): 1-25.

Doddy, Hurley. "The Sit-In Demonstrations and the Dilemma of the Negro College Presidents." *Journal of Negro Education* 30 (Winter 1961): 1-3.

Fisher, Isaac. "Ten Years of the Conference of Presidents of Negro Land-Grant Colleges, 1923-1933." *Proceedings of the Annual Conference of the Presidents of Negro Land-Grant Colleges, 1923-1933, 1935-1938:* 93-107.

Fleming, Cynthia Griggs. "The Plight of Black Educators in Post-War Tennessee 1865-1920." *Journal of Negro History* (Fall 1979): 355-76.

Fouse, W. H. "The Proposed Merger." KNEA *Journal* 9 (Jan.-Feb. 1938): 22-23.

Frazier, E. Franklin. "Human, All Too Human." *Survey Graphics* 36 (Jan. 1947): 74-75, 99-100.

Harrison, E.C. "Student Unrest on the Black College Campus." *Journal of Negro Education* 41 (Spring 1972): 113-20.

Jencks, Christopher, and David Riesman. "The American Negro College." *Harvard Educational Review* 37 (Winter 1967): 3-60.

Klotter, James C., and John W. Muir. "Boss Ben Johnson, The Highway Commission and Kentucky Politics, 1927-1937." *Register of the Kentucky Historical Society* 84 (Winter 1986): 18-50.

Kousser, J. Morgan. "Making Separate Equal: Integration of Black and White School Funds in Kentucky." *Journal of Interdisciplinary History* 10 (Winter 1980): 399-428.

Lomax, Louis E. "The Negro Revolt against the Negro Leaders." *Harper's Magazine* 220 (June 1960): 41-48.

Meyzeek, A. E. "Arguments against the Merger." KNEA *Journal* 9 (Jan.-Feb. 1938): 24-25.

Parrish, Charles H., Jr. " Desegregated Higher Education in Kentucky." *Journal of Negro Negro Education* 27 (Summer 1958): 260-68.

———. "The Education of Negroes in Kentucky." *The Journal of Negro Education* 16 (Summer 1947): 354-60.

———. "Negro Higher and Professional Education in Kentucky." *Journal of Negro Education* 17 (Summer 1960): 289-95.

Porter, Amy. "Weep No More, Kentucky." *Collier's Magazine* 117 (March 30, 1946): 14-15, 57-59.

Reddick, L.D. "The State vs. The Student." *Dissent* 7 (Summer 1960): 219-28.

Redding, Louis L. "Desegregation in Higher Education in Delaware." *Journal of Negro Education* 27 (Summer 1958): 253-59.

———. "Harry Truman and the Election of 1948: The Coming of Age of Civil Rights in American Politics." *Journal of Southern History* 27 (Nov. 1971): 597-616.

Smith, H.S. "Kentucky State College and Its President." *Wilberforce Quarterly* 2 (July 1941): 77-80.

———. "Reconversion and Educational Opportunities." KNEA *Journal* 18 (Jan.-Feb. 1947): 13-19.

"The End of Uncle Tom Teachers." *Ebony* 12 (June 1957): 68-72.

Thompson, Charles H. "Administrators of Negro Colleges and the Color in Higher Education in the South." *Journal of Negro Education* 17 (Fall 1948): 437-45.

———. "Why Negroes Are Opposed to Segregated Regional Schools." *Journal of Negro Education* 18 (Winter 1949): 1-8.

Timberlake, Clarence L. "The Early Struggle for Education of the Blacks in the Commonwealth of Kentucky." *Register of the Kentucky Historical Society* 71 (July 1973): 225-52.

Wright, George C. "The Founding of Lincoln Institute." *Filson Club Quarterly* 49 (Jan. 1975): 57-70.

———. "The Faith Plan: A Black Institution Grows during the Depression." *Filson Club Quarterly* 51 (Oct. 1977): 336-49.

Dissertations and Theses

Bolin, James Duane. "Bossism and Reform: Politics in Lexington, Kentucky, 1880-1940." Ph.D. diss. University of Kentucky, 1988.

Coleman, Lena Mae. "A History of the Kentucky State College for Negroes." M.A. thesis. Indiana University, 1938.

Edwards, Austin, Jr. "History of the Kentucky State Industrial College for Negroes." M.A. thesis. Indiana State Teachers College, 1936.

Evans, Lamona Nadine. "The Administrative Styles of Presidents of Black Colleges in the Academic Novel." Ph.D. diss. University of Oklahoma, 1987.

Frass, Elizabeth M. "Keen Johnson: Newspaperman and Governor." Ph.D. diss. University of Kentucky, 1984.

Goggins, Lathardus. "The Evolution of Central State College under Dr. Charles H. Wesley from 1942-1965: An Analysis." Ed.D. diss. University of Akron, 1983.

Hardin, John Arthur. "Hope Versus Reality: Black Higher Education In Kentucky, 1904-1954." Ph.D. diss. University of Michigan, 1989.

Hudson, James Blaine, III. "The History of Louisville Municipal College: Events Leading to the Desegregation of the University of Louisville." Ed.D diss. University of Kentucky, 1981.

Johnson, Angel Patricia. "A Study of the Life and Work of A Pioneer Black Educator: John W. Davis." Ed.D. diss. Rutgers University, 1987.

Ramsey, Berkley Carlyle. "The Public Black College In Georgia: A History of Albany State College 1903-1965." Ph.D. diss. Florida State University, 1973.

Sexton, Robert Fenimore. "Kentucky Politics and Society, 1919-1932." Ph.D. diss. Washington University, 1970.

Skaggs, James B. "The Rise And Fall Of Flem D. Sampson, 1927-1931." M.A. thesis. Eastern Kentucky University, 1976.

Sullivan, John E. "A Historical Investigation of the Negro Land-Grant College from 1890 to 1964." Ed.D. diss. Loyola University, Feb. 1969.

Syvertsen, Thomas H. "Earle Chester Clements and the Democratic Party, 1920-1950." Ph.D. diss. University of Kentucky, 1982.

Venable, Thomas Calvin. "A History of Negro Education in Kentucky." Ph.D. diss. George Peabody College, 1952.

Wennersten, Ruth Ellen. "The Historical Evolution of a Black Land Grant College: The University of Maryland, Eastern Shore, 1886-1970." M.A. thesis. University of Maryland, 1976.

White, Mae Vaught. "The Development of the Program of Studies of the Prairie View State Normal and Industrial College." M.A. thesis. University of Texas, 1938.

Other Sources

Anderson, Blanche Atwood. Interviewed by Johnnie Nelson, n.d.

Bunch, Ralph J., Jr. "A Brief and Tentative Analysis of Negro Leadership." A research memorandum prepared for the Carnegie-Myardal Study of the Negro In America. Sept. 1940.

"Factual Brochure of Kentucky State College Home of the 'Thorobreds,' 1886-1952." Comp. Office of Public Relations. Blazer Library.

Fisk University. General Anniversary Program, 4 Apr.-27 May 1920. Special Collections, Fisk Memorial Library, Nashville.

Hine, William C. "South Carolina's Challenge to Civil Rights: The Case of South Carolina State College." Unpublished paper presented to the Southern Historical Association Meeting, Lexington, Kentucky, Nov. 10, 1989.

Kappa Alpha Psi, Alpha Upsilon Chapter. "Biographical Sketches of Kentucky State College Presidents, 1887-1937." n.p., n.d. Blazer Library. Kentucky State University, Frankfort, Kentucky.

Index

CPSIA information can be obtained
at www.ICGtesting.com
Printed in the USA
LVHW091927180120
644128LV00002B/6